# Entanglement:

## A True Story

### Claire Thomas

**BALBOA**
PRESS
A DIVISION OF HAY HOUSE

Balboa Press books may be ordered through booksellers or by contacting:

Balboa Press
A Division of Hay House
1663 Liberty Drive
Bloomington, IN 47403
www.balboapress.com.au
1 (877) 407-4847

Printed in the United States of America.

ISBN: 978-1-4525-1134-4 (sc)
ISBN: 978-1-4525-1133-7 (e)

Balboa Press rev. date: 01/07/2014

# *Introduction*

*I*t was hard to decide, as I recall, whether it was darker outside or in. Certainly the night was black as jet, a rarity in that clear inland climate and under such stupendous night skies, so perhaps those ever-longed-for rain clouds were gathering that evening. Even so, inside the car, even under the mournful glow of the dashboard lights, my father and I seemed to be shrouded in an inky mist of the darkest feelings.

He was enraged with me, his anger fuelled by fine white wine, and even now, recalling such a long-ago moment makes my guts roil with fear. In the hour preceding, I had finally broken down in the face of the constant bullying of my brother and assorted cousins, become hysterical during an overnight stay at my grandparents (his parents). I had demanded (unthinkable) to be taken home despite knowing the likely ramifications of such a wilful but desperate act.

I wish I could remember the particular class of brutality that led to such desperation, but I can't, no matter how I wring my brains. All I can recall is becoming inconsolable, weeping copious tears with my head upon my arms upon the kitchen table and then seeing my father arrive at the front door, ashen with anger, shouting at me to get in the car and shut the hell up.

Then came the tight-lipped monologue that made up the first third of the journey. It went along the lines of, "How could you humiliate my parents? How could you embarrass me in front of them? How could you be so ungrateful? Who are you to turn your nose up at them and their kind hospitality? Who do you think are you? Why do you always have to be so bloody difficult?" and on and on.

It was hardly unexpected, so I sat wordlessly, staring out into the dark, praying my silence was the right thing to do and would not be likely to inflame his bitter fury. I felt the one thing in the world he longed most to do on that long drive home was to lash out in one sublime act of freedom and smash my head into the nearest hard object, in this case the front passenger seat window.

He finally ran out of huff and puff (though never out of contempt), and we drove silently for a while, which struck me as a huge relief, as a silent suggestion that I was perhaps out of immediate danger at least. Then, after a few miles, in a cold, cold voice he said, "I've heard you like to write stories."

"Yes, Dad," I said, confused.

"So you think you have imagination, do you?"

"Maybe. I just like to think of stories."

*"Right then, Miss Smarty-Pants-Too-Good-for-Your-Own-Grandparents, tell me a story."*

*"What?" I said in horror. "Now? What kind of story, Dad?"*

*"Make one up," he sneered, "seeing as you think you're so clever you can look down on other people."*

*"But what about?"*

*He sat silently for a minute as he drove. "I know," he said eventually. "Tell me a story about them." He pointed outside into the murk.*

*"What?" I said in a flat panic. "I can't see anything."*

*"Are you blind, girl? The roadside reflectors. Make up a story about them if you think you're so smart."*

*If I'd known of Scheherazade then, I'd have known just how she felt on at least one long Arabian night.*

*"Well," my father said while I sat silently, trying to gather my wits, "get on with it."*

*And so I did. I found a story as if it had been floating in the ether, waiting for just such a moment when I might need it.*

*With barely a pause for breath, feeling as if only words could stave off the looming chaos, I said: "One day two little aboriginal children, a brother and a sister, were lost in the bush at night—a dark, dark night like this one. The brother thought home was one way, but the sister thought it was to be found in the opposite direction. They talked about this and then decided the quickest way home was not for them to go together but to try both directions separately. But to make sure they didn't lose each other, they decided each would set fire to a branch and stick it in the earth as they went along—to light their path so that whoever arrived home first could then just run along the fiery track to reach the other and lead them home.*

*"And so they did. As it turned out, the brother found it first and then ran back by the light of the burning branches to find his sister and lead her home, and the story was often told afterwards because so many people found it such a good idea. Then when the white people took over the country, they heard the story of the brother and sister and designed reflective sticks to act like the branches to help guide everyone home."*

*As my voice trailed off, I think we were both in shock, for until that moment I had not even known they were called roadside reflectors and also because white kids then were taught nothing about aboriginal people and were given no clue that anyone was here before us.*

*After a few minutes of silence that stretched endlessly, my father growled into the dark, "I told you to make up a story, miss."*

*I wailed, "But I did, Dad. Where would I have read a story about ... about ... roadside reflectors?"*

*And to that, thank God, he had no answer, silently acknowledging, at least, that roadside reflectors were indeed a most-neglected subject within children's literature. Not one more word did he say, in fact, but I felt his eyes upon me at times during that long drive home, glittering in the darkness.*

*I had no idea where the story came from (though I do now), and I look back on this and wonder if I was perhaps given both a life-saving piece of inspiration as well as a glimpse into the future, for this is that story of a brother and sister trying to guide each other home.*

*Not that I knew then, of course, that funny little story would become the story of my life. Then I was simply pleased to have shocked the tyrant into silence and be allowed to live.*

# Chapter 1

# Claire

Do you believe in evil? It's such an old-fashioned concept now, is it not? Almost anything—any behaviour, any derangement—can be explained away by childhood torment, maladjustment, or a psychological disorder. Or perhaps we believe in it only when it looms enormous. Maybe we think of it as secretive, hidden, afraid of the light, but from experience, I can say not only that evil exists but also that it can hide in plain view, right out in the sunshine, sheltering only behind wide smiles and empty gestures and words like *love* and *God*.

It can take root through small, bad choices and small, vicious acts that accumulate over a lifetime until all there is, is evil. I should know. It's been part of my life from the beginning, but it has come from such an unnatural quarter I've had little defence against it. Although it cost me dearly, it killed my brother.

And still now, when he went his way home and I search on, still the evil continues, the whispering and slander, the thwarted rage, the urge to destroy, and sometimes I am afraid. Sometimes I fear for my life too.

*Would she kill me*, I wondered at times, *this mother of mine? I know she aches to do me harm, but could she actually raise her hand against me? Could she run me down in her car as I walk along the street? Set my little flat on fire? Could she poison me with a piece of cake? Or do such fears merely act to make her more powerful than she is?* Perhaps. She'd always loomed so large in my life it was difficult to know her true size, her true capabilities.

Perhaps she would simply limit herself to spiteful backstabbing, to the destruction of the few remaining family relationships I still retained, assassinate my character in lieu of the real deal.

If you could see her, you'd laugh at this, for she is a matronly, plump old lady, a soft-spoken grandmother, a church fanatic, a Catholic holy roller. You'd have to know her to believe it, know her for years, and you'd have to search her eyes whenever she spoke to see the sheen of malice lurking there. I've seen it, and it is a look that could wither roses. Certainly it is a look designed to strike down opposition, to enforce submission, for hers, when she chooses to reveal it, is an endless midnight gaze.

But you'd rarely get a glimpse of that because for over seventy years and more she has become adept at keeping the stones rolled across the gateways to her soul. Only rage can move them, and she is enraged at me. It's lucky I don't see her or my father anymore or I fear I would be turned to stone.

So I've decided to write our story—the story of us, my brother and me, and them, my parents. I want the truth to be known in case she finds a way to silence me—and therefore him—forever. Yet to know us you must know me, so that's where we shall start.

I am somewhat psychic. I have another voice inside my head that belongs to someone else I call Thomas, and for the life of me, I know not whether those two facts are connected. No doubt you think me deceitful or misguided, and all I can say in my defence is that I am not deceitful.

Trust me, for me it is not easy to say I think my mother harbours murderous intentions or to admit I have a separate voice inside my head. You try asking people if they have someone else in residence and you'll see what I mean. Years of sensible behaviour fall away like so much dust, I have found, when you pose that particular question.

But still it's true. I say *voice* because we have to start somewhere, but it is much more than just a voice. It is, or belongs to, a personality, a separate consciousness, yet it is a voice I do not hear. No. It is not audible, is not of the ears at all. It's more like communicating through pure thought.

I know it sounds crazy, but still, Yung knew all about it. In his childhood he described having personality one and personality two, one of this world, one of a far deeper origin, so perhaps we all are two. Perhaps we all start with two and I just never found a way of getting rid of one or the other.

And later, as an adult, he wrote of holding internal nonverbal conversations with a numinous other, a sage, a mystic guru, and Yung wasn't a nutcase. He called his person Philemon, which is obviously far more imaginative than plain old Thomas, but he was Yung and I am me.

Yet although it's hard to explain, this I know: It belongs to a he. He is much wiser than me, and he tells me things I could not possibly know and offers useful advice when I am too upset to think straight.

For many years, given that it is all I have ever known from three years old, I thought everyone had two people in their heads. Then I realised after some early discrete enquiries that they didn't. Then I thought both belonged to me. I thought perhaps the voice was the voice of my subconscious. And perhaps it is, but if it is all I can say is that it isn't very sub.

At one stage, like any rational person would, I thought maybe I was deranged and tried to silence it, him, whoever, shut it out and shout it down. But that didn't work. That in fact was crazy making. So I gave up fighting it—with all the strength of my rationality and reason—a few years ago when I literally had nothing left to lose.

Then after my surrender—or should I say our detente—he asked a favour of me, but lo what a favour.

He said, "Let's write a story together, Claire."

I said, "That would be absurd."

He said, "All you have to do is relax and write down what I say."

I said, "That way may well lie madness."

He said, "Please. What have you got to lose now?"

Well, what could I say? He was right. I am involuntarily childless, a voluntary orphan, and I'm single and alone, a tiny, barren twig on the luxurious family tree of humanity. With no career, money, or assets, I am in this material age almost a nonperson; certainly I am a woman with nothing much left to lose.

And I have to give him that. Thomas is, when he chooses to speak as plainly as he can, almost always right. So I said yes. After forty years of infighting, I said yes (which proves his patience if nothing else).

But don't think I'm playing for pity because strange as this may sound, I've never been happier. Not in all my life. I wake up every day these days tingling with delight, for there is great arm-stretching, heart-easing, mind-expanding freedom to be found at the fingerpost marked nothing left to lose.

It's only the journey here that hurts. And if all you have left is freedom, you'd be mad not to embrace it. So now I'm going to tell the truth. Or my truth at least. Or his.

Now I can say at last that I know this is not rational, reasonable, or normal, but still it is. To have two minds in the one noodle is not reasonable but still it is.

Besides, the more the scientists dig into the brain with their probes and electrodes, their scalpels and microscopes, the greater the mysteries of consciousness appear to be. Where is it actually located? What system drives free will? Where does the concept of "I" originate?

No one knows. It is a mystery, and I love mysteries as much as I love science. But science doesn't love me.

To be in two minds, so to say, and to be somewhat psychic is, from a scientific point of view, impossible. And that means that the world I love—the world of the physicists, the chemists, the biologists, the psychologists, the world I gaze into through my reading like a child into a toy shop—rejects me outright.

Which isn't very nice, is it?

Psychic phenomena cannot be, yet I know it is. I cannot be, yet I know I am.

Over the years I have received information about the future, or psychic flashes as I call them, in the form of an electrical-type fizzing (at a handshake, say), still images, moving pictures like a film reel, prescient dreams, the receipt of absolute knowledge of a future event that takes less time to know than it takes to think the thought, and the dim sound of bells, which I call the doom bells.

I have known (for better or worse) who I would love. I have known who I would lose. I have seen accidents waiting to happen. I have even seen a ghost, who gave me such a fright I thought I could vomit up my heart. Yet obviously never have I been able to do one thing about anything.

In many ways, it is a useless, confusing, paralysing ability, and only now, after all these years, have I been able to understand that, for me at least, it is without a moral component, without intrinsic meaning; it is simply an element of time.

That is to say that when I felt the fizzing handshake of a future lover, I did indeed see it as destiny and so it proved to be. But in most cases I should have run. Do you see? I thought the feeling meant that it—the love affair—was *meant* to be but in fact all it meant was that it *was* to be, which is not much help at all.

Yet perhaps the greatest mystery is that these glimpses can create a time loop in which knowing the future can create the future or even stranger, that the future can intervene to create a past. And that means time may not only and ever flow in one direction.

The quantum physicists know all about this—that a future event can create its own past. It seems that subatomic particles are doing it all the time. They, for example, can be both a wave and a particle, but they exist only as a potential wave or particle until they are measured or observed. Only after that do they become one or the other with their own past as one or the other, a past that is created only *after* they become one or the other.

And stranger still, they are only either a wave or a particle if or when we look, meaning that the very building blocks of the universe interact with human consciousness. And that means our minds matter to matter, to everything.

Here's how it is often explained. Imagine you go to a remote village and the witch doctor tells you he can do magic. He chooses a man and a woman, has them stand before two huts, and places a blindfold over your eyes. Then he says, "Choose whether you think the man and woman will be in one hut together or in separate huts."

You think, *You call this magic?* You make your choice. You say together, and the witch doctor takes off your blindfold and indeed they are together. You say apart and they are apart.

The magic comes in when you finally realise that whatever you choose is the correct choice, that there is no time delay and therefore no history to the activity of the couple and you are never wrong. You choose and there they are. How do they know which choice you will make? What happens with time? Where were they before you chose?

In quantum physics, this phenomenon means if you look for waves within an atom, you will always find waves; if you look for particles, guess what you'll find? Every single time. But what were those tiny masses of energy before they were observed, and what was happening with—and in—time? Mystery upon mystery.

Here's how I once experienced this time shift. Once upon a time when I was living in a small inner-city terrace, I decided to clean the glass sliding doors that opened from the living area onto the small inner-city courtyard. Though a rare thing to decide to do and an even rarer thing to actually do, this is not the spooky bit. No, the spooky bit came later on that long, hot summer evening when I took a glass of wine outside and slid closed the doors behind me.

It was beautiful out there, I remember, and I was peacefully listening to the birds settling down for the night and the crickets starting up when, to my surprise and with my eyes wide open, a film reel began to run in my head.

First it showed me turning in the direction of the brightly lit living room. Then it showed me walking straight into the freshly cleaned glass doors with the hand holding my wine glass taking the force of the impact. Next I saw that wine glass shatter, blood from my hand dripping onto the bluestone below, my partner leaping to his feet in alarm at the sound of the splintering glass and me standing frozen with a look of profound and utter shock upon my face.

Then in the film I saw him open the door, lead me inside, grab a towel to stem the bleeding, take me into the bathroom and hold my hand under the cold water, pick some glass from the wound, check that it wasn't so bad, wrap it up securely, and seat me on the couch.

Now here is the strange bit.

In the film version I did not say a word because I was so shocked, literally speechless. My eyes were like saucers, and I, as the viewer, thought this was hilarious. I knew I'd never react that way, being a hardy sort and more than passingly familiar with broken wine glasses. That, I thought, would never happen, so I put it out of my mind.

Then, in the dying light, as I bent down to do a little weeding of the small inner-city flower bed, the phone rang, whereupon I stood up, grabbed my wine glass, and yes, walked straight into the door.

I was utterly shocked, just as the vision had shown me I would be, but I was shocked not at what had happened but that it *had* happened. The look on my face, my speechlessness, was a direct consequence of having seen the future. More, it was seeing that look that made me dismiss the vision and thus even ordinary caution that had allowed the event to occur, as if the future had intervened to create itself.

If I hadn't seen that absurd look upon my face, I might have paid more attention. I couldn't speak for ten minutes. I couldn't believe it just as I had foreseen I couldn't believe it. But I have the scar to prove it.

So you see, this time-shift sensitivity is a useless gift and unlike all I have ever read about people with psi, I have never been able to use the information for any useful purpose.

I've never been able to head off catastrophe, never been able to save those I loved, never been able to extricate myself from an emotional disaster sooner rather than later. I've lived in a haunted house and felt only terror and sorrow and have been more often than not paralysed by the future rather than galvanised into preventive action.

It is useless. But still it is.

And having Thomas in my head is an added complication. For example, he wants to start this story at the beginning, and I want to start at the end. I want to write a murder mystery, and he wants to write a morality tale. Do you see how confusing this situation can be? (Easy for him to say, "Just go with the flow"; it's me who has to do the heavy lifting. See why I think he's a he?)

Anyway, I shall try to accommodate us both. Clearly to make this reality of mine believable to you, gentle reader, I know it would be more dramatic to write with two vastly different voices. But I (Claire) can't do that. He (Thomas) comes through me, you see, and so is limited by my limitations, which must be quite exasperating for him I'm sure.

From the little I know of his views, his cosmology, his reality is beyond my knowledge and way beyond my spirituality, for I am an earth-bound soul. But I have given him my word at last that even when I panic and hesitate, even when I plead against it, when he says, "Write this down, Claire," I shall write it down. And I can say that after years of squabbling and argument, there is a certain peace in surrender.

To finally say, "This is what happened. This is the world as we know it." To feel both sorry for it all and amazed at the wonder of these, our fleeting years amongst the billions. To tell of the sorrow and the joy, the brokenness and repair.

So welcome to my world, and when it gets strange, picture me saying, "Oh Thomas, I can't write that." And then imagine a voice in your head as familiar as that of your best friend saying, "Now Claire, you gave your word. You made a promise."

Well what can a reasonable person say to that? And should I tell you at the outset how I came to name him Thomas? (He says yes—and so it starts!)

One Christmas, so long ago now, I drove to the country to spend the festive season with my family. While I was away, two friends stayed over at my place with my housemate after their apartment mysteriously caught on fire on Christmas Eve.

A couple, they slept in my room, and upon my return to the city, I felt both sorry to hear of their misfortune and glad that my absence had proved to be of help. On my first night back, we all went to the pub, whereupon Joe, one half of the pair, said to me, "I had the strangest experience of my life a couple of nights ago in your room, Claire. I woke up in the middle of the night feeling like there was something odd about your room. I opened my eyes and sat up and saw this sort of glowing man standing by the window, looking out.

"I don't think we actually talked like people talk, but when he turned to me, he let me know he was with you, attached to you somehow, but he couldn't be with you for some reason. He said his name was Thomas, he said that all was well, that I should go back to sleep. And do you know, Claire? Although it felt absolutely extraordinary, I did as directed and just went back to sleep."

Joe stared at me, at his partner, at my housemate, and we all stared back.

So I call the voice Thomas, and while I get the impression that is not his original name, he has never objected. Neither has he shown himself to me, which seems a bit unfair, for every woman could do with a sort of glowing man in her life, don't you think?

He wants to go next, but don't blame me for what he has to say. I gave my word, as you know. Yet perhaps as you get to know him, you can answer the question that has long, long baffled me: who, or what, is Thomas?

# Chapter 2

# Thomas

God exists. I should know. I've been around (almost) from the beginning.

Yet while I honour his holy name, I've got to say sometimes this experiment of his—this effort with humanity—looks more like a catastrophe to me than a good idea. And so long in the making, so much trouble to bring forth your stream of life, yet always you cause him more grief than joy. And so little understanding between the two of you when, as far as I've been able to determine, the whole human affair was designed so he could be known.

If you think of him at all now, you seem to think of vengeance and retribution, of violent, thunderous judgement, of ironic unreason, of playing favourites, of pedantry, of cruelty, of indifference.

Some of you think of him as a force but not a consciousness. Some of you think of him as a principal. Heaven help us, some of you even think of him as the sort who supplies virgins to the worthy.

God as a panderer? Really, people. How offensive.

If he wasn't God, I tell you, he would have turned his back on the plan ages ago. And though you've been told he is love, you just don't seem to understand this central, guiding principle behind all things, as if you think that just because true and perfect love is hard for you it's hard for him.

So ask yourself: What is love? Is love to care beyond all things for the well-being of the beloved? Is it to put yourself second, to be subtle, to be patient, to be hopeful, forgiving, forbearing, kind? Of course it is. It is to want the best over the long term, not just this four-score and ten years you worry over so. Take it from me, that is nothing. Nothing.

To love and be loved, just exactly the same desire that drives most of you almost as if you were created in his image. To love and be loved.

It never seemed such a complex notion then and certainly not impossible, but I'll let you in on a little secret that has been going around our circles for a while now. Some of us think, from what we've been told, seen ourselves, and overheard, that while he knows now how hard love is for you, he didn't then. Not at the beginning.

Then he thought that it would be a natural, evolutionary development. But that was right at the start, at the very flaring forth, the birth of the idea of you, you might say.

Meeting you was another thing altogether, and it is true, there were times earlier on when he was angry and did destroy, but it was only the shock of the new, you understand, the disappointment, and not a permanent state. And of course, it didn't fix anything, those floods and fires, the pestilence and plague, or not for very long.

He hated doing it anyway. Destruction, really, is not in his nature. But you were new to him, as I said, and he'd been waiting for so long.

Perhaps it was only to be expected, and he hasn't done anything like it for millennia. Besides, even in those far-off days, he brought forth sublime, subtle, and fabulous wonders too (as always), but the patriarchs gave such stories scant regard, finding in them no useful lessons in terror or retribution, and I've often wondered over the years and years what view you'd have of God now if women had been allowed to tell the tale.

But they were kept quiet, and his gentleness goes mostly unknown. He suffers that unknowing as a sort of cosmic heartache that to us throbs through the universe in waves of pain. When so little of his power, his splendid creativity, is understood or appreciated, when to give eternally *is* his defining feature, only to receive such rare gratitude, must be heartbreaking.

And his heart is so broken, let there be no doubt. I bet you never think of God as sad. You seem much more comfortable with angry. Perhaps thinking of God as sad makes you feel responsible. Well, you are.

He should have stuck with us, or those of us who were left. But no. Without spelling it out, he made it clear, as only he can, that we were perfect as far as we went, but that the challenge, the purpose of the experiment, was to work with the imperfect, to see if he could turn clay into gold from a distance, using only the power of love.

And sometimes it does work. Sometimes it does, but not often and not often enough.

I'd describe him as the wisest, most benevolent of kings abandoned by his people, but that doesn't even come close. For, of course, he's nothing like your old kings of myth, legend, or history.

How many of them set the stars in motion, gave each element and particle a desire to be, to form, to cooperate, to create, and waited for time beyond time just for you? Though they were good times then, before you, so much excited anticipation; all of us innocent, hopeful, wanting the best for him, for you.

For you.

But you probably reject the notion of kingship, of authority, of majesty because you believe in democracy. So I'll spell it out—so does he. So does he, for there can be no love without choice.

Then, in those early days, before you, when his grand design was rolling itself out across the universe, free will even then was at the very centre of it all. What risk that carried but also, as I said, great excitement.

As you know, not all of us agreed. Some of us felt very keenly that it was a monumental demotion. Having you at the centre of it all? It filled them with rage (surely you are at least familiar with this story), and they chose not only to go but also to work against him forever to pay him back, to revenge the slight.

How traumatic that was, I remember, our world descending so rapidly from harmony to chaos when it became clear what he had in mind. He tried to talk them round, but they were filled with so much hate and thwarted pride they could not stay, not with him, so they turned towards a new master, his most beloved, his greatest betrayer.

Just for you, to be, in case you missed it, democratic. To give you a choice.

I've spent so much time down here, this time in particular, wondering if he ever really understood what you would do with that choice, for it was, as I said, an experiment. Yet a glance through your history is enough to make a soul scream (not least for the traces left always by the others).

And even now when you have almost destroyed the planet that took billions of years to create just for you, did he see that coming, that greed and thoughtlessness? Did he know?

I tell you truly, you have not seen heartbreak and disillusioned horror if you haven't seen God.

And here's another point. What other king of your myth, legend, history could blot out this catastrophe in a heartbeat? Go back to before? Start again? None. But he could. Yet he doesn't. It's called love. It's called hope. He is nothing if not determined to play this whole thing out to its finale.

Many of us tried to talk him out of you—both at the beginning and at the first signs of trouble—but he gently rejected that advice. But that was then and this is now. Now we don't even mention it, not wanting to add to his sorrow. We just go about our duties as best we can. And while we do our best, our best is never enough because of the limitations placed upon us at the outset, which he simply refuses to revise.

For example—our shouting of guidance down here is heard as a whisper if at all, bad will makes us ill, and we cannot communicate with each other to boost our flagging spirits or combine our voices because if we could, I can assure you, things on planet earth would be very different indeed.

But that is not allowed (have you got it yet?) because it would impact on your free will. We can't impose our will, we can't (at my level) engage with the others, and we're so very rarely asked for help.

We can stand right in front of you—we know you feel us—trying to impart some wisdom, some aspect of a deeper truth than is found in your frantic, distracted lives, even to give solace and strength, but to very little purpose. We try so hard to help (not only to please him but to avoid being sent down here again too soon, always too soon), but you shut your eyes, close your heart, or switch off that part of your brain purposely designed to aid communication.

We're here to guide you through the dark, to protect you from the others, to walk beside you through the valley of the shadow of death, so to speak, but we cannot do much if you won't let us in.

But most of you don't believe in us or the others, or good or bad. But how can you choose good if you don't believe in bad? Which, in case you're still confused, is the point of this fourteen-billion-year exercise.

Bad is. Evil is. Trust me. Evil is and has ever been since the others made their calamitous choice. That choice means bad is simply and only and ever about choice. Only and ever, and it has two defining features.

One: It has to prevail. It has to win, to get an advantage, to impose itself upon others, which means the fight between good and evil is never, can never be, a standoff because it *always* seeks to win. If it didn't need to prevail, it wouldn't be evil, it would be weak, and God has a soft heart towards weakness. (Well, we all do. We couldn't function down here on any level if we didn't.) People corrupted by evil have to win, and if their will has not prevailed, all they do is bide their time, waiting to regain the advantage. Within that time, all that is, is hate.

Two: It is based solely on individual ego. No one ever, ever does evil out of altruism. Bad people don't do bad things because it makes them feel bad. It's not the malicious, conniving people who are lying awake at night, worried and anxious about their shortcomings. Trust me. They are some of the best sleepers ever born. They thrill to the pain of others and ache for domination because they like it. Bad action suits them. It delivers (money, power, sex); it boosts their self-importance and makes them feel like … God.

You all think you know this, that you were born with the knowledge wired into your DNA, but these days you just don't seem to want to believe it. It's another inconvenient truth. But if you don't believe in bad, you can have no heroes, and honestly, you could not find a more effective way to bland out your existences than to kill off the heroes.

You can't cheer on a goodie doing battle with a personality disorder, can you? But don't you miss the magic? Don't you want your lives to be rich, thrilling, to count?

You people had far more spark, more jazz about you when you believed in an entire pantheon of Gods compared to now, when it appears to be beneath you to even believe in one. I hesitate to even mention the word *evil* because you're so confused philosophically, psychologically, you think even evil is a joke. Some joke.

I know I sound angry. I know I should be more empathetic, but I'm tired. I want to go home and be close to him and add my small voice to the choir of consolation. But he's not angry. Not God. Not anymore. He is just despondent—well, almost inconsolable on a monumental scale, I should say. But the key word here is *almost*.

I know it's hard for you to imagine him—given that whenever you knock your heads on the ceiling of your own limitations, you blame him—but I wish you would try.

You say, "God can't be universal and personal."

Yes he can.

You say, "God can't be all powerful and gentle."

Yes he can.

You say, "God can't be a loving, just God and allow cruelty to exist."

Yes he can.

Of course he can. How else could you choose one over the other or stand up for your brothers and sisters or bring about justice? How, if not this way, could you choose love over hate, him over the other?

His tears exist. They are real. But perhaps I should mention that so too is his laughter, his joy. I bet you don't think of God as easily and readily and warmly amused either. But what is love without laughter? And there are days, even I must admit, when he thinks you are hilarious. But they are few and far between now. All he wants is to be known, but you're as ignorant as ever.

Let me make this explicit. The part of you that he cherishes is your soul, and yes, you do have a soul. Haven't you seen anyone die? Haven't you felt the absence, the departure?

Just because you can't poke it with a stick, measure it, describe it, pin it to paper like a dead butterfly does not mean it does not exist. It exists. It is the point. And it is like a garden.

Think of it that way—a soul garden, your own tiny plot of paradise. Every time you act outside the framework of love, it is as if you have poured poison on the flowerbed. Depending on the act, really, it could be a few drops of acid to the dumping of the rusting chassis of a broken-down car.

Big and small, but all ugly, building up over time until nothing good can live there, some people creating such garbage dumps, such eyesores, that even they feel compelled to close the gate and abandon it altogether.

But cleaning it up is so easy.

All you have to do is look at each piece of rubbish, of rusting junk and rotting refuse, and be sorry for it. That's it. You just have to be sorry for it, and it is gone before you've even finished thinking the thought. Though I know how confused you get with time, so I had better make this clear: the bigger the junk, the longer you need to look at it, from every angle, acknowledging the ramifications and being sorry for it all.

Then it disappears, as if it had never been.

God wants to be with you. He is on your side; he leans towards you. It couldn't really be easier, could it? But you think that to love him, you need to sign up to come creed, some credo, some cult.

You think God belongs to the Jews (the law) or the Buddhists (transcendence) or the Muslims (responsibility) or the Christians (compassion), that he is the power behind the Hindu pantheon, the honour in Shintoism. Well, he is. He is all of this and more, but it is the more that is the central problem inherent in all your religions, for each one seeks to contain him, to set his limits, to pin him down and draw his outline even though the most definable quality of God is his absolute uncontainability.

He is bigger than the universe and smaller than an atom; he is everywhere and nowhere, observable in all things and invisible to the eye. How on earth can you think to contain him? But of course, this does not mean you cannot know him. To know him, just follow his lead made manifest from the beginning—that is, choose creation over destruction, beauty over ugliness, good over evil.

All you need to do is thank him and love him for his wonders, for waterfalls and rainbows, for your gently sleeping children, for a day without pain.

That's it. Could it be easier?

Every time one of you says, "I love you, God," or "Thank you, God," his heart mends a little; just those two phrases—nothing life changing (though in fact it is), nothing that costs anything.

Just try it, I beg you—if not for him, if not for yourselves, then for us because his pain is almost killing us down here now.

I wish I could go home, but I've still got a fair way to go here. Or I think I do, for we, like you, are never really sure. We have to wing it too.

But while I've got this rare access (dear Claire), I want to explain why it matters, these choices that you make, but to do that you need to understand evil beyond the vague grasp you have of evil writ large. You understand the horrors of the Hitlers and the Stalins, but you seem to think they are not you.

But who gave them support, these superstars of hatred? Who carried them on their backs and raised them most high? Yes, you know, people just like you.

Take it from me, who has seen enough down here over centuries to make your blood run cold, bad is bad is everywhere, and it can begin in such tiny, inconsequential droplets as to be able to settle on others as softly as dew until it weighs like lead. It is manipulative, it is deliberate, it seeks the weak spot, it thrills to suffering, and it can only exist within a framework of deceit, for it follows, like sunflowers the sun, the urgings of him, the prince of lies. You know the one.

When the prophets and the thinkers said the truth will set you free, take it from me, they meant it absolutely literally. Bad cannot coexist with truth because with truth (no matter how horrible) comes understanding and the ability to resist. When labouring under deceit and manipulation, of course, you can never untangle the chains.

Yet from my your-world-weary perspective, one of the great flaws in this experiment, one of the very many in my humble opinion, is the working of your minds or that particularly frustrating aspect of them that means that all of you (it seems to me) see the world and others through the prism of your own characters.

The greedy people only see others trying to rip them off; the egotists see only others trying to hog the limelight; the cruel and vengeful see only slights and reasons to hate. I'd leave them to it really if I had my way, for there is a place waiting for them, but the problem, the central, crucial problem, is that the good souls (yes, there are a few) see only good.

They give the benefit of the doubt, they accept shortcomings as aberrations, they deal with others gently, and they forgive. In a word, they are often absolutely hopeless when confronted with evil; wounded, confused, maddened, the best at times destroyed by the worst because they cannot see or believe in cruelty. They cannot comprehend that there are people who can say love and mean hate, people who can promise loyalty and deliver treachery, people who can look others right in the eyes and lie and lie and lie.

And without the goodies, the baddies flourish, and that makes us sick, physically sick (so to say), because those of us at my level are not made for this malice, this harm. And that means that if we are to be of any use at all, we too often have to remove ourselves from bedrooms, from kitchens, offices, schools, churches (!), and on and on, from parliaments to playgrounds even whole provinces once or twice in your history.

Which leaves a gap, I'm sure you can imagine, certainly a gap wide enough for the others to get in, and only the most powerful of us can deal with them face-to-face, certainly not me, which means I've spent much of this lifetime hanging around outside, sitting under the veranda, leaning up against the trees.

Yet while I think of it, here is a tip. If you ever walk into a place, a house, a public building, even a forest glade and it feels good then it is good because it means we are there. Conversely, if you enter space and feel a fluttering malevolence in the air, rest assured we are not. That will be them, not us.

If you have created a warm and loving atmosphere anywhere, anywhere at all, don't let the bad people in, for they bring the others with them. It takes a long time for us to feel it safe to come back in, and really we're sick and tired of hanging around outside.

Think about us for a change. We're here to help. I'm pretty sure we were designed for that purpose.

But perhaps I shouldn't be so cranky, for now I am inside, now Claire and I are one again and I'm guarding her space like her life depends upon it, particularly as we tell this story, for there is so much hate and thwarted domination directed towards her now that sometimes even I get the shivers.

But we are powerful if you let us be. All you have to do is choose.

# Chapter 3

# Claire

Now it's back to me, Claire, and if I could whisper on paper I'd whisper this: *Who the hell is Thomas?*

He's rather spiritual, don't you think, profoundly God-ish, and I can state with some authority that sharing your head space with a metaphysical, elliptical, spiritual consciousness is not as easy as it may sound. Ha!

If I'd ever been given a choice in the matter, I'd have gone for a sardonic, droll, agnostic voice to share my noodle with, but I wasn't. No, he's been there since I thought my first thought, and we've just had to make the best of it. Still, I know that whatever my disappointment in him has been as nothing to his in me at various points along the way.

Yet we're very close now even though writing his contribution, for a nonreligious person such as myself, involved quite a lot of horrified prevarication. Even now I am not sure I would have given him my word had I known he wanted to write that. So you must take it or leave it; that's all I can advise. That's what I have learnt to do.

Anyway, now that I know he means to tell a mystical tale, a sort of *Pilgrim's Progress*, I'll try to keep my side more earthbound and practical. Consider it a metaphor for the yin-yang of life inside my head. Still, my story is a murder mystery, as I said, and it is true so it will be dark. How else could it be?

Yet I'm afraid to say that telling my brother's story requires telling my own because so much of his was kept hidden from me, and those who know the truth refuse to tell it. I also know now that what was done to him was (almost) done to me and what was done to me was done to him. We were soul mates. We were connected. We were like twin electrons smashed repeatedly within our nuclear family.

In other words, we were entangled. Have you heard that phrase before? It too comes from the crazy world of quantum physics and describes a phenomenon once described by Einstein as "spooky action at a distance."

He was referring to the puzzling phenomenon in which twin subatomic particles interact with each other instantaneously no matter how far apart they are. Change the oscillation of one and you change the other—instantaneously. Change the spin direction of one and you change the other over fractions of a millimetre or across a million miles at the exact same moment in time.

My brother and I were entangled, the macrocosm of human life on planet earth to the microcosm of the invisible substance of matter. What is above, so it is below. Or that's how it seems to me.

Anyway, as I said, Thomas wants to start at the beginning and I at the end, but given that I'm the one holding the pen, I'm going to start with how I came to be here, a woman alone, a little twig, a nonperson, and that, gentle reader, starts with a story about other nonpeople—yes, a ghost story. Hoorah!

Two years ago, I wasn't alone. Two years ago, I was living with a man we shall call Mark for no reason whatsoever. Two years ago, we had been together for seven long years. We were in a very dark place by then, and I'm not speaking architecturally.

In the few years preceding, it had felt to me as if Death had sidled up beside me, taken a seat on the couch, and begun to pick off my dearest people, one by one, in no particular order. By the time this story takes place, I had lost three beloveds in traumatic, tragic circumstances in four years, with another dear friend, only thirty-six, slowly dying of a rare, incurable cancer.

In between, in a totally shocking twist, I'd also become so sick that I required surgery, which made me unable to have children before I'd had a family, the future and the past dead, dying, lost.

It was harrowing and unrelenting and you might despise me for saying this, but it also felt sort of personal. None of the dead or dying knew each other, none moved in remotely similar circles, and all their loved ones (well, almost all) felt their loss as unique and dreadful as if a meteor had slammed into their world out of a clear blue sky.

But I, on the other hand, the only common denominator, felt it as an almost constant cosmic bombardment, and every time I found the strength to stand up and gaze upon the ruins of my life upon their passing and to contemplate the process of rebuilding, there came another phone call.

Even as I write this, it seems to me that I may still have post-traumatic stress disorder from my visitation from Death, for even now I cannot pick up the phone without a gut twist of fear, and it's been three years since I've wailed at a graveside.

Still, such an experience does change your life, so perhaps it is to be expected, particularly for one such as me, or as I was then: an autonomous, educated ruler of my universe like so many of us believe ourselves to be.

We think the worst can't happen, but it can.

We think disasters won't strike us, but they do.

We think the sky will never fall, but it does.

It can, and it does.

And I learned two things then in that time of darkness that felt almost as earth quaking.

Other people who knew me then also felt it, this unfortunate series of events, to be, even on a subconscious level, personal. That is, many of them gave me the distinct impression that they thought my misfortunes, my sorrow and loss, might be … contagious.

Instead of finding shelter, I was shunned. Instead of finding comfort, I was cast out into the cold to limit the possible spread of infection.

It was an eye-opening experience I can tell you, and I felt like Job without the faith or patience.

I mean, I know people don't like losers, but still, I had no idea this aspect of human nature could possibly play itself like that in terms of actual, blameless loss.

Even my family turned their backs and looked the other way while leading me to believe I was more than welcome to tap them on the collective shoulder when I had cheered myself up a bit or when the crisis had passed, which was a bit rich given that the greatest cause of grief then and now has always been my family and the shocking death of my brother.

But we did not speak of that for that, as one of my sisters informed me, was the rule. We were to bury his memory as efficiently as we had buried his body, and that was an unspoken but direct order from the management.

I would have had a nervous breakdown to be honest, but I didn't know how. I just kept going, but I did think deeply and frequently about the merits of suicide. How could I not? All my dearest people, it seemed, were on the other side having found this one unbearable, and I knew just how they felt.

But to state the obvious (Thomas is laughing), I didn't.

First I said I'd do it tomorrow, which meant I could survive today. Then tomorrow became next week, next week became next month, and so on. It's a somewhat-grim survival strategy, I know, but still, it worked.

Another reason I resisted that particular siren song was the family. Consciously, I thought that after my brother I couldn't do it to them. Actually, however, I think it was more that I knew if I did take up that option they would say it was only to have been expected, that I had always been unstable, that perhaps it was for the best—everything they had said about my brother. They would have buried me and the thought of me just as profoundly as they buried had him, and strangely, I seemed to find just enough stubbornness to offset the allure of nothingness.

So I stayed, but here's the other thing I learned: when you're weak, you're prey, and the predator in my case was my partner, the man I loved and trusted, for bad and troubled times can bring out bad and troubled traits. For many reasons, we should never have been together in the first place, not least because when I first laid eyes upon him, Thomas began positively shouting in my head, "No, Claire, no. Don't even think about it."

But I wasn't listening to him then.

Also the somewhat romantic and peculiar nature of our meeting all those years ago made it hard for me to resist him at the start and walk away at the end, to turn my back upon him, on us, even on what we had become. It seemed destined, you see, oh foolish woman I was then, seeing signs and wonders when they were actually signs of warning.

How hard we struggle for meaning.

We met within the very first minutes of my birthday, which in itself is often enough to turn a girl's head with thoughts of fate. I'd been taken out to dinner the night before to a posh restaurant by a gay boy friend (oh sigh), all frocked up (me, not him) and feeling kind of groovy as I waved good-bye to my housemate, who was also leaving for a big night, a binge night, with friends she had not seen for years.

They were happy days in that house with her—before Death arrived—with the only fly in that sweet ointment being that the house was slowly falling down around us; rising damp, sagging ceilings, slugs in strange places, and a front door that no longer shut because of the warping of the wooden frame from the previous long, hot summer.

We made do with locking the metal security door instead, but note, the main door had not closed or come near to closing for four long months. So off we both went out into the night.

Frustratingly, my date (so to speak) was a self-confessed nanna who dropped me home at about 11:00 p.m. in a hurry to enjoy the comforts of his robe and slippers.

Still, it was a glorious autumn night, with a warm, restless wind sighing through the red and golden leaves of the plane trees that lined the street, possibly, by late April, the last such one for five grey and dreary months.

I couldn't settle. It wasn't my birthday yet, so I kicked off my heels, poured a glass of wine, and took it outside to the front porch to see it in. *How lovely*, I thought as I watched the trees and the passing cars, curled up in an old lounge chair we kept out there for just such a night until—have you guessed?—yes a gust of wind, not very forceful, simply blew the front door shut.

I could not believe it. I could not. I stared at the door in utter bewilderment.

So there I was, stuck outside with no shoes, no keys, no money, and no expectation of seeing my housemate much before 5:00 a.m. on my birthday. If I'd had shoes, I could have walked somewhere. If I'd had money, I could have hailed a cab. What to do? What to do? What would you have done?

I went to the pub. It was only three doors up the street (fine for tender bare city feet), and surprise, surprise, I was known there. I explained my predicament to the barmaid, and she let me use the phone, but it being a Saturday night, no one I knew was home.

Then she said I could stay there at least till closing time and run up a tab that could be paid on the morrow. It was a better plan than any I could come up with, and as I made my way from the lounge to the bar, I saw him. I saw Mark, and simply thought him the most handsome man I had ever seen.

Oh foolish woman.

He noticed my lack of footwear, he made me laugh, he wished me happy birthday, he bought me some champagne, and I just melted like an ice cream in the sun. He was drunk, which should have been a warning, but it was Saturday night so a lot of people were, and I was lonely and perfectly ripe for trouble.

So I took him home with me, which I must say impressed my housemate to no end for the rare feat of leaving home with one man and returning with another, so at least it was good for a laugh at the start.

I wouldn't go near such a scene now—not least because I now listen to Thomas—but also because in those days, those salad days, I thought I knew all there was to know. They say it's an ill wind that blows no good, yet while we had some good times, still the balance would suggest that was one ill wind.

And seven years later, I knew nothing, absolutely nothing, not even how to leave. But he thought he knew a thing or two. He thought me beaten by the sorrow. He thought me cowed by pain. He thought I'd never leave and that knowledge in the wrong head can eat away at love and respect like a cancer.

So what had once been thoughtless disregard in the early years of our union became deliberate emotional abuse in the latter. What had been occasional lies and evasions became outright betrayals. What had been social, chatty drinking became rage-fuelled, hate-filled drunkenness.

And I had been so lost in the fog of sadness and madness that it was as if I'd awakened to a different man.

Like other people then in my life, he thought me a loser, so all civilised bets were off, all for the simple, enormous thought that I was too fucked to flee, as I too felt myself to be, using what scarce resources I had to find a way to forgive, to believe, to accept his flowers, for I did not want to go.

I did not want to have to start again. I did not want to lose someone else I had loved. I did not wish to be pecked alive by my buzzard family, and I could not, would not accept another defeat.

What a foolish woman I was.

So on those nights when he said he'd be home by six and staggered in at eleven, itching for a fight, I fought but I stayed. On those nights when he started the fight at six so he could leave, I fought but I stayed.

The nights he smashed dishes, coffee tables, when he screamed that I was a barren bitch, that I should have done more to save my friends, when he showered and changed for a big weekend on a Friday night and did not return until Sunday, I fought, but to my great shame, I stayed.

And he, of course, saw me stay and was glad at what he saw, for here's something else I learned in that precariously steep learning curve. When you love an alcoholic, you, as the partner, man or woman, think yourself deserving of more gratitude and respect for putting up with so much crap.

They think you deserving of less respect for putting up with so much crap. A very hard lesson learned that one.

But don't get me wrong. I was no innocent victim in all this misery. I was by then a shrew, a termagant, a screaming banshee, a change that had come over me on the very day it had dawned upon me that his behaviour was not a function of weakness (as it had been) but of strength and power, that it was not thoughtless but thought out and that still I could not leave. Then my self-loathing reached a pitch or depth that not even I, an old hand, had thought possible.

By the time of this story, he and I were sleeping in separate bedrooms, me, on those nights of betrayal with my door locked, not, as you might think, to keep him out but more to keep me in, even just to put the turning of a key between us because my imprisonment (self-imposed, the very worst kind) and his exploitation of it (having come to relish the owning of a slave) were taking us into murder-suicide territory, a very black place indeed.

And I could have been the murderer, which is not a very nice thing to know about yourself, is it? I could have stabbed him through the heart with a kitchen knife, but then I would have had to go through with the suicide part right then and there or spend the rest of my life in orange overalls, and orange has never been my colour.

Some nights he'd have his hands around my throat, and I'd be screaming inside, "Do it! Do it! If I can't leave and you can't love, just fucking do it."

He was quite a vain man, though, tall, dark, and handsome, and I don't think he relished the thought of orange any more than I did. Do you think so many countries choose orange for their prison garb for this reason? That it's capable of stopping people from committing atrocities just because no one wants to wear it? God knows. I don't know.

We were the neighbours from hell, with both outside walls adjoining other happy homes, which added no end of misery to me, a usually quiet person. I feel nauseated even now thinking about those people, what they must have heard, how dreadful it must have sounded, how tempted they must have been to call the police. They probably expected to be woken up any night with body bags being removed from our house. Wretched, wretched days.

But what was even stranger than all this baleful, hateful bitterness is that in between the raging anguish, we got on quite well. What a piece of work is (wo)man! He'd offer a halfhearted apology, I'd give it a halfhearted acceptance, and on we'd wrestle, to paraphrase Tennessee Williams, not so much living together as sharing the same cage.

So for you lucky souls who have ever wondered, like I once did, how domestic violence begins or continues, well, now you know. It's simply fear (me) and loathing (him), very old hat.

By then, of course, the house, like the universe, was filled with so much dark energy pushing us apart while keeping us in motion that, well, it would have been a surprise if ghosts hadn't popped in, don't you think?

Still, it was a shock, even for me, who was then still spending a large portion of my thinking time thinking about the dead. But that was to be expected under the circumstances, and they were known to me after all.

Dead strangers were of a different order altogether.

But wait. Thomas says it's his turn. He's being a bit impatient, if you ask me, but he says he has waited a very long time to say what he wants to say and so wishes me, to put it simply, to let him. Oh well, I gave my word.

# Chapter 4

# Thomas

Her birth was no cause for celebration, I can tell you. It should have been (as for all new life, so much time in the making, from dinosaurs to dragonflies, etc.) but it wasn't.

Looking back I think I was the only one in the least bit pleased with her arrival, but then I'd been waiting a fair while, it must be said, and had been led to expect big things. It was a bit disconcerting because it wasn't just a strange anticlimax, a "thank God that's over with"; it was more menacing than that.

I remember I felt queasy. Not a good sign.

How can I explain it? Think of longed-for births, the tummy holding, the crooning, the wonder and fear, the miracle of the universe coming wrapped up as a tiny bundle, and then think of the opposite. And by that I mean it wasn't the despair and exhaustion of a mother with too many children and not enough resources. It wasn't even hate, I don't think, looking back. Not then.

It was not: "Oh no, not another mouth to feed. How am I going to manage?" It wasn't even a feeling of worn responsibility. It was a nothing. A blank. A poverty of spirit I wasn't prepared for.

As the baby was handed to the mother, the child certainly did not give rise to that numinous moment of first-ever eye contact or spark that ageless question asked by post-partum mothers everywhere and in every era of: "So where did you come from then, little one?" Or "Who are you then, I wonder?"

No. There was nothing like that at all. This birth was met by a monumental yawn, with the mother keeping her eyes tightly shut, praying for the nurses to take the thing away.

From what I was able to gather, even then, right at the beginning, even in those first few moments of life, the cause of this cold indifference could be summarised by the following: It happened in rural Australia in the 1960s. It happened in a rural 1960s Australian Catholic family. The baby was a girl. She was the second girl.

And oh so many reasons, she had kept her parents waiting for a whole month after her estimated time of arrival, which was an unforgivable sin, perhaps her original sin, because these parents did not like to be kept waiting, not by a child and certainly not by a girl.

And last, that extra cooking time had given her a large head, so large in fact that it would take two long years for enough white blonde hair to cover it, making her look like a strange little alien, which, of course, she was.

To sum up this arrival, then, the creature was a daughter, a useless second daughter, she was late, and she was ugly.

As soon as it was decent to do so, the mother begged the nurses, her prayers having gone again unanswered (ha!), to take the baby away to the nursery, and then fell fast asleep as if nothing at all had happened.

Later, when the father came to visit with his beloved firstborn son and pretty curly-headed first daughter, he took one look at the swaddled bundle and seemingly confused himself about the time anomaly, stared at his wife and said, "Not much to look at."

"No," said the mother, "not much."

Looking closely, really I think for the first and last time, the father said, "It doesn't look like the others."

"No," said the mother, "it doesn't."

They stared at each other, her just daring him to express his intensely jealous suspicions. The butcher? The baker? But he backed down, as she knew he would. She went to mass twice a week, after all, meaning it would take a bigger man than him to accuse her of immorality. So he redirected that thwarted passion towards the child and chose to hate her instead.

As simple as that, a minute's decision scraped out of the hot ice of their marriage and one he never, ever revised.

"Oh well," said the mother finally. "It's God's will. We can always give her to the church."

Another silence stretched across the bed and out into the maternity ward like a bitter gust of winter wind until, in a rare moment of unity, the two said, "A closed convent."

And that helped dispel the tension. An ugly girl: embarrassing but funny. (Standing in the corner of that antiseptic room, I was becoming seriously freaked out, as you say, already.)

"She's got a big head," said the four-year-old boy.

"She does indeed, Son," said the dad.

"She's cute," said the two-year-old girl.

"But nowhere near as cute as you, sweetheart," said the dad, scooping her up in his arms. "You have no competition there, love, I can tell you."

Then, with not even a backward glance, he grabbed his son by the hand and fled the scene.

Left alone—well, virtually alone—the mother closed her eyes, having yet to cuddle the child who lay so quiet in the wheeled crib beside the bed, and thought of all the broken sleep, all the effort, the feeding, the filth, the washing, the *caring* this useless creature would require and the ever-present pilot light of resentment that flickered right in the centre of her heart flamed up blue and white.

And this, as I later learned, is why.

She did not love her husband and never had. She had married him because he was handsome (tick), because it meant beating her two sisters to the matrimonial prize (tick), it meant never having to make her own way in the world (tick), but most importantly, most crucially, because he was weak (tick, tick, tick).

She had resisted his ardent sexual advances for four long years before the eventual wedding—not hard in that time and place—and in so doing secured the double win of seeming virtue and actual control.

Of course she pretended she felt the same urgent desire as he did but piously held that her faith forbade the act—which, in hindsight I think (given the success of the ploy), was when she first understood the true deceitful power bestowed by wrapping herself (and trapping others) in the glorious, impenetrable shroud of religion.

She even prevaricated about the wedding at times, claiming she was drawn to be a nun—which was preposterous given her need for control—but which she knew made her all the more elusive, untouchable, and therefore desirable. As if her holiness could bring down a band of angels (ha!) to pluck her from his grasp.

It was smart. She was smart, even I have to give her that, because one of the many things fake piety can hide—behind the incense and the kneeling and the bead work—is coldness, a bitter, frigid emptiness where love should be.

All you have to do (and this is as old as the hills, I might add) is mention the word *God* enough and people believe you believe and forget to check your actions.

She was glittering with resentment too because (I later learned) she detested sex but being a woman of God—well, I should say, a Catholic—she had to put up with that most unpleasant coitus and of course, the consequences.

Even more she hated being pregnant—hated any living thing to be close (including her husband), and no one is closer, of course, than a baby in the womb, sucking her dry, ruining her figure, destroying her teeth, swelling her up like a big, doughy pudding.

Luckily for her, she was going through this before the modern push back towards breastfeeding because she would never—did never—do that. She said once, or let slip many years later, in reply to an adult daughter's enquiry, that she had never had any intention of becoming a cow, no matter what anyone said.

As is probably clear by now, she loved no one above herself, not even the first two born. But then he, the husband, loved them. They were his.

But she was nothing if not pragmatic, knowing children were a necessary evil if she was to fulfil her small-town, small-time goal of becoming the second-biggest-fish (after the priest, of course) in a very small parish.

"What a wonderful mother," the other churchgoers would say over the years as three, four, five, six arrivals arrived, all tricked out in their Sunday best and herded into mass at the earliest possible opportunity. (They had to be good for something, and public display of her moral worth was as good as anything.)

No one knew, not even her husband, then, of this white-hot resentment, this black egotism, this total inability to love that lay behind the fecundity. The question of love, of having sufficient love, of understanding and nurturing those sent reeling into her orbit never occurred. She would have thought it an inane and ridiculous idea. They were hers to do with as she wished.

A lot of this that I am now relating I only learned later, but as I said, I had been waiting. For months I'd been watching.

I'd learnt that he had married her not only because of desire (she was petite and voluptuous then, a moment in time she never forgot. A size-ten wedding dress, she used to tell her daughters, with a size fourteen bust!) but also because he was profoundly sexist and fell for her seeming bent towards self-sacrifice.

And because she was strong. He liked all this—a comely, capable, second-class consort. What on your earth is not to like about that?

Of course the reality, for both of them, was somewhat less than they had led themselves to expect. And when she arrived—this new creature with her great big head—it was all starting to unravel.

But at the heart of it all, all that was to come, was the mother, reclining there in her hospital bed but really, it seemed to me, already sprawling at the heart of a dark and sticky web. No one knew what she was like; it would take years for that to become apparent. Well, no one but me, and I couldn't speak a word. It was a bad start, for her, that baby, and for me.

But throughout this, her first day, the girl child slept as if she was still safe, still quietly becoming, still and only reliant on her mother's physical heart. And the mother slept too while I watched over them both, but even then I got the impression menace was still afoot, that she was somehow even plotting in her sleep.

Yet also it must be said that nothing was preordained then. She was, after all, only twenty-four. She was not then bad all the way through because that happens over time, choice by choice, because there is no stasis in your world. There is only change, growth to decay, forwards or backwards, good or bad.

But something very bad happened on that no-account Wednesday, and I think looking back it was the idea sparked by the gleam of hatred in her husband's eyes as he glared at the child. As if that unnatural woman thought, *Now that's interesting. What can I do with that?*

Bad through and through takes a lifetime, but the journey often starts at moments such as this. Destiny set in motion by just a look.

Scary, isn't it?

While all was quiet, I spoke words of love, trying desperately to change things even then, to fan the tiny spark of divinity still there before she snuffed it out as being too much trouble altogether.

Sometimes I hate this job.

★★★

At that time, when this child was born, the father cared for the other two while the mother lay comfortable, so much happier in the clean, sterile surrounds of the hospital ward. Later, as other babies arrived, the children would be farmed out to relatives for as long as the mother could reasonable get away with it.

This served two purposes. One she got a break from them (halleluiah), and two, much more importantly, by the time they returned, the new baby was already in-situ (so to say) and therefore, crucially, *no cause* for excitement.

Each new baby, she made clear in a sort of address-to-the-nation announcement, represented only extra work and more responsibility. It would wake them in the night, it would create mess, and it would drain her to the bone, so they had better not expect anything from her for the next ever-so-long. It became one repeated lecture, expertly delivered, that in minutes smothered their natural childish instincts to kiss and cuddle and love a baby. Each one became to the others an inconvenient intrusion, even a threat, the cause of resentment fed by the fear of maternal neglect.

Have you figured out why she did this? What possible benefit was to be gained by setting them against each other from the minute they all met? Well, thoughtful malice, you will find (like its opposite), always achieves more than one goal.

In this case, most obviously, the technique gave her control (divide and conquer, anyone?) while it also ensured love would never, ever be the fulcrum of this family's life. And then when she added into the mix her Christian piety (such a fabulous weapon!) and her lectures on love, love, love, well, you can imagine their colossal confusion and weakness and discord.

I know I'm getting a bit ahead of myself here, but I mention it because it was this birth that triggered the dynamic. It would not have worked with the first two, of course, not only because they were too young to be affected then but mainly because the father loved them. They were loved, really.

They were welcome.

He would have stopped there if he'd had a choice, which he did, in a way, if he was prepared to choose a lifetime of celibacy, which he certainly was not. He was the man of the house, the boss, the petty tyrant. She'd meet his needs whether she liked it or not, whether he liked it or not, whether the consequent children liked it or not.

And she let him think that, of course, that he was in charge, and met her conjugal obligations by closing her eyes and thinking of … herself, actually. Oh they were such hard people; a perfect match.

Maybe some of you by now will be asking yourselves this question: what happened in her childhood to make her like this, to be so cold and calculating? And the answer is nothing. No, not one thing.

Her parents were down-to-earth farming folk, nothing fancy or flash, a bit emotionally tough, as such people were back then (had to be, really, to survive what they had to survive), but fair, decent and warm, churchgoing and charitable.

But to her, this daughter, they had one glaring, combined, never-fixed fault. That is, they did not adore her passionately enough, bow to her will frequently enough, place her, as the eldest, above the others far enough. And she never forgave them for it.

She had the choice, you see, even then, as a little girl, of curbing her ego, but it was a choice she refused to make. Instead she thought she'd bide her time, be as pleasant as she had to be, always knowing that sooner or later she would show them. They would learn.

Bad is a choice.

She envied one sister her beauty, the other sister her lightness of heart, and despised her brother simply for being a brother, the heir to the farm, her father's little mate. But she kept all of this close to her heart and presented, mostly, a smiling face, only launching into action if she could (quite secretly and safely) queer a childhood pitch or two, make them suffer without consequence to herself.

Bad is a choice, a choice that becomes easier every time it is made until it becomes quite second nature, and then, ultimately, entirely natural. All those years of hidden malice—a perfect apprenticeship.

And because her parents were not looking for it, really could not conceive of it they saw no sign of it, and were left simply wondering why she was so hard to get close to, so difficult to truly warm to, this daughter of theirs.

Only once, I believe, from a story I overheard much later, did the mother of the mother think something was mal-aligned with her child and that came the day she found her little daughter playing with a snake under the dripping tank stand. For the life of her, the mother of the mother could not understand the absence of the natural, primordial aversion that exists between humans and snakes.

It seemed, as she stood staring in horror, her hands held above her eyes to shield them from the glaring inland sunshine (thinking the light was creating a horrible mirage, that it was a thick piece of rope, a stick, a hose) profoundly unnatural. It looked like they were friends, the snake and the girl, not just inhabiting the same place at the same time but playing.

So as not to alarm the child, she gently coaxed her away and inside. But I suspect, from what I now know, that the child would never have felt one ounce of alarm.

You probably think I'm giving too much significant to this little incident, but really, I ask you, isn't it strange? When most children shriek and shout and run and panic, isn't it strange?

And what can I tell you about him, the husband and father? A few things, perhaps, stand out as important.

First, he was the younger of two brothers. No girls. Second, he was sickly as a child and so was doted upon by his submissive, brutalised mother. Third, his father was a small, ill-educated bully who left them all, after lying about his age to make himself younger, so desperate was he to go away to war and bully about on a global stage. Fourth, upon his return, the mother, who for the first time in her life had been given the freedom to act as a sentient human being, was martinetted back into the kitchen and back into servitude.

After four years and much dimmed memories, the two brothers found this shocking. They also found it exciting. *So this is how a man is*, they thought. *So this is how men behave.* It was a lesson neither of them ever forgot.

What it meant for him, this future husband and father, is that, really, he hated women. Well, maybe that's not fair. He didn't hate all women. No, not all.

He only hated women who were not wives and mothers—that is, women who were independent people. He hated them intensely and saw them only and forever as grotesque, ridiculous parodies of men. *Who did they think they were or were fooling*, he asked himself a million times. *What a bloody joke.*

If he had thought for one minute as a young man that he would end up with four daughters, all he would have thought was, *Oh well, domestic labour.*

You can imagine his surprise, then, when he fell in love with his first daughter, but he thought of it as an aberration (and besides, she was so placid and docile) and made sure it never happened again.

For all the others—well, all except one—he thought, *If they do as they're told then we'll all get along fine.* He couldn't, he thought, be fairer than that.

He was as smart as a whip, and I use that phrase deliberately. As a whip, he used his intellect as time went on with brutal arrogance but only, please note, against the clearly less intelligent. God knows, he'd never risk a showing up.

What else can I tell you? What else do you need to know?

Oh yes, I almost forgot. At this time (swing back to the hospital with me), he was slowly but absolutely surely becoming an alcoholic. Surrounded, as his ego forced him to be, by people who he thought were really quite stupid and worn out by nappies and night-school (taken to increase his income in an effort to feed the metre of his marriage), he was, to put it mildly, monumentally bored.

Drinking beer, talking bullshit with the blockheaded boys of a tiny country town, and avoiding the wife and kids until it suited not only dulled the frustration but fed it. A perfect circle. A snake biting its tail.

Yet no matter the Saturday night, he always made mass on a Sunday. Perhaps, in a way, that was their strongest link; they both worshipped, truly, at the altar of public perceptions. And although she hated his drinking, his boorish, repetitive ranting, she also quite loved it because it gave her an advantage.

It almost made her moral high ground unassailable. Indeed, after such a night, when he looked slightly crestfallen (because he could not remember the details of what he had said, to whom, or where) and offered some sort of half-baked excuse, she would merely raise her eyes to heaven and say, "Oh well. I'll just have to pray harder for you, won't I?"

She loved it, and besides, it gave her more time alone to mould and manipulate the totally defenceless little souls placed into her care. As a trained primary school teacher (though never employed—saved, praise the Lord, by the wedding bell), she knew all about that, all the techniques to quieten, to terrify, to control.

Perfect that he was out so often, really, for what she had in mind.

So the birth of this latest child, though an enormous irritation on the one hand, came with blessings on the other because two was not enough. To create a group dynamic, to stand above in total control, really, you do need more.

As I stood watch in that eerily quiet hospital ward (unaccustomed as I was to the lack of that timeless, sweet crooning we all adore), there was much I did not understand then.

Later, of course, I came to realise that what this child's birth absolutely represented was the birth of a tiny, private cult.

# Chapter 5

# Claire

It's Claire now, and just as an aside, writing about myself like that has to be one of the strangest experiences of a rather strange life. Honestly, he could have eased off on the ugly baby bit, don't you think? Yet still, Thomas was right. I did have a big head—I have a photo to prove it—and he was right too about the writing. All I had to do was get in the zone.

But I'll leave him to tell his tale, for obviously I can't confirm or deny what happened on my first day on planet earth. We'll just have to make of it what we will. But that's all I'll say about his literary contribution, for he can, as you see, speak for himself (with my cooperation).

Oh, except for one thing. I understand that what follows might be a touch confusing in terms of my mother, but keep in mind that while Thomas seems to have seen her clearly from our earliest days, I never did or not until recently. I not only believed in her but in everything she said.

I ask Thomas now while I write why he didn't heal my blindness, clue me in if he was such a know-it-all? He says he tried but during my childhood he couldn't get close enough to help me and that later I wouldn't listen.

That's true. For years and years I wouldn't have heard a bad word about her, for to question her was to question everything and to see her clearly would have required more courage than I possessed until I had no choice but to look and look and look.

But now back to me and the ghost story that took place when Mark and I were living in a 1890s Victorian terrace. As you would expect, the house had a long shotgun hallway with the two bedrooms and a bathroom off to the right as you walked in off the gorgeous tree-lined street, with the hall opening onto first the living room, then the kitchen and out into a modern high-ceilinged sunroom, which in turn opened up onto a wooden deck and courtyard. Spacious and elegant, it deserved better inhabitants—well, those of the "alive" variety anyway.

At the time of which I am writing, Mark and I had been in residence for about eighteen months, and although I'd had my reservations about the state of our union before signing this new lease, I remember feeling compelled to see it through to what, even then, I feared might be a very bitter end. In that first year the house felt good but odd.

I was working from home, with my desk located in the sunroom, and very frequently I'd hear what I thought were footsteps down the hallway. I'd turn at my desk, expecting to see Mark walk into the living room, only to wait and wait and wait, shake my head, and get back on with whatever it was I was doing.

So it was odd, but it wasn't scary, menacing, or malevolent. Not at all. And even though I am a little bit psychic, I didn't feel anything awry. Such a helpful gift, as I said.

I loved that house then, in those early days, the ornate fireplaces, the leadlight doors and windows, the ceiling roses and arches in the hallway, but the deterioration of our emotional life in there had a poisoning effect on the place, as you could imagine.

Anyway, after more than a year with only domestic disturbances occurring within those walls, mischief of an altogether different kind began.

One night as I was sitting in the back sunroom watching the night descend, listening to classical music, longing for my dead friends and both waiting and fearing Mark's return from the pub, a clear beam of light grew across the darkened room from the middle of one wall to the other, which was, to say the least, a most startling development.

I put down my wine glass and looked and looked from one end of the thick beam to the other and back again and again from end to end before it sort of simply melted away. I remember my heart was pounding, but I wasn't scared. I was more curious, I think. I got up and checked the wall, thinking that as a terrace, there might have been a hole into our neighbour's property (oh dreadful thought) but of which there was no sign (praise be!).

I went outside into the courtyard feeling rather intrepid, actually, to see if anyone was out there, a burglar perhaps with a torch that could penetrate brick walls, but no. No burglar, no torch that could defy the laws of light and physics.

It was a mystery, but it was also a start. When Mark came home, pretty much when expected, that entire night felt odd indeed. I hesitated to tell him, of course, never being one to bring scorn upon my head willingly, but I did and was much surprised at his response.

"There's something strange about this house, baby," he said. "Don't you feel it?"

I was tempted to say I was beyond feeling any more than I was already feeling but I didn't. No point looking for trouble, is there?

That remained a tranquil night, I recall. No fighting. No chaos. No more surprises, nasty or enigmatic, but in hindsight I think it was the last such night. The following one, in the very witching hour, we were jolted awake in our separate cells by the ear-splitting shriek of the house alarm. We rushed into the hallway—more in addled fright than in search of an intruder—bolted into the living area to the control box, shouting at each other over the din to see if either of us remembered the code when what we did actually remember was that it was not turned on. We never set the alarm, ever. Life in there was alarming enough. We stared at each other, we opened the box and hit buttons at random, and we looked for batteries before realising it was electric.

Then it stopped, and the sudden silence felt frightening.

That happened three more times over the next six weeks until Mark finally took to the control box with a knife (better it than me), cutting every source of power into it he could find.

Almost from that first night of the weird laser-like light, the atmosphere in the house began to change not so much for the worst (that may well have been impossible) but as if it were becoming charged, like the air was filling with electric particles, like that acrid sense you feel before a thunderstorm.

Then objects began to disappear and reappear—cutlery laid out for dinner gone in a blink, freshly washed work clothes gone from the hanger and found under mattresses. The night thumps down the hallway grew louder while during the day we felt the increasing need to almost shout through thick air to have our voices heard in conversation (not just conflict), and all the while we refused to entertain the thought of a haunting.

For one thing, we'd been there for more than a year without incident, so why then? And what could we do about it anyway? We didn't even use the word.

But then there was an incident that forced me to say it. One night I was sitting in the living room watching the TV curled up in a big red chair in the right-hand corner of the room, and it felt like almost an ordinary night like happy people have.

Mark was sprawled on the couch but almost fell off—a move that posed a grave risk to his precious pinot—when he saw me catapult myself off the chair and begin jumping up and down as if a horrible, hairy spider had crawled all over me.

"What is it?" he shouted, but I couldn't answer immediately, shaking as I was both voluntarily (to rid myself of the sensation) and involuntarily.

Finally I said, "I just felt a cold hand on my head. I could feel the fingers and everything on the left side of the back of my head. Oh fuck, oh fuck. What the fuck is going on?"

Later, calmer, sitting on the other side of the room, I said, "I think we've got ghosts. I think this house is haunted." I must admit that when I said it I half expected the alarm to shriek into life as confirmation, thereby triggering a heart attack, which in turn would have made any suicidal intentions totally redundant.

But it didn't. All was quiet. We went to bed, and we carried on (in all manner of ways). We thought our house was haunted and we didn't think our house was haunted, being experts as we were at such conflicted thinking.

Then all my electronic work equipment began to fail, one by one, as if something was draining the power, and given that I worked from home, that was a most serious development. First my phone, a newish system, only about one year old, simply stopped working. It had a dial tone (I'd paid the bill), but the numbers would not connect to the outside world.

Then my printer stopped printing and my computer stopped computing, which, given the state of the phone, meant I could not even ring for assistance. This technological breakdown occurred over a matter of days, and during that time I had an experience I can hardly bring myself to write about.

For some time leading up to this time—maybe weeks—I had thought the very strange thought as I was going to sleep in my self-imposed exile in the second bedroom that something, some small someone, was lying down beside me as I settled for the night. It was such an unsettling thought that I allowed it to gain no traction in my head, mainly because I had nowhere else to lay my head—well, nowhere safer. Consequently every time I thought the thought, I un-thought it pretty sharpish.

Until one night when I had turned off my bedside lamp and was lying thinking sadly of my life and what was to become of it, when I saw a little girl standing by my bed.

Clearly dead.

Clearly dead. I had seen dead by then. I knew what dead looked like.

She had lank brownish shoulder-length hair, sunken eyes and cheek bones, and pallid grey skin and was maybe nine or ten years old. I have never written of this before, have barely talked to anyone of it, and now my heart is racing just to remember it.

She had her arms outstretched towards me in mute and desperately mournful supplication (what living child does that?), and I thought I was going to vomit up my heart. She looked so lost and sad but also truly terrifying.

In one movement I'd turned on the light, sat up, and clutched the doona, as if it could provide some protection, staring wildly about me like a crazy woman, but she was not there. No one was there, but from that night on I left all the hall lights on, the lounge lights on, the rear courtyard lights all on, all blazing, and I hated Mark more—much more—for those nights when he left me there alone.

So by then I couldn't sleep, I couldn't work, and there was a building sense of desperation (outside my own) that made me feel that had I still cared enough about our happy home to bring flowers into it, they would have been dead within hours of arrival.

And you might mock the notion of ghosts, but for the life of me, I could not think of another theory that would cover all the events. Mark saw balls of light fly in through a wall and out through a window, odd misplaced objects were placed on coffee tables or benches, and the movement censor lights began to flicker almost constantly when no one we could see was moving anywhere at all.

What would you have thought? What would you have done?

This is what I thought. I thought how tragic for anyone or anything to be trapped or lost in there, with Mark and me, when not even we wanted to be there. I at least had a choice even though I seemed to be incapable of making one, and on those nights when the two of us were screaming at each other, that house felt truly hellish. I felt great compassion for them, it, whatever, as nutty as that sounds.

And this is what I did. One sunny morning I went out in search of new equipment, but as I walked up and down the local shopping strip in search of a new phone, a new computer, a new printer, or even a technician to sort them out, I kept noticing a new age crystal shop with an advertisement in the window for psychic readings.

That's why I was going up and down, to be honest. It lured me like an oasis in the desert, but I felt too embarrassed to go in. I'm a rational person really in spite of what you must think. But finally my fear of home won out over my fear of humiliation, and in I went.

I asked to see the psychic. The crystal-bedecked woman behind the counter, in no hurry to respond, glanced languidly at me and said he wasn't there. I asked when he would be there. She said soon, which I thought, in the world of the new age, could have meant any time at all. I said it was urgent, and that got her attention, I can say, psychics rarely, I presume, being needed in an emergency.

"Seriously," I said. "I'm not joking. I need his help."

She pointed across the street to an outdoor cafe. "He's just there. That's him in the dark shirt, having a coffee."

Well that threw me. What was I meant to do about that?

The crystally woman saw my confusion (she didn't know the half of it) and said gently: "He's a lovely man. Don't worry. His name is Michael. Just go over and talk to him. Say I pointed him out to you. He'll help if he can."

I said, "Oh I don't know. It's a bit strange …"

She said, "He's a psychic, love. Strange is his core business."

She had a point.

So knowing she was watching through the glittering window display of beads, birthstones, potions, and incense, I felt compelled to see it through although the idea of discussing the matter with a stranger in public on a sunny street was not quite what I had had in mind (which was more back room, dim lights, purple curtains, and patchouli, if you know what I mean).

*Dear God, can my life get any weirder?* I thought as I took a deep breath and crossed the street.

But before I could squib it, I went up to him (half joking to myself that as a psychic he was probably expecting me), and standing at his elbow, I blurted, "Hi, Michael. My name is Claire and I'm sorry to interrupt you, but the woman from the shop pointed you out to me and said you wouldn't mind but I need some help because I think I have a ghost in my house and I don't know what to do about it."

A man sitting and sipping his coffee at the next table almost choked, I remember, while I almost began to hyperventilate, but Michael?

Michael looked at me with solemn composure, as if he was regularly accosted by strangers having trouble with the supernatural, motioned me to sit, which I did, leaned over, and placed a hand on my forearm. Then he closed his eyes and said, "Yes. You have. But not just one."

The poor man sitting nearby almost snorted his cappuccino out of his nose.

"Yes," said Michael, "more than one. I can feel them all around you."

"All?" I said, both relieved at the lack of mockery and alarmed.

He said, "Describe the house."

I said, "Victorian terrace, shotgun hallway, living at the back.

He said (still with his hand upon my arm), "There's an old man in the living room. He's the strongest presence. I think he must have lived there, but there are others." He sat back, removed his hand and took a sip of his coffee. "Has someone close to you died recently?"

"My brother died a few years ago."

"You loved him very much?"

"Yes."

"Yes," said Michael. "I can see him now, actually. He's just sitting over there—a young man, yes? Less than thirty, I would say."

My head nearly did an exorcist-type manoeuvre then even though I knew I would see nothing (hope, loss, and longing being so very powerful), which is exactly what I saw.

"He's fine," said Michael. "He has a dog."

(A dog?)

"The reason I mention that is that I think the spirits are in your house because of you."

"Me?" I said, thinking, *Right, great, now I truly have been blamed for everything.* "Why me?" I asked. "I don't want them there." The conversation was becoming increasingly surreal.

He said, "Because you've been thinking so much about the dead. You're more in that world than the world of the living." He had a point. "When that happens, you can shine like a beacon to them, especially if a spirit is already attached to the house."

"But what do they want of me?" I asked in plaintive voice.

He laughed at my ignorance. "They want your help, of course."

"My help?" I squeaked. "How can I help them …" I trailed off then before blurting, "when I can't even help myself." Instead, I finished lamely with, "Help them how?"

"To help them go where they need to go."

"I can't do that," I said.

"No," said Michael. "But I can."

"You can?"

"Of course. What do you think I do?"

I didn't answer that. Never having had the need of a professional psychic, I didn't really know. Answering "make bogus predictions" seemed a bit like cutting off my nose under the circumstances so I wisely said nothing because, despite all the scepticism and rationality in the world, I did feel in desperate need of his help.

And so, apparently, did Michael.

"I think it's quite urgent," he said. "Has the atmosphere been building?"

I nodded, feeling queasy.

"Yes. There is a great deal of dark energy around you, and that is not good. You live there with a partner?"

"Yes, Mark," I said, meeker and meeker.

"Yes. I thought so. They're not just living with you—excuse the phrase—they're feeding off you."

"Oh," I blurted. For want of anything better, I finished with, "That can't be good."

"No," he said. "It isn't. So the sooner we move them on, the better. How about this Sunday?"

"What about Sunday?"

"To do the clearance. I'll bring my team. It'll take a couple of hours, costs about one hundred dollars, just for travel expenses and such, and we'll get it done."

Dear god. When I had approached Michael, I had no real expectation of receiving help, though that is what I had asked for. I hadn't really thought the matter through—possibly because if I had, I'd never have gone through with the thought.

I asked, "How do you do it?"

He said, speaking as if he were a pest exterminator, "We go in, we feel who's there, we get a sense of who or what we're dealing with, and we call on the powerful righteous spirits to come and get them."

Right.

"What if they don't want to go?" I asked nervously.

"Almost all ghosts or spirits want to go. That's mostly why they try and attract attention from the living."

"So they're stuck?"

"Well yes, but lost is a better description."

It was such a sorrowful thought. "How do they get lost? Surely … things … the other side … is better organised than that?"

Leaning back and gazing at the sky, he replied, "Some don't know they're dead. Some didn't understand that they needed to go into the light. Some are too attached, to people or a place, like the old man in your house, I suspect, to want to leave and some"—dramatic pause—"don't want to go where they need to go because they're fearful of punishment for the things they have done."

Fucking hell. Literally. I stared at him.

"We call on the powerful spirits to take them—almost like asking God to send the elevator back down—and sometimes many, many lost spirits rush through, and—Claire, isn't it?"

"Yes."

"And Claire they are very, very grateful."

"But not all?" (I'm such a scaredy cat.)

"No. Not all. But they are a very tiny minority."

It wasn't much consolation. What if I had a not-want-to-go one?

"So Claire. Sunday?"

"Yes, Michael. Sunday."

So Sunday it was, only five more sleeps. That didn't seem so bad then, but it's hard really to explain how dreadful those nights were.

One. The air felt thick, heavy and agitated.

Two. Mark's contempt reached new highs or lows, I should say, and not just for me. Twice that week he awoke too hung-over to go to work, instead rising at midday and only leaving the house to go to the wine shop across the street to bring back expensive bottles he could not afford as a way to convince himself he was a wine aficionado and not an alcoholic. Then after a few, or after enough, out he'd go again into the night to carouse with strangers.

It was desperately depressing, for I had loved him once and thought that once he had loved me. I would have thought twice about living opposite a wine shop had it not been for the fact that when we had moved in, Mark only drank beer and despised wine and all who sailed along in it. The day he fell in love with wine, then, was a very dark day indeed, which even so felt weirdly familiar until I realised it was familiar. My father had done much the same thing, and that made me feel like a crazed rat in a trap.

Three. I couldn't work, Michael having advised me it would be best to wait to replace or fix the broken equipment lest they, the invisible people, drained more power. While it may or may not have been good advice, this created not only a stressful backlog of work but also a most creepy sense of isolation.

I couldn't sleep, couldn't bring myself to leave the bedroom at night to go out into the main body of the house for fear of what I might see and be unable to unsee, and most of all, I could not settle for I could not imagine how it was all going to end.

Now that I'm in such a happy place, psychologically speaking, it's hard to write of that time without feeling sick. Even now when I dream of then, those dreams of everyday life with Mark there in that house are nightmares, and I wake up sweating, heart-broken and afraid.

Can life be so hard and strange and hopeless? Well, yes, it can. But nothing lasts forever.

I remember thinking of our years together then, during that long, wearisome week, waiting for the spirit removalists. I thought of the time Mark had saved my life by belting me in the back when I was choking on a piece of roast lamb, of all the times I'd tried and failed to save him and us—wondering how it could all have gone so awry that I could barely find a shadow in Mark of the Mark I thought I knew.

I can only assume he felt the same about me given that on the Friday night before the Sunday he came home from work, showered, shaved, and put on the new shirt him I'd bought him for Christmas. Upon seeing my tears (for I was both definitely uninvited and too beaten to fight), he strode out down the hallway shouting, "Good shirt, baby. I should definitely pick up in this."

I didn't see him again until Sunday morning so I can only suppose he did.

There is a good reason people call it the demon drink, I now know, for when I looked into his brown eyes at moments in those days, they looked black.

I was so frightened that night and on Saturday, the atmosphere in the house feeling so desperate and agitated that I almost felt as if hemmed in by a crowd, almost as if something or someone was tugging at my clothes to get my attention. I would have left there in a heartbeat if I'd had anywhere else to go.

Finally, Sunday morning.

Mark stumbles in without apology or explanation and still drunk, asks cheerfully if I'd like to go out for breakfast. I cannot answer. He cleans himself up, says, "Suit yourself," and goes out anyway, ignoring my request for him to return in time for the exorcism. Ha!

Then an hour later the team arrives, Michael and two assistants, and while I am relieved and grateful for their presence, I am afraid and worried they may pick up on the misery of the living in chez nous and not just the dead.

At the front door Michael says, "You are right, Claire. We can feel them even out here. You don't have to stay. We can do this alone. Just come back in an hour so we can cleanse you too. And your partner. Is Mark here?"

I tell him no as I invite them in, and Michael shakes his head in consternation. "It's important that we get rid of all the dark energy from both the house and all inhabitants."

I say Mark will be there by the time they finished (hoping he'll need to come home at least to sleep off his hangover) and explain I will stay, that I am curious and interested, that I would like to see how it is done.

Again Michael shakes his head. "It's not very interesting," he says. "Or not for spectators. We just combine our energies and pray silently for assistance and deliverance."

By then all three of them are moving around the house, checking out each room in turn, sometimes muttering to themselves, sometimes nodding to each other, sometimes standing in odd corners with their eyes shut and their hands held out, palms facing up towards the ceiling.

Then at a shout from Michael, they join together in the sunroom, have a quick conference, and turn to me.

"Right," says Michael. "You've got an old man in the living room, in the right-hand corner near the red chair. There's also a very dark presence, an angry man, in the front bedroom and a little girl in the second bedroom."

The young woman in the team turns to me and says, "You've seen her, I think. She says you've seen her."

The young woman looks at me intently but I have no idea what to say. "There's bad energy in here," she says, and I think, *You don't know the half of it.*

"Right," says Michael, "let's go. You go outside, Claire. We can't clear the energy in the house if it's attached to you. We'll do the house. Then we'll do you and then your partner if he comes home in time."

I step outside, listening intently, yet all I can hear is a vague but comforting murmur as they move through the house, one with a book, one with a candle, and one with incense.

It takes about forty minutes. Then Michael calls me in.

I say, "So?"

He says, "All done. It went well."

I think, *How disappointing*—not that it went well of course—but that it was so subtle, no cracks of thunder as the cosmic door reopened, no smoke, no sulphur, no flashes of light.

I say, "Are you sure they're gone?"

He says, "Oh yes. Quite sure."

I say, "Did you see them go?" I want confirmation in the absence of evidence. I need reassurance if I am to stay in that house another minute, another day.

Michael says, "Trust me, Claire. They're gone. Now we need to clean you up and all will be well, though it's a shame Mark is not here. Doesn't he believe in spirits?"

I answer, "He's been as wigged out about this as I have been. He's seen balls of light and found things in odd places."

"Male pride then."

It's not a question.

We all shake our heads at such foolishness (they don't know the half of it), and then Michael asks me to sit. The three stand around me with hands linked and pray silently over me, as if I am on my death bed and though utterly peaceful and nonthreatening, the tableau feels uncanny and unsettling, and I pray for them to get on with.

"Right," says Michael. "I think you're good now, but I've got to say that there is way too much misery around you. You've got to let go of the dead, Claire. You've got to set them free. Their destiny was theirs—not yours."

I cry. I can't help it, and the young woman has me stand and holds me tight and says, "You're alive. You have to live. You have no choice if you choose to live."

I cry some more and then pull myself together and remove myself in a tangled rush from the arms of the stranger.

Michael says, "It is important, Claire. I think you're somewhat psychic, which means if you don't find a way out of this grief, this darkness, spirits will find you again."

That got my attention. And so they leave, with no sign of Mark and with Michael assuring me that while the atmosphere might take a day or two to lift, lift it will, and he is right.

★★★

By Wednesday it felt like a different house. There was light, for one thing, in places that had long been dim, settled, peaceful, ordinary, so wonderfully ordinary, supernaturally speaking, that even by then it was hard to imagine how dreadful it had seemed.

Even my work equipment just switched back to life, the hall thumps ceased, and the movement sensor stopped sensing movement. It felt amazing, fresh, and clean. But life on the human plane was not so good, and although Wednesday felt like a blessed day, atmospherically speaking, all hell had broken loose by Thursday, dashing my hopes for my own miraculous deliverance, though in hindsight that may have been exactly what it was.

I was home alone, surprise, surprise, on Thursday night, relishing the newfound tranquillity even to the point of sitting in the dark, in the sunroom, looking out into the night and listening to my music, a favourite combination I'd not been brave enough to indulge for what seemed like an eternity.

By then I was back, in a sort of weird advance, to being only afraid of Mark's presence, and I pondered that night about what it would take to make me leave. In that thinking, I made a very grim discovery, and that is that if you have chosen for any length of time to sink below your bottom line, it's very hard to reimpose it.

What could he do, I asked myself that night, that could make me walk out the door, that he hadn't already done? If I was so hopeless, so cowardly, so afraid of being alone, what could possibly galvanise me into action, put some steel into my broken soul?

I was thinking and thinking, trying harder to hate him than myself, for there is, of course, great shame in accepting abuse, when I heard a knock at the door.

At first I assumed it to be Mark, too drunk to manage his keys, and I would have left him out there had it not been for the lead light glass panel in the door that I knew he'd smash if his knocking went unanswered. I walked down the hall with spirits sinking and anxiety rising, opened that damned gorgeous door, and was met not by him but by two uniformed policemen.

My guts lurched to see them. I had lived in fear for some years of such a visit by the police telling me that Mark had been hit by a car on one of his drunken zombie stumbles through the city. I didn't love him anymore, but I didn't want him dead. No. I definitely did not want another dead person in my life, so I looked at the coppers with frightened eyes until they explained that he was not dead but dead drunk, in the back of the van, having been found sprawled across a major intersection by a worried stranger.

They said he must have fallen because he was so drunk and knocked himself out.

Then I felt no longer frightened but monumentally fed up. After I said that yes, he did live with me, one copper asked me if I wanted him and at the asking of that question it was as if the earth stopped turning just for an instant, just for me.

I'd never wanted him like that. I'd never been given a choice. No one had ever asked. But now they had; now I had a choice, and I took it.

I said no. It felt incredible, simple, and profound.

I said, "No. I don't. I've never wanted him in this state."

Policeman One asked, "So he has a drinking problem?"

I replied, "He's in the back of the van isn't he?"

Policeman One said, "What I mean to ask is whether it's unusual for him to get in this state."

I said, "No, it's not unusual. He's getting worse, and it's destroying us."

Policeman Two asked, "Has he hurt you?"

"No, not yet, but it feels like that might be just one bad night away."

Policeman One said, "Right. That's all you need to say. We'll take care of him tonight."

Policeman Two said, "He's a bit of a mess. He fell on his face."

"Oh God, what? Blood? Vomit?"

Policeman Two said, "Yes. Do you have a change of clothes for him?"

"Of course."

Policeman One said, "No. Don't do that. If this is a problem, it might be better to let him do the walk of shame."

The walk of shame? I looked at Policeman One, distressed and uncertain. He said, "He's not your problem tonight. We'll put him in the drunk tank, and you never know, miss, it might be enough to set him right."

"Do you think so?"

"It has happened."

Oh it was so grim, and I gave the policemen a wan smile before they walked back to the van parked along the shadowed, quiet, civilised street.

Then a thought occurred, and I hurried after them.

"How long can you keep him?" I asked.

"Three hours," said Policeman Two.

"Oh no," I wailed.

"Why?" he asked.

"Because he'll still be drunk."

"Sorry, miss. That's all we're allowed."

So they left, and I was right. After a sleepless night, half hoping for a miracle, half grieving for his shame, in he crashed at 4:00 a.m. to stamp down the hall, to batter on my bedroom door (locked against just this eventuality), to scream, to rant, to terrorise.

I'll spare you the language. I'll spare you the abuse.

All I'll say is that vain, controlling bullies don't seem to much like regaining consciousness behind bars, covered in blood, filth, and vomit. And because he couldn't remember falling, or said he couldn't, he claimed first that I had called the police and second that they'd beaten him.

For four hours—four hours!—he smashed at the door, he psychotically played a ringtone of a police siren on his mobile phone as he ran dementedly up and down the hallway. He threatened to kill me, he threw pots and pans around the kitchen and rang a friend to tell him what the treacherous bitch had done (that, of course, being me), his pride so wounded that someone had to pay (that, of course, being me.)

Four hours. I couldn't leave my room, I couldn't get to work, and I couldn't go to the loo.

Yet finally, worn out by rage and hatred, he sank into a chair and once again into unconsciousness. I ran for the loo, then the phone, and then I fled.

Minutes before I made my escape, though, he woke upon the taxi driver's knock upon the door, and seeing me walking out with a small suitcase, he shouted, "No one else will have you, you know. You're old, you can't have children, all your friends are dead, and not even your own family like you."

And my footsteps slowed, for he was right.

He was right.

But upon seeing me pause, he said, "Come back, baby. I'll forgive you."

And that was enough. I kept walking, thinking that even if I were to shatter into a million pieces, I'd do it on the other side of that damned gorgeous door.

*So this is what it takes*, I said to myself. *That is exactly what it takes.*

Yet still I have so many other questions. Did the ghosts know? Did they know I was about to go? Is that why there was such a sudden build-up, such a sense of mad desperation, such a need for my attention? And did this mean that along with all my other troubles (as listed by Mark), I now had to fear becoming some sort of ghost magnet if I didn't cheer up?

And last, can life really be like this? Well, I can answer that one. Yes, it can. But nothing lasts forever.

# Chapter 6

# Thomas

Come back with me now to the first day.

Just when the nurses were starting to wonder at the complete maternal disengagement and really, feeling somewhat put upon at having to feed, change, and cuddle the infant themselves (as if they didn't have enough to do), the mother, ever aware of the power of small-town gossip, announced herself ready to go home.

It was a move that, while clearly expected, I'd still been dreading, for though the experience in the hospital had been unsettling, depressing, there was worse. I really hated the town they were living in then, and while I'd be forced to digress completely if I were to try and explain, trust me, I've seen some horrible places in my time (slums, dungeons, the holds of ships). There was just something godforsaken about the hamlet, stuck as it was miles from anywhere on the edge of hard and bitter plains that, really, began there and stretched west almost across the entire continent (taking in a desert or two).

The very edge of nothing. Can a place be toxic, wretched, for no apparent reason?

God knows. I don't know; I'd never encountered such before. Most places have at least one redeeming feature, but this place? None that I ever found—though now that I'm thinking so hard about it, looking back over time, I must at least allow that the night skies of the southern hemisphere in that region were splendid (made me feel wistful, oddly homesick).

So there you are—one redeeming feature. If they had razed the town, leaving nothing under that enormous sky, it would have been infinitely better.

It was such a strange settlement. Young, it had only come to be in the wake of mass road transit, yet still it felt old, corrupt, hopeless.

Assembled primarily to meet the needs of the truck drivers passing through and the occupants of outlying farms, the town boasted a large and gaseous fuel depot, a general store, a sub post-office, a barely manned police out-station, a church, and a two-roomed school.

Oh, and a ramshackle pub that reeked of hatred for anyone stupid enough to have had the misfortune to be born outside that honoured template of the weather-beaten, proudly ignorant, and justifiably brutal white Australian male.

All really it was missing was a broken-down brothel so the truckies no longer had to run the risk of not picking up at all over the tedious, mind-numbing five hundred–kilometre run. But back then the idea of paying for it, when they could simply take it (the missus had to be good for something!) would have struck the menfolk as a ridiculous waste of beer money.

So that was the town's infrastructure.

Spread between stood a scattering of houses, all of which sat or leaned or drooped only on one side of the highway. This, as you could imagine, gave the hamlet an ugly, unbalanced appearance. It was as if no one wanted to look at each other, as if everyone was pretending no one else was there. But there was a reason for this bizarre town plan, and that was the hill that rose upon the other side of the road, the only hill, I suspect, though I never fully checked it out, for hundreds of kilometres, at least to the west.

Looking back and knowing much more about Australia now than I did then, I am wondering whether this hill had significance to once-local, now long-gone Aboriginal clans. I am wondering even if something cruel and barbaric happened there. (Note that I did not say inhumane. From all that I have seen, I'm sorry to say I don't know what that word means.) I wonder if the memory of that something may have lingered over the land like a poisonous miasma, hanging over the town as it assembled.

God knows. I don't know, for once we're here we can't ask questions. But it's as good a theory as any, and besides, the hill lent itself to such speculation being as it was, weird and uncanny. Rising abruptly out of nowhere, the western side was green and damp and shady with large, moss-covered boulders scattered under the trees, providing evidence of its ancient volcanic genesis.

Here the children were allowed to play.

Over the crest, though, was a barren, blasted landscape, the tortured, spare, and desperate scrub clinging to life through and around the pulverised rocks. In shallow gullies on this side, cattle, sheep and even goanna skeletons lay bleached white and picked clean.

A mystery. Did they die there, or were they dumped there?

I don't know, but I do know many things died on that hill—not all of them physical—and I have good cause to hate it.

The town also had one other feature that should have been good in this parched place but wasn't. It had a water source, a creek, which, if left to run its course, would have been quite pleasant.

But it wasn't.

It had been dammed (man triumphs over nature again, hoorah!) to retain recreational water, given the creek's annoying habit of drying up in summer. So the village had a waterhole, known as the billabong, but it also had plagues of mosquitos, legions of leeches, snakes (there I go again), slime, and a smell of putrefaction that rose and fell with the water level.

When the creek was running well, it would have been a good enough place for a dip, but that only happened in the crystal cold of inland winter. But in the desperation of summer, in that pre-air-conditioning era, the people felt almost forced to take the plunge.

Oh, what a town. In summer the temperature climbed to over forty degrees by early December and stayed there pretty much until late March, melting the bitumen, baking the fuel depot, scorching the landscape, burning the people.

In winter a frigid, bitter wind raced across the plains, battering the place on its way through. Even the tired and dismal gum trees that dotted the town looked like they wished they had grown up somewhere else.

I was dreading going back there, and for one tiny moment in the hospital, I prayed that they might put her up for adoption, save us both. (It's not just you, you know, who hope for miracles.) I felt bad at the time, thinking such a thought, but now …

I suppose by now as I get underway, I should give all these people some names. They won't be real names, of course, though that would not bother me, but Claire is loyal even now. So if she wants anonymity, I have agreed that she can have it. So let's have some fun.

Let us call the mother Faith. Yes, that's a good one. And something strong but gentle for the father, just for a laugh. (I bet you never think of us as being sarcastic, but Lord knows we need all the coping strategies we can think of down here. And really there is so much more to us than is dreamt of in your philosophy.)

Anyway back to him, the father. Strong but gentle. I know. We'll call him Joseph.

And the children. Let's think. We might call the oldest boy Peter (that's good, upon this rock, etc.), and the first daughter, placid and tame, she might be Deborah (oh I'm good, named for a warrior, too funny).

The new child I've already dubbed Claire simply because it sounds like clear, which is me being sarcastic again because nothing was ever made clear to my dear Claire—well not, at least, for a very long time.

So there they all are then, mother, father, children all together at home—in hell.

What were they doing there, you may be asking yourself. How does anyone find themselves in hell? Well, metaphysically everyone chooses to be there. More prosaically, in this case, they were there because Joseph ran the fuel depot/general store. While Faith had begged him not to take the job after she'd taken one horrified look at the settlement, he had dismissed her with what he considered justifiable contempt.

"You're the one who insists on children. They've got to be paid for."

The job came with a considerable pay rise plus the use of a portable house trucked in for them and dumped on stilts at the end of the line, right near the pestilential billabong.

There's not much to be said really about those first two years of Claire's life. She was fed, she was cleaned, she was wheeled out for public display—mass, of course, and family functions. But still the message of her role, her position, was already getting through to the other children, even though they were such babies themselves.

Isn't that amazing that such tiny humans can pick up on emotional neglect, dislike, insipient hatred? What absorbent creatures children are.

So when Peter pulled Claire out of her crib and let her fall onto the floor, where she lay a bit too long wailing and hurt, only to have the mother berate the baby ("Can't you stay quiet for a minute?"), he got the message.

Or when Debbie asked to hold her and was told no, that the baby was best left alone and trouble-free, she got the message.

"Your dolls are so much prettier. You should play with them," Debbie was told. "You don't have to worry about her."

But Debbie wasn't worried; she just wanted to love the baby. And the baby loved her back, would raise her plump little arms up to the curly-haired tot in the hope of a cuddle, some physical contact. But the older sister was always swept away, distracted.

The mother would say, "You won't find her so cute when she gets a bit bigger and wants your toys. She'll annoy you then too, believe me."

"What," the sweet little thing half wondered, "did this baby do to make Mummy and Daddy so angry?"

After a short time, though, she stopped wondering, stopped puzzling over this conundrum not because the question was ever answered but simply because it became a natural part of the family scheme, though one that was never articulated, never consciously acknowledged.

No one ever said, "Mum and Dad hate Claire."

In some ways it didn't need to be said; in others it could never be.

Still, much like the blasted eucalypt saplings that held on to life outside the house, the child clung on and grew despite such a hostile environment. Not that her tenacity was appreciated.

When she took her first steps early, she was not greeted with cries of delight but heavy sighs of disappointment.

"She's so ungainly," said Joseph.

"I know," said Faith.

"Her head is out of proportion," said Joseph.

"I know," said Faith.

"Is one of her feet turned in?"

"I don't think so."

"Look, she's bumping into everything."

"I know."

"Is she blind as well?"

"Surely not."

In contrast, when she spoke her first words early, she was met with a breathless, appalled silence. Faith and Joseph looked at each other. The child's words formed a sentence, and given that there had never been any coochy-cooing, any play or practice, they came out of the absolute blue. They'd never heard anything like it, and by then, in their catholic world, they had been around a lot of children.

*Oh no*, they thought, *the child is smart*. Without one word being exchanged between the adults, a pact was formed, a decision made. The child must never know, for how could she fulfil the role of the ugly village idiot if she was smarter than half the people in it? (Thanks, Thomas! C)

You'd think it couldn't be done, wouldn't you? But it can be, trust me, in a closed-circuit family.

Instead, Faith and Joseph decided the child should be made to feel stupid, foolish, a burden in a conspiracy that worked so well that even now, more than forty years later, if you asked her siblings if Claire had brains, they'd look at you like you were mad.

At this time it was, then, about all the parents agreed upon. Well, almost all.

With all their youthful hopes (individual and combined) withering before their eyes, they had hammered out one other lock solid agreement. They would not fight in front of the children. The reasons behind this were complex even then.

Both people were by nature secretive and they were egotists, so the idea of their children ever being in a position (some time in the future) to look down upon them, to roll their eyes, to think they or their marriage were not perfect, was quite repugnant.

But they could not admit that. No. That would signify pride, and pride was a sin when they wished to be seen as sinless. Instead, they said it would be best for the children. That felt righteous. They went with that one. So all their arguments, the sarcasm, the emotional brutality, was played out late at night in hissing undertones.

They were, I've got to hand it to them, fine actors, rising in the morning after such disputes with neither resolution nor forgiveness but smiling, as if nothing in the world were wrong. So went the nights (frequent) that he stayed at the pub and trudged home, to be met with a freezing chill and burnt chops. So went the nights that he fell asleep in his chair, leaving lights on and windows open, letting in swarms of insects (various). So went the nights after the days she had played tennis, laughing and flirting with *other men* (she had returned to her pre-pregnancy shape swiftly after Claire, a fact she thought of as her only blessing in the whole grotesque affair). So went the nights she refused his advances.

"But you don't want another baby!"

Hissing rage at night. Sharp, smiling silence in the day. And all after only five years of wedded bliss. They were so young to my old, old view, to be so black, so bleak, so hopelessly locked in such marital misery.

The atmosphere was so acrid even then that I could not stay inside. It made me sick. So I set up outside while staying as close as possible to Claire, guarding, watching, hoping.

The house they were living in then had a deep veranda that wrapped all the way around. That's where I stayed (with my colleagues, I suppose you could call them, five of us by then, though we could be so little comfort to each other). Faith used that space for drying the laundry, white nappies, white business shirts, white tennis and cricket clothes.

I just mention this, as I look back, because I know that Claire saw me out there when she was just a little thing. Children can, you know, see us before their minds close as their skulls fuse, as if so much of what is true just can't seem to fit into adult human heads. As she grew older and remembered, she put it down to the whites wafting in the breeze.

But it was me. Watching, waiting, trying not to look forward, into the dark tunnel of the years and years that stretched before us both.

What a house, a hamlet, a time we had of it.

Then, just when I felt the situation couldn't get worse (you'll hear me say that a bit as we go on), the day came when Faith told Joseph in hushed, imploring tones that she was carrying again. She said it after dressing up and accentuating the rosy glow of pregnancy.

She said it after cooking his favourite dinner (steak and eggs). She said it after the children had been fed, bathed, and bedded without bother to him. But she did say it.

He stared, stood up, and walked straight out the door, past me on the veranda and down the road to the pub. To spend money they didn't have to spend.

For one black and bitter moment, it looked to us outside like he might punch her in the stomach, resolve the issue that way. But we shouted, "Don't do it!" and miraculously, he didn't.

When he left, she sank to her knees, clutching her rosary beads, praying for strength to carry the cross of married life. Really, though, her prayer more closely resembled "take this cup" than "thy will be done."

And someone must have been listening that particular night, though I wouldn't necessarily say it was God.

As Faith became heavier with child, Claire became, at about the same speed, aware. By now capable of delightful play with her sister, the two little girls thrilled at the idea of a baby. And even though Faith and Joseph tried to disabuse them of any notion of joy or excitement, their gloom couldn't really penetrate the innocent perfection of two good little hearts.

Faith was at her wit's end. She had a drunken husband who wasted their money, she lived in a hellish hamlet, and she had a fridge barely coping with the amount of food needed even then. She still had one child in nappies, and she was growing huge this time, which utterly threatened her girlish, tennis-playing figure.

She was filled with anger. It was never meant to turn out like this. She thought, but never said, over and over as a sort of mantra, "I do not want this baby. I do not want it. I do not."

But the two of them were so freakishly fertile, no natural birth control system seemed to make one egg/sperm of difference. But what she hated most was how vulnerable it made her. Yes she was the pride of the parish, with her ever-growing flock and belly and that was good, but it only worked on Sunday. How to get through the rest of the week?

Clearly she couldn't express hatred for him, her husband, for the twin reasons of no-divorce and economic need. But she had to hate someone.

And he? He felt like he was drowning in glue. But what could he say? He knew the deal, had done most of his courting before or after mass, at catholic community dances. He knew the deal; he just didn't know it was going to be like this, a father of four at twenty-eight. How the hell many would they end up with?

As the day of arrival neared, the three children were handed over (in what would be an exciting, reasonably frequent break in routine) to Faith's parents on the farm about a two-hour drive away. The children (mostly) loved it there. Peter got to be a pretend farmer but was not given free rein to express his increasingly manic bullying streak.

"The strong don't hurt the weak," Pop would say. Or, "I put down farm dogs that can't control their behaviour."

That brought him up short, I can tell you.

And the girls? They loved their Nan and Pop, collecting eggs, taking all morning to walk on little legs down the road to the mailbox just to check.

I loved it there too. I could come inside for a change.

Knowing as much as most women do about childbirth at the tender age of twenty-six, Faith determined she would not be left hanging around for another mad, inexplicable month this time around, so determined that she was prepared to go against a lifetime of conditioning and stand up to the male obstetrician to insist she be induced.

He said, "But hardly anyone goes into labour on the exact date."

She said, "I don't care."

He said, "It would be better for both of you if we at least gave it a few days."

She said, "No. I have three other children; I have enough to cope with. I can't just sit around waiting. I am begging you, just bring it on."

She looked so fraught, what could he do? He booked her in. He hooked her up to the drip and let it roll.

Joseph, while she was labouring, was out and about reacquainting himself with old pubs, old pals in the large regional town that had previously been their home, and after not such a bad delivery, the two of them became the less-than-euphoric parents of a boy.

A boy. It softened the blow considerably.

And he was pleasing to look at, they thought with detachment, with his dark hair like his father (what a relief), a normal-sized head, clear skin.

*Oh well*, they thought. *We have had worse.*

Meantime, Faith's father left the farm, suddenly, unprecedentedly, and drove his truck all the way to hellsville without a word to anyone and left there one enormous fridge.

When Joseph saw it upon finally going home, he had a good mind to reject it. How dare his father-in-law think him a poor provider. But upon reflection and a few quiet beers in the luxurious quiet of his home, he thought better of it.

He thought, *Standing between a woman and a family-sized fridge is more than my life's worth.*

And laughing at women put his ego back together and made everything all right. Or as all right as it could be.

Back at the hospital five days later, Faith's mood had not lifted much. Yes, he was a boy, yes, he looked as he should, but still, really, all she felt was horror at the drudgery lying before her. If she could have run out of the place without him and without scandal she would have, but everyone knew of their happy arrival. The birth notice had already been published.

She did ponder the idea, though, yet in the end no such drastic measures were needed. For one night as she slept rocklike, as she always did, the little boy, named Sean by then, developed a mystery fever and died. Just like that. No one even woke her. Isn't that incredible? They simply waited until the following morning when she was sitting up ready for him in makeup and morning jacket.

The nurse came in and said, "I've got some bad news."

Faith said, "What is it?"

The nurse said, "I'm afraid your baby died last night."

Stunned, Faith for once was without a socially acceptable response. She stared at the nurse, who took the look to be one of anguish and trauma but which was, really, reflective of this thought: *God heard me.* But "oh" is all she articulated, not even asking how or why.

The nurse, a kind woman, thought she was clearly dealing with a mother in shock.

Over the next hour, various professionals came in to explain. They didn't know the nature of the fever. They would have to carry out an autopsy. Would she like them to tell her husband? Funeral arrangements would have to be made.

She found it all incredible. Could prayers be answered like this?

At the time I had completely conflicting feelings about this sad development. Was the child spared by God through such a rapid arrival and departure? Did he die of neglect—hospital or maternal? Was it good for that precious soul or bad?

What I do know, however, is that together the parents made the decision to bury him in what was known then as a pauper's grave (three other infants, no headstone), and that they both despised each other for it—Faith because she would have quite liked to play the full sentimental role as the grieving young mother if he hadn't drunk away their money and Joseph because it made that apparent.

A bad provider.

They held a service, though, but she didn't go. She gave the impression she was too distraught, but really she was simply unable, too tired to summon up the appropriate public feeling. It would be another thirty-five years before she even enquired as to where his little body had been laid to rest.

Yet while she got a fridge, a rest, and attention, she also got the first sparks of guilt that flared, only occasionally, if she stayed still enough, long enough. Rationally it was: Did I have something to do with his death because I did not want him so desperately?

You might think that's not rational, that it was simply an illness that took him back, but I'd dispute that. You people have a greater impact on each other than you will ever know.

Still, that thought was not frequent. More common, more irrational was this: Am I so powerful, so holy, so beloved of God that he answers my prayers? Like this?

In case you don't know, haven't read much history, this is among the very worst thoughts you people can think for really, there is no limit to what you can do if you believe God is on your side.

She thought herself special—of course she did—but when you start thinking you are particularly special to God, designated to a higher rank than others, well, then hell looms, for it is a shudder-making thought.

That poor family. Those two strange people. My heart went out to them then.

I don't mean just then, at the death of this child, but in all the time I'd known them. I wish they had just been able to hold each other, to put aside the sexual frustration, the holy bleating, the fear and suffocation, and reach out to each other, for they did have warm feelings for each other once.

Religious dogma, I have to say, has a great deal to answer for.

I don't know whether to point this out or not right now. Still, I might as well say what I have so longed to say just in case Claire finds this all too hard and severs the connection. God designed sexual union as a gift, yet you, in all your muddle-headedness, mistake the pleasure for the gift.

No, the gift in the deal is intimacy, to have the capacity to be as close to another as sex allows, as close as is physically possible to another human being, to be able to unite body and heart, mind and spirit. (How we envy you that, when it is done well, which is far rarer than it should be.)

All creatures (well, except us and the others) are designed to procreate, but you are designed to love. In God's plan, sex plus love equals good. Sex without love is counterproductive, self-defeating in a cosmos where your self, for a reason that often eludes me, is of paramount importance.

I'll spell it out. Being so intimate, every incident of sexual union completed without love drips a drop of poison into the soul garden, hardens the heart, dulls the senses. It's not that hard to understand, but you have turned it, over millennia, into a complex mess. It has been designed—as a gift—to strengthen love, not destroy it.

He doesn't care what you do with your bits as long as you do whatever you do with love, as long as you do no harm to your partner, to any interested third parties, to yourself.

So same-sex sex with love yes, loving sex with contraception, yes, sex outside marriage, outside the church, just outside with *love*, yes, yes, yes.

God is love.

It isn't that hard. Most of the rules you once followed but have since mostly rejected were written by men, conceived via the minds of men, which of course is a very limited medium.

But now you've swung the other way, thrown out all the fears and restrictions and embraced sex just for the sake of sex. You've gone from being told to abstain on feast days, saints days, Lenten days, and menstruation days to being told (via your modern media—the new religion) to do it all the time, that you're a loser if you're not a lover, expert, indefatigable, senseless, and stupefied.

Honestly, you people and your eternal capacity to miss the point. Your bodies are the least interesting part of the trinity of each one of you. Trust me, the human mind is far more fascinating than the clumsy machinery it calls home, and the spirit, the human spirit—well, what can I say? It's everything. Really, to put it simply, it fires the entire universe.

So as Faith's and Joseph's marriage was descending into civil war, all of us outside were shouting, "Put a condom on! Love each other!"

But did they listen? No they did not. They seemed to feel incapable of turning back, of finding a different way. Too much left unsaid, too much that couldn't be said.

When they brought their little brood back from the farm, they didn't even speak of baby Sean. They buried the idea of the child as obscurely as his body. They simply told the children that the baby wasn't coming home ("Why not?" wailed the little girls. "Where is it?") and carried on as if (a pattern, you will note) nothing at all had happened.

Was it planned that the children would take from this the idea that babies could just disappear? Was it planned that they would be left to constantly internally pose the question, "What did this one do?" God knows. I don't know. But I do know they were very big thoughts to leave knocking around in (relatively) little heads.

And now all these years later, I still feel like weeping for them, all these children, big and small. It was such a complicated, painful start, and I kept begging for guidance, wondering what on earth I was meant to do about it, any of it, what any of us were there for when our voices were so wilfully ignored. "To witness," was the only answer I ever received, and like you people do, I wished for somewhat less-obscure assistance.

Slowly, Claire grew into her head, which was both good for her (less obvious cause to find her freakish) and good for me (more soon).

Yet still, her infancy was tough viewing. Within weeks of the disturbing demise of the last baby, for example, Joseph began, without hesitation, to make his feelings clear on the matter. Now spending less time and money at the pub (haunted and humiliated by the pauper's grave, though not the child within), he began to drink at home.

He'd sit in his chair drinking cans of beer with the children playing at his feet and say such things to Faith as, "Old Huey sure is some joker, don't you think? He took our son and left us this. Look at her. She certainly is some kind of joke." He'd stare at Claire morosely and then shout, "Can't you put her to bed? I can't stand to look at her."

These days people would explain such cruelty as the effect of unresolved grief, but they weren't in grief; they were in relief. All Sean's death signified was another excuse to hate and to blame. Bad is a choice.

Such outbursts were always met with silence, but everyone in the room knew who he was talking about—everyone, even then. And that in turn encouraged Claire to cling to her mother. Not a good idea. A bad idea indeed because as her character emerged from the fluffy clouds of babyhood, it soon became clear that Claire had all the makings of the perfect private victim—the family scapegoat—which to Faith and Joseph seemed the least she could contribute to the smooth running of the family home.

What a made-to-measure miracle they thought, particularly given that the choice had already been made on that first day of her life.

She was trusting. She was sensitive. She was gentle, and she was compassionate. All of this was perfect because there is no point, no satisfaction, in bullying the coarse and the stupid because they'll either just bully right on back or miss the point altogether.

Even then, in those early days, Claire knew something serious had happened when the baby had not come home. She had overheard aunties offering comfort, the ladies at mass offering prayers. And she heard Joseph. She thought it was her fault, that she should have swapped places with the baby somehow, that the mistake was cause for misery. So did Peter and Debbie.

She did, then, the only thing she could think of to try and make up for the upset. She loved more, following Faith around the house, cuddling her legs when she stood still, running to meet Joseph as he trudged, hopeless, down the road, drawing pictures for them, singing little songs.

Faith and Joseph found her repellent.

They wanted to shout, "Get away from me," but that seemed too brutal (without drink), so they just shrugged her off, told her to go and play somewhere, anywhere, and turned their attention warmly to the other children.

Faith knew what was going on in that largish head and found it good. Claire was so easily affected. Nothing even had to be spelt out.

In fact, the dynamic seemed to work better when nothing was spelt out, for then, even then, it seemed Claire's heart and mind would do all that was needed, understanding just enough, feeling bad enough, feeling responsible for anything and everything, her thoughts and emotions in perpetual useless motion.

I can tell you, it was the stuff of madness, and I shuddered for her future as I looked on.

Faith would be nasty, then deride Claire's tears, and then pat her on the head, telling her to cheer up, that she looked ugly when she cried, that she should not be so morose and sullen. Then she'd give her a treat. Really, Faith was turning her into a spinning top.

She'd say, "It's such a shame you're so clumsy."

She'd say, "It's a pity you're not as pretty as your sister. Oh well. There's nothing we can do about it, I suppose."

At times, when the two were alone, as Faith did the ironing or folded the washing, she would even say things like, "Do you want to hear a secret, Claire?" Such a wheedling tone she'd use I'd feel like being sick and would call to Claire to come outside, but she couldn't hear me over the malice.

She'd say, "You've got to keep it a secret. Do you promise? Well, I hate your father. I do. But we're stuck with each other. I do hate him. Oh don't look at me like that. What a face! Are you trying to make me feel worse? Honestly, it's a good thing I love God or who knows where we'd all be. You children are so lucky to have me. He doesn't care, your father—not for you, at any rate. You know how he feels about you. Imagine what would happen to you if I wasn't here. Just imagine."

And feeling better for having vented to the only person possible, she would send Claire off to play, and off she'd go, the sweet little thing, traumatised, confused, harmed. Even then Claire could smell the hate and misery seeping from her mother's skin but it was the only maternal smell she knew, and what could be done? Who was to blame?

How could she make them happy, these parents of hers? That was a question she would ask herself for decades. It was about now that Claire began to develop insomnia. She was only four years old. But as the Jesuits used to say, "Give us a child up to seven and we will give you the man." They knew a thing or two. Emotional maiming can never start too early, an early start being even more crucial when grooming a scapegoat, preparing the sacrificial lamb.

Do you know the concept of the scapegoat? It comes, of course, from the Old Testament tale of Isaac choosing a goat to carry the sins of the chosen people into the wilderness, as far away as possible. Honestly, it was an idiotic idea even then. Why can't you just be sorry, take responsibility, change? It's all that's asked.

Throughout history there has been the scapegoat. Jesus, of course, the Jews, so dreadfully afflicted from pogroms to the Holocaust, and now the Moslems, gentle Moslem women having their scarves ripped off, young traumatised African immigrants, boat arrivals. Anyone, really, who is vulnerable or different.

It's such an easy thought—it's all their fault—which never seems to lose its appeal to you people, no matter where it leads. Sadly, the same process can occur in particular types of families. They have to be big families (you need numbers to make it work). They also have to have a measure of dysfunction, usually caused by the demon drink (so aptly named) where there is great resentment, which in turn gives rise to a great need to blame someone, anyone.

And it particularly happens in Catholic, isolated families—especially then—where no divorce means no escape, where public virtue is paramount and private vices necessarily hidden (given the small parish), and where the idea of an agonising individual sacrifice (Jesus) for the salvation of others is the central guiding philosophy. It is an ancient idea, and really you'd think you would have moved on.

In effect, in the bosom of the family, the chosen sacrifice becomes the hub of the wheel, the central focus of all the hate, the unhappiness, the frustration. This has the following benefits.

- Everyone has someone to blame.
- Everyone is in agreement (if on only one thing, which is infinitely better than nothing).
- Everyone is in collusion, so everyone is compromised, silenced.
- Everyone feels better in comparison to the object of derision, so privately, profoundly grateful that it is happening to someone else and not to them and acutely aware of the object of that lesson.

Yes, it works for everyone except the one.

And that one becomes, by design, completely defenceless, particularly in an isolated environment, where the chosen one does not even have access to other families who could act as a guide to what is normal, just, and loving. They have nothing to measure their lives against. If this is the only family they know, then all families must be like this. If everyone thinks they're ugly, so it must be. If everyone thinks them stupid, that too must be so.

If they are told (to general agreement) that they are difficult, impossible, hopeless, or hard to please then it all must be true because parents don't lie, do they? So the one hears from the minute that she can hear that she is too loud, too quiet, too passive, too aggressive, too needy, too distant, too soft, too hard, too smart for her own good, too stupid to believe.

That, my friends, is the making of the scapegoat.

And there's another word. I mentioned it earlier, do you remember? The word is *cult*.

You might think of them in terms of tambourine-jangling innocents waiting for the end of days that are always just around the corner (and who knows, they may be and that may be a blessing, at least for me), the small rictus-smiling bands who claim to know the answer but to what question has always been the question.

They are not always comprised of strangers, such cults, people preyed upon, picked up in public. But they all pivot on the axis of power and control. Every one of them punishes dissent, demonises outsiders, uses guilt, shame, mockery as a weapon. Every one.

They offer idiotic beliefs, and to make them stick, they use such timeless thought-reform methods as chanting and group sin sessions while demanding absolute obedience to the leader, as far from God, the greatest of democrats, as it is possible to get.

Yet don't they all love God? Don't they use him as the power behind their throne? Don't they love to prop him up to sit at the right hand of the cult leader?

In this case, God was right beside Faith, a looming, ominous presence, terrifying and incomprehensible to her confused little brood. For Faith by this time had decided that if she was forced to endure this marriage, this terrible mistake, this horrifying drudgery, fecundity, and low-status misery, she would be obeyed. She would have power and influence and control over, at the very least, her own creations. Just like god, she thought, only with less room for manoeuvre.

So at about this time, she began her lifetime practice of placing a religious image on every wall of every room in the house (weeping Marys, tortured saints, bleeding Jesuses). Even then, the idea of God and Faith were so inextricably linked in the minds of the children they might as well have been portraits of their mother in various scenes of suffering and anguish.

She put them everywhere. They pulsed, "Don't forget. Don't forget my maternal sacrifice. Don't forget you are being watched. Don't forget who has the power." And then, with the children still so small, she imposed upon them a daily rosary.

Are you with me? Thought control? Chanting?

Before they began, she made each child admit a sin from the previous day. If they couldn't think of one, it didn't matter. Faith would wait. They would all have to wait while the sun shone outside calling them to play or the night sounds echoed and the little heads drooped in need of sleep, all turned so effectively one against the other in their hurry to have it over. Until a sin was found, real or imaginary, it didn't matter.

It was repugnant and preposterous, and I tried not to look, listen, wail.

Then on their knees they'd say the rosary, one decade for each sinner, one for Faith to help her with such children, and one for Joseph who, to give him credit, hated this new practice and refused to participate. I think he would have put a stop to it at times but felt incapable of imposing his will to stamp out something so seemingly holy, devout, worthy.

The children, so little, had no idea of the words, the meaning, the purpose of the prayers. They just rattled them off, trying hard not to fidget or jig, not to hate it, her, each other, God. It was a cult of personality, the cult of Faith.

While all that was going on inside, outside they looked picture perfect, particularly within this godforsaken community. Faith (what a saint!) cleaned the church and provided what flowers she could manage to grow in the wasteland of her garden, baked extravagant cakes for the local priest, the Catholic ladies, the fundraisers. And on Sunday morning, the little troupe would be paraded at mass, so neat, so quiet, a credit to them both.

Joseph worked hard, joked with the truckies and the farmers (indulging his misery only in his own time, a credit), and played cricket for the local eleven; a good bloke, a good family man, smart, an asset to the district.

Peter was at school, and Debbie and Claire played quietly, gently outside most days, so careful, even then, to be no trouble (perfect girls).

Then Faith, as was to be expected, became with child once again, but this time, having had a precious four-year interval, she and Joseph accepted it with stoicism and a certain resigned decorum. The new baby was added to the prayer list, a room made ready, and the children warned of less attention, more work, the usual routine, that timeless address.

Faith, feeling ever more powerful, really, in that house, omnipotent, thought she had better want this baby just in case God's love for her played out again so literally. She was beloved, so she had better be careful. As a sign of gratitude for her exalted status, she offered him (or the souls in purgatory, whichever he preferred) the pain of this labour.

Again, miraculous, he seemed to her to be listening. She almost died. The umbilical cord wrapped itself around the child's neck, the obstetrician could not be found, she began to haemorrhage, and it all looked lost. A midwife asked if she would like them to bring in Joseph, who was standing, like all men then did, out in the corridor.

But she said no. She said no.

Many years later she would explain this as not wanting to upset him. Really, what rubbish. She blamed him. No, she said no because she did not want him to see her agonised, helpless. She did not want him to see her ugly, to leave such an impression, not even to hear words of love or comfort, not even to say good-bye. How she believed in appearances, even up to what could have been the end.

Finally the baby, at almost the last minute, twisted, freed itself, and slid blindly, bloodily into the world. Three things came of this. One, Faith became totally convinced of her central role in God's life. Two, she never made the same offer again. Three, she felt a bond like no other to this child who had almost killed her. Curiously, the child never felt the same. She was born in her mother's image, did not feel much, and certainly had no need for cuddles or closeness. Faith felt cheated. Isn't that ironic?

# Chapter 7

# Claire

It's me again, Claire, and I've got to say I'm feeling more and more unsettled by Thomas. Who is that mysterious "I" who seems to have been eyeing me?

I'll tell you what I think and have only thought since we began this mad collaboration, never really having put myself in this zone before—well, not to the point of channelling anyway. He clearly believes in God, speaks as if he knows him, seems to have been around forever, and talks as if we are deeply, even cosmically attached.

I'm trying to whisper on paper again, but do you think he could be an angel? Can other people hear their angels? And when he speaks of the others, is he talking about demons?

He's never made himself known to me as an angel that I can say. Whenever I ask him who he is, he laughs and says, "I am who am" or "Who do you think I am?" Even when I'm desperate and refuse such nonsense, he says, "You wouldn't believe me if I told you." All of this is frustrating and useless and raises so many questions of a biblical nature that I've given up asking.

This also I will say. Thomas knows much more than I do. He has an understanding of the world, of the meaning of our lives, way beyond mine. I quite like the notion of God with a capital G, a sort of grand designer, but it is a relationship defined by Doubt with a capital D. Thomas just seems to love him and suggested I use the lowercase g to help move away from the idea of God as Great and Grim and Gruesome to God as gentle and gracious and generous (but strangely that felt a bit disrespectful, even to me).

And he may be gentle and gracious, but that's not been my experience, I can assure you—though Thomas says that attitude says more about me than it does about God.

And well it might, I suppose, given that I lost what little faith I had in a benevolent universe when Death came to stay. Don't get me wrong. I think life is amazing—perhaps for the simple reason of having seen so much of it come and go—and I am cheerful (no more ghost attracting for me). Yet, knowing that so much can be lost without warning is a tempering experience that tends to wipe out thoughtless optimism, replacing it with respect.

I'm afraid. Thomas is confident. I feel as nothing. Thomas says I'm fourteen billion years in the making and should be more appreciative of the effort. Ha! He thinks our time on earth to be short and almost excruciatingly precious. I feel it to be long and strange. I think meaning is hard to find. He finds it everywhere.

And one last thing I'll say about him—he sometimes leaves me when I need him most. That is to say I am not in charge of us, and I hate it when he goes.

When that happens, I can make all quiet in my world and wait and wait and wait, and not one word do I receive. Not one, and though, as I said, our conversations are not of the ears, still the silence is deafening and I feel bereft. Never once has he explained where he goes or why he remains so quiet.

Then when I think all is lost, that whatever it was is no more, there he is again, chatting, laughing, advising (do you see why I think he's a he?).

But back to my story.

Question: what is murder? Is it only the taking of a life, the destruction of another in a moment in time—a bullet to the heart, a knife to the throat—and does it always require a weapon, a physical agent, poison, strangling hands, a candlestick in the library?

I used to think so once upon a time. I believed murder to be defined by premeditated violent action at a specific instant in time, you know, as in the judge intoning, "I put it to you, Bill Smith, that on the night of the third, you did knowingly and with malice aforethought enter the abode of one Bob Rustbucket with the clear intention of bludgeoning said Rustbucket with a broom handle until he was dead."

But now I'm not so sure. Now I think you can murder with only malice if you're powerful enough, if you're patient enough, if you're cold enough. You need to be able to isolate the victim, to demonise him to ensure his cries of anguish go unheard, but if you can do that, if you're prepared to play the long game, then I think malice aforethought is more than enough for murder.

It could indeed be the perfect crime—to make the victim do the deed. No blood on the hands. No fingerprints or evidence or accusations. No need for alibis or answers. If you hold the right position in the life of the deceased, not only will you be spared sharp scrutiny but you will rather be treated gently, with the timeless honour and respect given to the grieving.

But perhaps I'm wrong (it would certainly not be the first time), perhaps I'm too close to the subject, too upset to see it clearly, so I'll let you be the judge.

I can't remember exactly when I fell in love with my younger brother, Luke, but fall in love I did, and before you get any weird ideas and with apologies to those wanting a very dark tale, there was no carnality in this affair. It's not a love much talked of is it, the love that exists between siblings. The poets don't muse on it much, do they? The songwriters don't sing of it, and if they do it's usually about sisters and sisters or bands of bothers rather than one of each.

I wonder why? Does it automatically give rise to thoughts of illicit passion, of unnatural attachments, of dysfunction?

If so, it says more about our limited notions of love than it does of love, for I think there's a wonderful yin-yang to the love between a brother and sister for it offers frank and fearless access to the oft-incomprehensible "other" and creates a magical safe space that can be filled with tears and laughter, dreams and sorrows, sports and flowers, beer and bubbles.

I don't know why it's not more common, more valued, but perhaps it only arises in bigger families, now so rare, where there are enough babies made of the same genetic soup to increase the chances of finding two kindred spirits among the brood.

Luke was mine, and while there had been a certain distant affection between us when we were children, we had the freedom to become friends when we were both far away from home, when he arrived in the city to study science at university.

He was one of the funniest people I had ever met. He was the kindest person I had ever met, and he was smart. He was good at everything, and he was just good. He could pick up a golf stick and outplay the fanatics, and he could sit at a piano and create music. He was a star cricketer, a handy footballer, a talented photographer, and a loyal friend. No wonder the vainglorious people disliked him so.

But the rest of us didn't. The rest of us felt like the sun came out when Luke popped in. And though our friendship began long after our initial meeting, I thought it would last until we were funny old people, but it didn't.

It didn't even last until his death, for to my eternal shame, I turned my back upon him when he needed my love, which was before other people turned their backs on me. Karmically speaking I know what I did. I know how I made him feel, and if it were possible to snatch back time with a desperation born of knowing, I'd do it in a heartbeat.

I know why I did it. I wanted to be like other people (the very worst motivation ever dreamt up by woman). I didn't want the responsibility of loving Luke alone, and I was afraid if I did, we could both drown in anguish.

But I don't know how I could have done it. I don't know how I thought I could do such a thing as betray my brother's trust and not pay and pay and pay. I was innocent then, I suppose. I didn't really know regret, remorse, and the endlessness of death.

Also being somewhat psychic (have I said?) I became paralysed with knowing. I knew he was going to die—I had a vision—and I knew the second his dying began even though we were hundreds of miles apart, as if we were physically entangled somehow over time and at a distance but to so little positive effect.

Two days before the beginning of his end, at a time before the broken wine glass episode but after the appearance of the glowing man, I was pottering around my bedroom when I came upon a photograph taken and framed for me by Luke lying face down, neglected, forgotten, covered in dust.

I picked it up and cleaned it up, trying not to think with sinking stomach that the state of the image was symbolic of my care of him, though I knew it was. I'd simply become useless and hopeless in the face of his misery, variously diagnosed as severe depression or mild schizophrenia depending on the day he was having or the professional consulted.

I sat on the bed looking at the image of a giant Christ crucified, built by monks on a hillside behind a monastery and photographed by Luke at dawn so as to capture a resurrection light slanting in from the bottom left-hand corner. He had taken the photo when he was dreaming of taking holy orders before the church rejected him, before society rejected him, a decision that had catapulted my mother into ecclesiastical ecstasies before it all went wrong.

It was such a noble idea, so wildly countercultural and hugely amusing given his good looks (think Paul Newman in *Cool Hand Luke*), and while I tried to take it seriously, I couldn't rid my head of thoughts of all that future fluttering in the female congregation.

Can you say your brother is handsome? Does that give rise to freaky notions? Should a sister never think that? I don't know. It was a fact, and it seemed marvellous to one such as I who had always felt herself to be so plain. Why not acknowledge beauty when you see it? Girls swooned for Luke, but Luke being Luke, he kept them at a distance—or most of them at least—fearing he could not love them back to the degree they deserved. What an unheard-of notion.

I'd say, "You don't have to marry them, Luke. You can just have some fun."

But he'd just grin that shy grin and go on about his business.

An honourable man. A rarity in time. But there was one woman, a delightful young women named Beth, who I think he loved in his own quiet way. She was a woman he let in at any rate, the two of them laughing, chilling, feeding the ducks together in the local park.

I was mad about Beth and was sad for her when he told her he wanted to be a priest, for she had more substance and meaning about her than any church could offer, in my opinion. I thought, *That poor girl. This could scar her for life.* I thought, *She'll always win at the dinner party by saying, "I was dumped by a man who preferred celibacy."* I hope she didn't suffer too much, and I hope her life has turned out to be a good one.

So given Beth and given that I hate religious dogma, the idea of the priesthood was one I tried to talk him out of with all the antireligious bigotry I could muster.

I remembered, as I sat upon my bed looking upon that strange image, coming home from work one evening from one of the most godless of places—a tabloid newspaper, no less—to find Luke sitting on the doorstep, smoking a rollie, the photo in a plastic bag lying beside him on the stoop. It had been a torrid day—filled with murders, betrayals, lies, and exploitation, half committed by them, the public, and half by us—and so to see his dear face was a balm to my weary spirit.

"Hello, you," I said. "What brings you here?"

"I've got your present," he said as he stood.

"What present?"

"Your birthday present."

"Luke, my birthday was three months ago."

"Better late than never," he said, grinning.

"True," I said as I fished in my handbag for my keys and opened the door.

He walked behind me down the hall and into the kitchen, clutching the plastic bag.

"Well," I said after standing there some time.

"Well what?"

"Is that it?" I asked, looking at the mangled bag.

"Yes."

"Are you going to give it to me?"

"You might not like it."

"So you've bought me a gift you don't think I'll like."

"I didn't buy it," he said.

"You didn't buy it."

"I made it."

I was delighted. "If you made it, Luke, I'll like it more."

"Maybe not."

We stared at each other.

"You're being very weird and enigmatic, my dear. Why don't you just give it to me and I'll see?"

He made no move to hand it over. "Because I have to tell you something first."

The two of us were still standing through this strange exchange, though I had at least put down my handbag on the kitchen table and kicked off my shoes.

"Okay," I said. "So tell me."

"No," said Luke. "Perhaps you should see it first."

"Luke!"

Shyly he handed over the bag, and now, all these years later, I can't for the life of me remember what I'd expected to find within it. I can say, however, that a framed photograph of an enormous crucified Jesus was not it. I stared at him, at it, at him.

"I know it's not a normal birthday present," he said.

"You got that right."

"But I've been told to save your soul."

"My soul?"

"Yes."

"You've been told to save my soul?"

"Yes," he said with a grin.

"Luke, it's a Tuesday night."

He laughed.

"It's been a long day."

He laughed.

"My soul is the least of my worries."

He just laughed.

"You're not going to go away, are you?"

"No."

"You're not going to let me be until you've said what you've come to say?"

"No."

I sighed and put my shoes back on. "Right then, to the pub. If you're going to try and save my soul on a Tuesday night, I want a pint of Guinness while you're doing it."

And so with great good humour, he tried. Luke said my soul was important. I said I doubted it. He said God had chosen me for a particular purpose. I said I doubted it. He said I'd understand in time. I rolled my eyes.

He said, "All I'm asking is that you don't become too dark as to not be able to find the light."

I said, "Luke, sometimes I can't even find the door."

I tried to talk him out of the Catholic Church, and he tried to talk me out of agnosticism, both of us unsuccessful but happy in defeat. He even wrote a song about that day. I have it on a CD, which I am still only brave enough to listen to occasionally, that dear voice from long ago being both a comparative comfort and a lifelong sorrow.

Have a guess what the song is called? It's called, "Maybe Today We Will Not Argue."

That ratbag. It took me two years of tearful listening to be able to find enough emotional distance to be able to listen to the words, not just the voice, but when I did, and when I realised it was the soul-saving song, I laughed and cried and laughed, for he got the last word after all and is still at me one way or another.

Such days we had of it, talking of God, the universe, the stars. But oh that day looking at the dusty picture, that day those days seemed like a lifetime away, for Luke hated me then. He hated me, and I, being the naive fool I was, put that down to mental illness instead of asking the far better, far more practical question of why. Why did he hate me? What had been said? What had he been made to believe, and by whom? Those questions didn't occur to me for years and years, but I wish they had occurred to me then. Then perhaps all could have been different.

And as I sat cradling the crucifixion, I thought of him coming to find me when I lived in a little cottage by the sea, looking so sad and beaten after having been rejected by the prelates because of a failed psychological test of which he would not speak.

I tried to make light of it. "As if the catholic church can judge! You're probably too sound, Luke."

It wasn't helpful at all. He didn't smile or respond. He looked, at only twenty-five, like a man without hope.

For two days we talked and talked about everything, with one profound omission. We did not talk about our family, and even now I find that incredible. What were we afraid of? What could we not bring ourselves to say?

I did, however, talk him into seeing a doctor. It did no good, however, for about three weeks after this, he went missing in his work van and was found two days later by my father, sitting disoriented, penniless, and in a sort of fugue state under a tree in his favourite forest.

And what did my father do? Did he gather up his son with words of gentle comfort and protection? Did he suffer to see his son suffering so? Did he even just pick him up and take him to a doctor?

No. My father berated him for causing trouble, he gave him petrol money to refill the van, and sent Luke back to the city alone. Yet later he told anyone who would listen of his tremendous fatherly fear of walking into that forest to find his son hanging from a tree.

I didn't know then that actions are truth. I believed my father's words.

Upon hearing that Luke had been found, I raced from my cottage to the city to gather him up myself. Yet having spoken to my parents—both of whom were quite happy to hand over responsibility—I was consequently horrified to find that they had neglected to tell me that dear, gentle Luke was psychotic.

A mad man.

His eyes, circled by darkness, were sunk into his head. His movements were those of a marionette. He hadn't washed for days, and my father had seen all this and sent him on his way, handed him over and washed his hands.

It hurt so to see him like that. He was my friend, my brother, and as I drove him back to my house—him telling me that he was John the Baptist, that I was Mary Magdalene (so few roles for women in the scriptures) and him seeing the number plates of passing cars as acronyms of divine import—I swear I felt crow's feet forming around my eyes, as if burning wires of grief and fear were being laid against my skin.

I was then only thirty-two, but I thought as I drove, not knowing what in the hell to do when I stopped, that the next time I saw myself in a mirror, the face of an old and troubled woman would be looking back at me.

I had always feared madness, had often felt myself to be only just outrunning it at times by a lurch or two, so to see the dearest friend of my unsaved soul caught in that tentacled grip made me feel like screaming. But instead of standing by him, instead of finding courage, instead of offering comfort in his darkness, to my great shame, I ran. I ran to the other side of the world.

But before I fled, I took him home to the family for Christmas and was utterly shocked to see my clan, that unit I still blindly believed in, split and fracture on the subject of Luke. My father and the rest on one side, and me on the other, with Faith, as usual, playing her cards very close to her chest.

My father, who you know as Joseph, gazed upon Luke with contempt, as if to say, "I knew it. I knew it. He's been hopeless from the beginning." He made a point of walking out of the room when Luke walked in. To anyone who'd listen he'd say, "He's a disgrace. He won't even shower. He's always been a lazy little blighter, and now he's here to bludge off us again."

It was horrible and hateful and now I realise only to be expected.

Peter said, "I told him when he was staying with me that physical exercise is the key. I told him to take up running. I even bought him the gear. But would he listen? Would he get off his arse? No. And now look at him!"

But Ruth was the worst, as usual, for she was there that Christmas with her brand-new first-ever baby, and Luke was stealing the attention—shifting that ever-desirable spotlight away—and that to Ruth, then and now, was an unforgiveable offence. "He's always been useless. He's just looking for attention. He doesn't care about anyone but himself. I don't want to hear one more word about him."

And she imposed her will upon Grace and Debbie, as she always did, leaving me to feel much like I imagined Luke to be feeling. This brother of ours who was idolised by others, who had taken the children of his siblings camping, fishing, and skylarking, this brother who had brought sunlight and joy and a gentle spiritual masculinity into all our lives, was written off over Christmas dinner just for being sick.

I thought they simply didn't understand mental illness. I somehow convinced myself that they couldn't see his crazed and anguished eyes, his awkward movement. I tried to defend him. I tried to explain mental illness as best I could, but I was looked at by the others as if I was cut from much the same cloth. Certainly I was not worth listening to, an empty drum.

And Faith agreed with them in public and me in private, as she always did. Is it any wonder I ran away again? No. It was not surprising, but neither was it excusable. But there is something deeply frightening about an irrational, vicious group dynamic, and I was afraid. I was afraid they'd turn on me.

How hopeless we can be.

In my defence, I can say I'd already bought the tickets for an extended stay in Ireland before the madness descended. I'd given my word to my dear friend and travelling companion, Kate, yet I did think of cancelling. I did say I would, and I told my mother that perhaps I should.

But she, for the first time ever when presented with my plans of further peregrinations, urged me on and away. She and my father, even, for the first time ever, gave me money to aid my escape.

She said, "Luke is our responsibility, not yours. You have the right to live your own life. You must go."

All of that sounded entirely reasonable, but her words rang so false, so hollow, being unprecedented as they were, that they rattled in my head as a confused jumble rather than as a warning. I didn't have the wit then to realise they were perfectly designed to appeal to my weakness, but I should have; I should have. I'd been around her long enough.

And when I returned from Ireland, Luke hated me, would not speak to me, and upon the rare occasions of eye contact, he looked at me with eyes so wounded and betrayed that I lost the power of speech or critical thinking.

Why didn't I ask him why? Why didn't I sit him down and untangle the hurt?

I asked my mother (big mistake), and she said, "It's just the illness. Don't bring it up with him. You'll only upset him. Leave it. Let it alone. Leave him to us."

And I believed her, and I obeyed her.

Even when Luke accused my father of abuse and my mother of monstrous egotism, accusations that were met with barely controlled rage and pious, longsuffering patience, I did not believe him. I believed them.

I didn't even ask him. I didn't want to know even though I knew there was a world of darkness at our core. It was much easier to trust them and think Luke mad than to turn the world upside down by trusting Luke and thinking them bad.

Even when my mother displayed her perfidy with open confidence, still I trusted her. It is the power, I suppose, of the mother, but still, it shouldn't be so powerful as to shut down the brain, should it? Even when I knew she had lied, I could not conceive of her as a liar.

I could not think of her that way even when she rang one day and asked me to drive her and Luke back to his caravan in a remote country town to collect his belongings. It was a request I gladly obliged in the constant hope that each development could be the crucial one, the life-changing one, the event that could turn it all around. Of course I said yes.

But one hour into the drive she said that bringing Luke home was not actually the purpose of the trip. With him sitting quietly in the back, staring vacantly outside, I tried to keep my voice low.

"What do you mean we're not bringing him home?"

She said, "Well, we might. That might happen."

"Might?"

She said, "We're going there to meet someone first, and then we'll see."

"Who?"

"The priest."

I was furious. "The priest? What on earth for? Haven't we had enough priestly nonsense? Isn't that part of the problem?"

She said, "He's going to conduct a ceremony."

"What the … what kind of ceremony?"

"Oh nothing. You don't have to come."

"What ceremony?"

"A healing ceremony, that's all."

"What, he thinks he can pray away schizophrenia?"

She laughed. "No, of course not. He's just going to pray. He's just going to see if there are …"

"What?"

"Nothing."

"What?"

"Demons, that's all. He's just going to try and get rid of anything evil, that's all."

I couldn't believe it. "An exorcism?" I hissed.

She said, "They don't call it that anymore."

"We're taking Luke to an exorcism?"

"You don't have to come."

"You can't let Luke think he's possessed."

"He agreed." And that was her final word.

I almost drove off the road, not only because of the idiotic horror of the idea but also because I knew she had lied, had known I'd never have participated had I known. Madness upon madness, and I was driving.

When we arrived, they went straight to church with the other crazy people, and by that I don't mean the sick or sorrowful. I mean the comfortable Catholic burgers who were all probably hoping for a bit of excitement to liven up their lives, a bit of green vomit say or some shocking Latin cursing.

I went down to the beach to stare into the distance, to smoke countless cigarettes, and to wonder where in fact the madness lay in our family. Part of me had been tempted to go with them, to protect him, to be a voice of reason, but my mother discouraged my attendance, probably for that very reason. I also felt I could not endorse such diabolical nonsense by participating in it.

Two hours later she found me by the pier to tell me it had not worked; no evil spirits had been found. Only my most respectful daughterly regard prevented me from saying, "No shit, Sherlock."

She said the priest had found no demons lurking in Luke's being, that it was all rather disappointing. She said, "Perhaps he's just sick."

Even now I'm not really sure why she embraced the extreme of an exorcism. To give her only the tiniest benefit of the doubt I still possess, perhaps she was desperate like I was then. Perhaps she really was searching for any mad solution, though I suspect she stage-managed the whole affair so she could get to play the starring role of the faithful mother of the afflicted. That she would have relished.

And she also got to drive Luke and I mad and madder, and she did enjoy that too.

That was the last time I saw him—well, interacted with him, I should say, begging him to wish to be well, to take his medication. I even scuffled with him in the car park, shouting and crying, crazed by it all. Not the best approach, I know, not a strategy endorsed by the professionals while she looked on from the comfort of the car.

I said, "You don't have demons, Luke. You're just sick. Mum's wrong to encourage such thinking. If you're sick, you can get well. You just have to take your medicine."

But he just stood there as I rattled him back and forth by the shirt front and with my words until I was spent and could think of nothing else to say. Then he slowly walked back into his caravan and shut the door upon us both. It breaks my heart all over again to write this down. Why didn't I hold him? Why didn't I offer comfort and love instead of anger? Why didn't I focus my frustration and confusion upon the constant cause of it—my mother, who sat quietly, gazing out upon the two of us absurdly wrestling in the fading winter light, calmly eating an apple.

If only I had known that would be the last time we were to speak, Luke and I …

Oh if only we knew the importance of the moment.

# Chapter 8

# Thomas

Claire could hear me in those early days much like she can now but with greater acceptance and less bewilderment. She thought it was normal, as, of course, it is.

You'd be surprised at our powers of communication if we are given a chance. We can talk to children as children, to presidents as advisors, to scientists as the thoughts of their rational minds. Listen now. Perhaps even now you are being spoken to. Can you hear it?

She thought it was so normal that she spoke her side of the conversation out loud until mockery made that impossible.

"Stop talking to yourself, child," Faith would hiss at her if she overheard. "Stop that muttering. Really, do you have to be so odd?"

But still we spoke.

Yet there were times when I could not shout loud enough to help. Oh Lord I hated those days in that pestilential village. (We had a much better time of it later, in Edinburgh and Rome, having fun, finding friends, when we finally made our escape, but those days of larking optimism were a lifetime away from the days we had then.)

In the burning, blistering, petrochemically poisoned summer in that place, the billabong was the sole relief.

Though crawling with creatures, no one could afford to turn their noses up at it, not at all, for it was all there was.

Peter, son and heir, had learnt much in his few years on your planet. He had learnt that boys were the chosen ones, the divine template against which all else was judged and found wanting. He had learnt that girls (like a variety of defenceless creatures) were very good for hurting. He had learnt that boys even rated higher than women from Joseph's defence of his bullying when Faith, upon rare occasions, thought he had gone too far. Most importantly, he had learned that he was loved and Claire was hated. Not hard to figure out but such a dangerous thing to know.

So let us all go down to the billabong, down the scrubby path that led off from the back of the house, past the drooping, exhausted gum trees, over the leaf litter, the bugs, and the trapdoor spiders.

On those burning afternoons, it was the arrangement within the village community that if one parent was present, all the children could go for a swim. One of the little people with a willing parent would run up the melting macadam and return with a hot, bothered, fractious band waved off by hot, bothered, fractious mothers.

Down they all went to the rocky bank, the stagnant pools, the foetid water, and in they'd jump, as only children could do faced with such a putrid prospect, gleeful and carefree. Only kids, really, who had never known clear summer water could have managed it with quite the same gusto.

Faith, when it was her turn, would find a spot in the limited shade to read a magazine, taking the chance offered for some blissful quiet time, her new baby sleeping quietly beside her. But rarely did that quiet last for long for every time that Claire went in, out she came again covered in leaches, on her little arms and legs, her back, her chest. Scrambling out, she would be screaming and hysterical.

It was the clarion call, her wailing, to the boys who surrounded Peter, his little gang, to scramble out after her, surround her, and pluck them off, one by one, watching with fascination the small rivulets of blood left behind on that delicate skin. But this did not happen by accident. Peter had told her, so kindly, so earnest and thoughtful, that the leaches only ever dug into people who moved in the water. If she could only stand in the water perfectly still, they'd swim right by her. Trust me, he said, and she did.

I tried to get her to move, made up water games and whispered them into her ear, but I was no match against that innocent trust and that terror. In she'd go, not yet five, her plump little limbs so perfect for the task, and stand amid the splashing of the other children as still as a statue.

Faith saw it all often enough to know what was going on and thought it most amusing.

At each hysterical emergency, an unholy baptism, Faith waited for the boys to pluck off the fat black shining creatures (which they'd turn inside out, burn, impale on barbed wire, oh endless tortures, endless barbarism) and then hiss at her daughter to hush, to stop making such a fuss.

Finally, by the end of that summer, Claire would no longer go in that wretched waterhole, but that only made matters worse. Get in and play like the other children. Stop being so difficult. You're fat; you need the exercise.

Really, in the end, she had no choice but to slide dolefully back into the water more determined than ever not to move a muscle.

Finally, on another parent's watch, (after her screams had subsided, after the parasites had been plucked) Claire was given the chance to explain what her brother had told her, why she did what she did, weeping that she just couldn't seem to stand still enough, long enough. That mother of a son was horrified. She marched the band of boys home to Faith and explained what had happened even as Claire begged her not to.

Faith feigned horror, said his father would deal with Peter, herded all her children inside, waved off the outsider, and turned on Claire such cold fury, so many tiny daggers of malice that the child thought the sting of the leeches nothing, really, in comparison.

Claire knew by then that she was detested, that the world was made up of people who were loved and people who were not. She knew particularly then because of the recent arrival of her new sister, for this new baby had been welcomed; this one had made it home from the hospital. It couldn't just be about babies.

It therefore had to be about her.

Once she'd asked Debbie who she liked better, mum or dad, only to be overheard by Faith and belted with a wooden spoon.

Faith said, "What a ridiculous question. You cannot choose between your father and me. There are no favourites in this house."

Claire's head was just about ready to explode. Claire knew that what her mother said was untrue—of course there were favourites—but could not then, not for ages and ages, think the next thought: *My mother lies.*

She couldn't do it. All she wanted, as all children want, was to love and be loved. If she felt her mother to be deceitful, nothing would ever turn out all right.

Not ever.

And of course the more Claire's need for love was denied, the more she craved it, an appetite fed on by Faith for years and years and years. Really, it is the perfect way to gain control and keep it—to hold out the promise of love and never, ever deliver on it.

You all know this. You do it to each other all the time, one way or another. It is hard even now, after all these years, to accept that an adult can relish inflicting such emotional pain on a child, to gaslight them, to make them doubt their sense and senses, to set them up as a sacrifice.

Yet of course it does happen, for it sets up an entire lifetime of confusion, of internal conflict, of misery and self-doubt, of vulnerability and anxiety. It is the creation of the victim who can later be exploited, a perfect circle.

Oh I longed to protect the child, to try and explain that she was in the eye of a very dark storm, the unwitting focus of a long, long game, but I couldn't for there are no words childish enough. Besides, our time together outside, even in that toxic dustbowl, was the only innocent happiness available to her then and I was determined to ensure that Faith and Joseph did not poison us too.

The least she could have was me.

Instead of the truth then, what she took from her life so far, at that delicate, absorbent time of childhood, was the profound belief, a belief that lodged itself in the very marrow of her bones, the core of her psyche, that if she just tried harder to please she would be loved as the others were loved.

It was a rational thought, it was optimistic, and it gave her some sense of control in the chaos—that she could do something, she could aim for something. It all might change some glorious day when she finally managed to absolutely nail it.

It was rational, but it was wrong. It was wrong, but it took her decades to figure out that glorious day sometime in the future was never part of the plan, was never on the agenda, would never arrive.

I mention this summer of leeches because it still gives me the creeps, so to say, when I think of it. We don't cope well with slimy and crawling kinds of creatures. Really, they seem to belong to the others. We are much more comfortable with tamed lions, unicorns, that sort of thing. Note: God finds this funny.

I also remember it so clearly not only for the misery of it, the barbarity, but also because such a patch was to symbolically occur later in her life, quite recently actually, when finally she heard me say quite clearly, "Pluck them off, Claire, these people, these parasites. You don't need to be hysterical anymore. You can do it yourself." And hooray, she did.

Also it was a public display of her status, which in those early days I would have preferred to have hidden, for the marked vulnerability of one can appear as an irresistible invitation to others.

After the summer of the leeches, Claire was sent to school. It was a life-changing moment not just for Claire (and so for me) but for Faith for letting this child, in particular, out into the world carried an element of danger. What if she told what life was like behind closed doors? What if she gave rise to doubts as to the holiness, the perfection of her parents?

(If this family had lived in another place at another time, Faith would have happily embraced homeschooling. Really, it offers such privacy, such power, so perfectly suited to the secrecy of cults. But that was not allowed then and there, praise be.)

Faith had to minimise the risks, it was quite crucial, so she reached into her bag of tricks and pulled out … (can you guess?) the rosary. So, on the child's first morning and hundreds of other mornings after, Faith made the three children recite the prayer as they dressed for school and as she sat watching.

The three little Australians chanted the Hail Marys as they put on their singlets, shirts, skirts, or trousers, as they struggled with their socks and shoes, as they brushed their hair and washed their faces. They were almost hypnotised by it all, almost maddened, even before they had left the house.

Faith said the rosary was to help them be good. She said they should pray to be obedient, and they should know that God (that terrible ogre) was watching them everywhere. Then she made them say a special Hail Mary for their mother and the wonderful gift of her love for them and sent them off.

Already able to read and write, Claire could not wait for that first day.

The two-roomed school, nestled amid the trees on the flats opposite the north-facing aspect of the horrible hill, beckoned to her like a calm oasis, but when her near-skin-bursting excitement was reaching its zenith, Faith popped her like a little balloon.

As she wheeled the pram down the road with the others running on ahead to let the morning breeze clear their addled little heads, she pulled Claire back to walk with her.

She said, "Don't talk in class."

She said, "Don't answer questions unless the teacher calls your name."

She said, "Don't annoy anyone."

She said, "Don't hang around your sister; she's got her own friends."

She said, "Don't show off."

She said, "Don't be clumsy. Sit still. Don't fidget. Don't hurt yourself, and if you do, don't make a fuss. The teachers have better things to do than worry about you."

Don't, don't, don't.

Claire, utterly bewildered, walked into the school room, spoke to no one, and gave every appearance of being autistic. She stood, in the midst of the delightful flurry of excitement of that first day, once again like a statue.

Finally, over the next few days, her fear and confusion were gradually calmed, particularly after the young teacher showed her delighted surprise to find a literate pupil so early, so young. Soon she found that Claire would participate if called on, that she liked to play with other children, that she could be chatty and funny. It was like watching someone gradually emerge from an induced coma.

When Claire was handed her first report to take home, the teacher gave it to her with a hug, so moved was she to have at least one bright mind on this godforsaken rotation. Faith told her to bring it straight home unopened, that it was written to her and Joseph, and that it was an extremely serious sin to read other people's letters. It was a system she stuck to for most of Claire's schooling.

It meant, of course, that any praise could be ignored so the child would never know from outsiders that she was smart. Claire had to think herself an idiot to allow herself willingly to be treated as an idiot, to be the willing sacrifice, not the wretched victim fighting, for unwilling, screaming victims can be a tad embarrassing. They have the potential to draw attention to themselves, to make other people look bad, don't you think?

So if it was written that Claire became restless because she was bored, she was in for it. If it was written that it might be best to move her up a grade, she was in for it. Really she was just in for it.

Before we leave this time and place (Yes, thank God, we did eventually leave, but to better or worse I cannot say, not even now. The natural environment was better no doubt—how could it not be?—but inside the next house, well, let me just say, all was not well), there is one more major event I must relate.

I am afraid of telling it, I am, but if Claire is brave enough to write it down then I am brave enough to tell it. As the children grew, their characters of course became more apparent but also, in this house, more crippled, bent out of shape, like saplings trying to take root in a bitter, hostile environment.

Debbie, knowing herself to be so beloved of Joseph and with no doubt as to what Joseph liked in little women, was becoming fantastically passive, obsessed with her prettiness, doll-like, and inert. Peter, knowing himself to be so beloved of Joseph and knowing also what Joseph admired in men, was becoming an almost pathological bully. This did not play itself out with other boys, where he might take a beating too, but only with his sisters. Punching, kicking, pinching, smashing into them on his bike, pulling them around by the hair, throwing stones—really anything he could think of that could possibly hurt.

Occasionally he was punished for harming sweet Debbie but only rarely reprimanded for his wounding of Claire if he left visible marks that might need explaining. Understanding, he felt compelled to keep it up, almost, you could say, encouraged. But he was just a child. Inside I sensed he ached for reigning in, but there was nothing for it, no internal or external control, no limits.

One afternoon during another endless, wretched summer's day, Peter surprised Claire enormously as she was playing quietly under the stilts of the house by asking her if she'd like to go up the hill to play on the rocks.

She couldn't believe it. She'd always wanted to muck around up there with the big kids but had either been refused an invitation or seen off by flying stones. She was delighted to be asked, still clutching as she was at the belief that if she tried hard enough, all would be okay. She thought Peter's invitation was proof of progress.

But I knew otherwise, could feel a certain foreboding, a rising static in the air, and first began to sing to her, then shout, trying to distract her, keep her there, safe. Surprisingly, I say sarcastically, it didn't work. She was too thrilled to have been included and ran off after him, over the boiling tar of the road and up the steep, stony incline of the hill.

I didn't want to follow, I didn't and silently screamed for some divine assistance, some help from someone more senior, even some guidance, but I was simply told to go and witness, my usual hopeless instructions. And this is what I witnessed.

As the children climbed, four other boys joined them on the path.

"Where's Debbie?" asked Claire. "Where are the girls?"

"They're up ahead, waiting for us," Peter said.

They made their way down into a mossy, tiny valley, hidden from view by the volcanic boulders, and then they jumped her. Two of the boys grabbed her arms and pinioned her to the biggest of the rocks. The two others grabbed her legs. She couldn't even fight; it had been too quick.

But she did cry. She said they were hurting her, it wasn't funny, and she wanted to go home.

Then one of the leg boys pulled down her knickers and she started screaming, but her cries blended into the throbbing din of the cicadas, the screeching of startled birds, the roaring of the trucks passing on the road below.

No one heard who could have helped.

Then Peter produced his red-handled bike pump (dear Lord, I can still see it now, all these years later) and shoved it inside her tiny sacred space and proceeded to pump rank, greasy air inside her, laughing and screaming, out of control, as if he knew he was crossing some terrible threshold.

So much screaming.

Then he gave the others a turn.

I saw. I saw it all, my anguished keening adding to the unheard uproar, hopeless, useless.

Little Claire fought, writhed in pain, wailing and twisting, but not one of those boys, all of good country stock, not one gave her a thought or were disturbed in any way. Lords of flies.

They thought it hilarious. What else was a girl's hole for, if not to stick things in? And besides, everyone knew Peter's sister. That she was hated. That it was okay. That if not her, then *who?*

When they stopped—when it was clear she was not going to blow up like a balloon (the scientific component of the assault)—they wandered off after catching their breath, in search of another distraction, a bike race, perhaps, or a search for bones on the other side of that wretched, haunted hill.

Before Peter joined them, he wrenched Claire to her feet by her shiny white hair. He said, "If you tell anyone, we'll hurt you more than ever. No one will believe you. They'll think you're a filthy liar. Mum and Dad will believe me. You know they will. They'll hate you more than ever."

And she did know. She did know. And she was broken by the knowing.

When Peter had seen acceptance in her eyes, or rather despairing resignation, he felt quite safe and light of heart and went off to join his mates.

Claire sat down. She sat quite still. She sat quite still while her mind spilt in two …

In one half she put what she could know, what she could think about, what she was allowed to remember, and in the other—all the rest, that is—the truth. But before she closed that door, which would remain shut for years and years and years, this is what she knew. She knew that if she told she would be blamed. She knew that if she told, her father would think her rotten, dirty, repulsive. She knew that if she told, nothing would ever, ever work out all right, that there would never be love, that she would never be loved. And finally she knew that she *was* now totally disgusting, a bike pump, so filthy, that she should have fought harder, that she must have deserved it or it would not have happened.

She knew all this as she wiped the trickle of blood from her thighs and sat staring at her knickers. Finally, she stuffed them behind the rocks, straightened her little dress, and began the long walk (that lasted almost a lifetime) back home. But before she got there, she slammed the door of her mind tight shut, locked it, and forgot it was done.

I'm traumatised by it still. No wonder Claire took almost thirty years to find the words, but even then she understood the hurt lay less in what was done and more in knowing that what was done would not have mattered, that it would have been held against her, that there was no protection for her. It could not be known and survived so she simply could not know it.

She went home. She became quieter. She began biting her fingernails, pulling at her hair. She began to sleepwalk and was found one night walking like an eerie wraith on a deserted country road. Visiting a school friend for her first-ever sleepover, she had wandered out of the house in the middle of the night in search of what, I wonder—home, peace, towards her parents or away from them all?

I saw it and whispered into a certain person's ear that it was time to go, to finish up, to make that one his last beer for the night. Finally, at last, finally I was heard. The friend's older brother, driving home from the pub, saw her on the road and got an enormous fright, rubbing his eyes, slowing the car to a crawl, winding up the window until he was close enough to recognise his sister's diminutive house guest, for she looked like a ghost in her long white nightgown, her bare feet seemingly insensible to the gravel, her long blonde hair floating in the night breeze, her eyes open but unseeing.

With his heartbeat slowing, he stopped the car, got out under that stupendous glittering night sky, and walked towards the shuffling figure. He spoke, received no answer, and understood her to be asleep. It was creepy, he thought. Should he wake her? Would she recognise him? Would she be frightened to find herself out here in the dark? In the end, not knowing what else to do, he picked her up, put her in the seat beside him, and drove like a crazy man to get her inside, safe, hand her over to someone else. I doubt he ever forgot that night, and because he never left the district, I bet he still sometimes thinks of that strange apparition when he drives home in the darkness.

The other mother was distressed by this nocturnal perambulation. Our mother was furious. She said how extraordinary in public, she said how humiliating in private.

She said, "Why do you cause everyone so much trouble?"

She said, "Now as if I don't have enough to do, I'll have to make sure all the doors are locked at night."

She said, "No more sleepovers for you."

There, a blessing. There is always a blessing if you look hard enough because Faith had been searching for an excuse for months to keep the child tethered more securely for fear, really, of what this daughter might see in other people's houses—love, that is, kindness, justice.

But all of this malice had opened another door. No matter how secretive, how disguised is bad, how long the long game, it does have a real-time effect. It opens the door to the others, quite literally. Every such choice invites them in, calls to them through the ether, a sinister siren song. Every such choice acts as a virtual offer of residency, and once they come in, we have to leave.

By this time, in that house, there were dark shadows everywhere, eating up the light, draining out the life force, an energy that was at once repressive, restless, ominous.

Faith, of course, still thought she was praying to God, but she wasn't. At best she was praying to herself, but really even by then I think she was in communion with someone else entirely. He loves liars and adores religious hypocrites even more, all the better to mock God with, all the better to show him the idiocy of the original plan, as if to say, "Is this what you had in mind? Are these the creatures you thought better than us?"

One effect of this dark presence was that very few outsiders liked to visit that family home. Not that they were, ever would be, encouraged or welcomed into the house of Faith and Joseph, but I can say that those rare occasions of an unexpected visit never lasted long.

The woman from down the road bringing home-grown tomatoes, a cricket friend, a school parent with books to lend, none of them ever stayed long at all. They felt uncomfortable. They felt vaguely threatened though they were offered a cup of tea or coffee, a piece of cake, or a cold beer.

It was confusing. Faith and Joseph were such good people, pillars of the small community, the children well-behaved and quiet, the house spotless, but still they could not stay and later could never explain their unease. Most did not return, which, of course, left the children in ever more desperate isolation and allowed the family faults and flaws to grow unchecked, as if under a rich, humid layer of rotting compost.

Joseph's drinking became worse, not just in quantity but in the quality of the morose, sneering contempt and black-hearted misery produced. Faith's resentment bloomed like a huge black rose. The newest baby knew only a cold and bitter internal environment despite the blistering heat, the burning light outside.

And the dark shadows looked on and liked what they saw, whispering, "Isn't he hateful?" whispering, "You deserve so much better than this," whispering, "One more beer won't hurt," whispering, "No one could blame you with a life like this." The house was almost humming with it, almost throbbing, and once they are comfortable, they are very hard to remove, for there is nowhere else in the universe as pleasant for them as your houses, offices, boardrooms, bedrooms.

All you need to do is invite them in, yet then we cannot help you. Then you are on your own.

If, however, you find the strength, humility, and good judgement to rescind the invitation by saying you are sorry—well, then, there we are back again before you've even finished the thought, offering protection, offering comfort. Then we prevail. They can't beat us when we are working together.

But before we leave this time and place, I ask you a question. Who was to blame for this assault, this rape of a tiny child? Peter? Well yes, he was a little brute, but who made him?

We aren't supposed to hate, and it must be said that we aren't very good at it. It goes against our natural inclinations. But that place, that time was perhaps as close as I have ever come to feeling hate for this reason. It was unnecessary, totally unnecessary—all of it.

Faith and Joseph had not been damaged, were not ignorant, and had not been brutalised. They had not one extenuating circumstance, not one excuse for the treatment of their children, all their children, including Claire.

Bad people do bad things because it makes them feel good.

They did it—they created this family mess—just for the sake of their egos, for Joseph to have someone to hate, someone so low on the pecking order that he felt almost a king in comparison, and for Faith to have someone to manipulate and control. Each created this misery only to feed their egos, the human ego, the very smallest thing in the universe.

I can't forgive them for it. Really, I can't.

Luckily, that's not my job.

# Chapter 9

# Claire

Before you go thinking the sexual assault brought Thomas forth as part of a psychological splintering, I'll point out again that I knew him before then. I knew him from the beginning.

Besides, I dealt with that years and years ago, though it was painful and confronting to write about, as you can imagine, even from an external perspective. True, it did take until I was thirty, at the end of a drunken, trustful night with a former paramour, to say the sentence, but still, I did say it. I did admit it had happened.

True also, I can't see a bike pump without breaking into a sweat, yet that brother gave me shelter when I needed it upon walking away from Mark so perhaps there is a balancing of the scales in that. They were barbarous times, and no one knows like I do how dark, crazed, and frightful we humans can become in barbarous times.

But it was also difficult to write not only for the remembering but because I keep trying to tell Thomas we should be writing of Luke, not me, but he just says, "Claire, you promised." Then he says, "Your story is his story, so keep your hair on and keep going."

He's tough, don't you think?

And angry, and though I could try to convince myself for the thousandth time that he is the voice of my subconscious, I don't feel angry, certainly not enraged. I let all the anger and pain burn me to the ground a few years ago in a phoenix-type manoeuvre, and now I'm just glad the worst is over and most pleased to have survived.

But on with my story.

Two days after I had cleaned and dusted off that neglected photograph of the crucified Jesus, Mark and I were preparing to make dinner for friends. The winter sun was shining, I remember, and our love affair in that first wild flush when you touch each other in passing, kiss for no reason, and dream of bed. It was the kind of day, the kind of heart space, where all troubles feel as if they are solvable and resolvable, and even now as I recall it, I wonder again if it is better or worse that we are trapped in time.

If I'd known the future of Mark and me, that dark and stormy descent, would it have been better or worse? If I'd known what was before me—even the significance of the sharp, knifelike pain that frequently cut into my hip—would it have been better or worse? Or does happiness depend on the not knowing, given that every life will have its share of sorrow—well, every life worth living? Would the knowing destroy the living?

I don't know, but I do know my psychic flashes only added to my confusion, for while I had seen Luke jump from a bridge, a vision that came to me on a no-account workday when I was distracted by professional banalities, still it had not happened. I knew and I didn't know.

I grieved the knowing, crying at the vision as if it had been fact, but still it had not happened. And though I thought of him every day—fearing he was cold, fearing he was hungry—yet still I did not act but was lulled by the passing of time, distracted by the love affair, wanting to be like other people, to be happy, thoughtless, comfortable.

And I was excruciatingly aware of my prophetic limitations too—or my ability to prevent disaster, I should say—having seen only six months previously a calamity approaching my dearest girlfriend. Yet I had—surprise, surprise—no capacity to head it off, to reroute the disaster train in time.

What a useless ability.

Her name was Jess, and I fell in love with her too over one glorious summer afternoon. Do you remember what that feels like, making a best friend in a matter of hours like we did when we were children?

To be so open, to be so free of care, to meet someone and simply allow yourself to be bowled over by friendship—that is my idea of the divine (sorry, Thomas). In our lives we meet hundreds of people, don't we? Yet still how rare and fantastic it is to meet a friend, the friend you've been waiting for, your friend.

She was hilarious. She was brilliant. She could sing high opera in German. She was a teacher who was too shy to teach, a singer too shy to sing, a shop assistant who preferred to socialise than sell, and she backed the underdog with a tireless, passionate devotion.

She was a natural comic and could do so many accents that it would make my head spin; the nostalgic Yorkshire man, the kind and overly polite Indian, the bad soapie actress staring into the middle distance, the Mafiosi and the Mafiosi's moll—all imaginary hair and fingernails—a lout, the queen, an American preacher, a black rapper, and various characters from the novels of Jane Austin.

In those roles she was not shy. Oh no. In the roles of her devising, she inhabited the stage like a glorious, hilarious diva, and often I'd have to beg her to stop just so I could breathe. It was as if she was comfortable in any skin but her own, as if she could play anyone but herself.

She was surrounded with laughter, but Jess was wounded. She suffered depression. She gravitated towards the darkness and was swallowed by it for love, all for the love of a bad man. Still for a time, for a short but glorious time, she gave out the wild light of a dying star.

She already loved him when we met, so like all good friends, I tried to love him too. I didn't succeed. He was menacing. He was controlling. He introduced her to heroin, and while you don't need to be Nostradamus to know that had disaster written all over it, still, not every user dies.

And she kept her growing habit hidden. She kept it secret. She kept her increasing need for it and so for him part of their dark and private passion so I didn't know, leaving me to behave in the friendship much like a gormless Pollyanna, not understanding her increasingly frequent absences from society, her increasingly scattered thinking.

I knew trouble was afoot, but I had no idea of its depth or nature.

I'd say, "I don't like him, Jess. He means you harm. I won't change my opinion of him, but that doesn't change my opinion of you."

Then she'd raise her doubts about Mark, which was only fair, and on we'd go until the day I was told she had been found drugged out and unconscious in her little ramshackle car on a quiet suburban street on a quiet afternoon. This, among other things, made it profoundly clear that this person I thought I knew, this person I loved, had a private life darker than my darkest imaginings even though we saw each other more than twice a week.

More than twice a week.

How I did not know I do not know, but then I knew. I knew she would die. I knew it as a fact rather than a vision, that she would become a statistic, all that glorious life reduced to a figure on a policeman's sheet.

So we went to the pub.

I said, "Why didn't you tell me?"

Jess said, "Because I didn't want to have this conversation."

She had a point.

I said, "You're going to die if you don't stop."

Jess said, "So?"

I said, "What, like Russian roulette?"

She looked at me in silence.

Then I wailed. I said as if it were becoming the chorus of my life, "You've got to care. You've got to want to live. You can't just throw life away."

Jess said, "Yes I can."

She had a point.

"Well yes you can, but please don't. Please don't leave me here without you."

Jess gazed at me with great fondness, took a sip of her wine, and said, "I won't die. Don't panic. I'll stop."

And me, being the idiot I am, took her at her word.

Why didn't I do something? The refrain of my life. Why didn't I get her into rehab or whatever it is you do? Who just takes someone's word for it, gives them a hug, and buys another round of champagne? Me. That's who. Knowing and not knowing.

Two weeks later she was dead while he, that dreadful man, lives on and on. And when I received the call to tell me she was dead, after leaving countless, silly messages on her answering machine while her body grew stiff and cold upon the couch in her little flat around the corner, all I could say was, "No. That can't be. We're going out for dinner tonight."

Honestly if there was a game show called *Biggest Idiot* I'd have to enter it because I'd win. When they laid Jess to rest in a green and pretty hillside, I felt like throwing myself in with her and had to back away from the open grave on trembling legs to avoid creating such a gothic scene. Though if I had and if I'd had to be lifted out all covered in roses and dirt and sticky tears to the horror of the dignified gentry, I bet I would have heard her laugh, for she did so love a dose of black, black humour.

Then as if anything could make this worse, something made it worse. It was the public revelation only months later that the smack she had bought, that last fatal dose, was fatal for the simple fact that it had been supplied to the local dealers by the local detectives. The poison was too pure. Why not? The supply appeared to be endless and secure.

One of those detectives is in prison now, and I hope he is haunted every minute of every day by the lives he destroyed, which is not to say I want Jess's spirit lurking around a maximum-security facility no matter how much that might intrigue or amuse her.

So many people think of hard drug users as subhuman, as if they forfeit the right to care or respect the minute they plunge in that first needle, for we do so love to find reasons to hate those who are not like us. Yet Jess died for love. She loved not wisely but too well. When I saw that horrible man at her funeral, I wanted to stab him with a knife, which isn't very nice, is it?

I wanted to shout, "She was worth ten of you, you fucking bastard," and make a huge commotion, but I'm an anglo woman, so I didn't. I stared at him instead. That surely showed him.

But life went on as it does one way or another.

Luke drifted in and out of psychiatric units, sometimes against his will and sometimes not, once walking out of one such dreary place, hailing a taxi, getting the cabbie to drive him two hundred kilometres back to the city, and simply getting out and walking off when the car stopped at a traffic light, which I'm sorry to say I found hilarious.

I know it's wrong, but really. What was the driver thinking? Luke had crazy hair and a crazy beared and wore crazy, twisted clothes, and I mean that literally. He wore layers of shirts and sweaters which he corkscrewed to the left around his torso, and he was picked up outside a madhouse.

I hope that taxi driver put that lost fare down to a lesson in greed.

Then Luke went back to the monastery of crucifixion fame, no doubt in search of sanctuary, but while the loving monks took him in to work on the estate for no wages, they soon booted him out again, giving in return for his devotion only the train fare back home to my parents.

They said he was unbalanced, but they did nothing about it. They said he didn't belong in their holy, contemplative company, but they didn't get him help. They didn't do anything to aid that troubled soul, a soul who only ever wanted the comfort of that church. They drove him to the train station and simply left him there.

By the night of the dinner party (I got a bit side-tracked, I know), Luke was back in the same town as my parents but was not living with them for he'd made it plain that he wanted to kill my father. But he had been taken in by people of the church. He had been embraced by those church-going sort of women who love a lost cause, and I love them for it. Thank God for them. They did more than I.

My help was pathetically limited to supporting my parents, who I thought were supporting him. I found and sent them books on schizophrenia. I sourced and sent them information on support organisations. I investigated the different drug regimes in the hope a better one could be found for Luke, him so hating the zombie effect of the drug he'd been prescribed. I suggested they raise different options with his mental health workers, his psychiatrist, anyone, to get it altered if they could. I told anyone who'd listen that I was afraid he would suicide, that we should do more, do something, anything, but as usual I was dismissed as an hysterical Cassandra and told to let it be.

And then in desperation I told my mother a secret; I told her Luke's secret. I agonised over it for weeks before I said the words, tossing at night or pacing in the dark, trying to think my way around all the corners of our family dynamic. I needn't have bothered, for while I thought in the end to have gotten it right, though I had made the right decision for all the right reasons, I was very much mistaken.

I told her (it makes me feel queasy still to think of it) that Luke had tripped out on acid some years before. I told my mother in the hope it would help him, so she and my father would have as much information as possible, so they could raise it with someone, thinking it might be the key to the mystery.

I didn't say, as I knew to be true, that Dad's contempt and hatred had been behind Luke's choice to fly away on LSD. I didn't say he'd been harmed by them—though I knew that too to be the case. I thought to spare their feelings.

I rang my mother and told her, "It's not the cause, but it might be a factor."

Faith, I can still hear her now, sounded breathily thrilled with the information. It gives me the chills to think of because now I understand why. But then I didn't.

I expected her to be sorrowfully horrified, as in, "My poor son, my son, what have you done?"

Instead she was subtly gleeful and said, "Really. How interesting. Did he really?"

She said, "Thanks for telling me. That's very useful to know."

I, being the nincompoop that I am, thought she meant useful in terms of his treatment, but she didn't. No she didn't, and though I didn't understand then, still my roiling anxiety, that close companion of my life, gave me to believe I had made a very big mistake, though what that was I did not know. I thought I was helping, God forgive me. I should have kept my big sister big mouth shut, but they were desperate times and I had no idea what I was dealing with or rather who, which begs the question: How can you know someone all your life and have not the slightest understanding of who she is? How can you be so blinded, so brainwashed as to not be able to see or, in my case, so devoted to an illusion as to not even be brave enough to look?

Dear Thomas is laughing as I write this. He's saying, "I did try. I did try, Claire," and he did.

But some truths are too monstrous to look upon, don't you think? It takes a brave or brainless person to look upon the face of the gorgon.

Much easier to create a fantasy family and stick to the dream no matter what, to prop it up, to defend it against all the clanging inconsistencies, bigotry, and false dealing and tell yourself, "They don't mean it." For if you look upon a family such as mine with an unshrinking gaze, then upon that day it simply vanishes.

I couldn't do it. Not for a very long time.

So I supported my parents over Luke, my brother. Talk about backing the wrong horse.

And by then two years had passed since I'd had the vision of his death so I thought all could still be well. The night of the dinner it felt like it, for it was Jess's sister and her husband who were coming to dine. At least that was something, to have some part of her, some subtle genetic reflection of her still in my life and someone who missed her too, of course.

As Mark prepared the meal, I arranged the table, the flowers, the candles, looking forward to a contented evening, but as I walked from the dining room into the living room, I fell into an abyss.

There's no other way I can explain it. One minute I felt normal, in search of music to play, and the next I was hit by a tidal wave of despair that felt like all the sorrow ever felt on planet earth.

I couldn't breathe. I felt like I was falling and slowly, slowly sank to my knees onto the carpet in the living room, sobbing. It was all I could do. I felt like all the darkness of the universe was washing through my spirit, and the hopelessness of it, the pain of it made my bones melt. It was the sorrow of humanity without a focus. It was outside time. It was ineffable and ineffably sad, and tears poured out of my eyes, as if I had oceans of salt water inside.

It was like falling into a wormhole and ending up in hell. I know despair now, but I didn't know it then. Then I didn't know such misery existed.

It only lasted minutes, maybe five, but it felt an eternity, and poor Mark, seeing me happily walk out of the kitchen and into an emotional collapse, had no idea what to do and neither did I.

Then it was gone. Then it was as if the vortex closed over.

My wracking, wretched tears dried up. My shaking stopped. My bones became solid again, my body and brain switched back on, and I just sat there without a clue as to what had happened or what to say.

Mark stared at me. I stared back.

I said, "I have no idea what just happened."

He said, "Why were you so upset?"

I said, "I don't know."

He said, "But why were you crying?"

But I could hardly say for all the sorrow in the world, could I?

It was only 6:00 p.m. That shouldn't happen until at least eleven.

I'd just gone into the living room to put on music. I was a touch infatuated. I didn't want him to think me a lunatic. I wanted him to love me. Ha!

It was an experience almost beyond words so I didn't try, which probably made me appear madder. I just stood up and got on with what I was doing, leaving him both relieved and confused, and said not one more word about it.

We had a wonderful dinner, we talked of many things, including Jess and Luke, but we did not speak of that. It was bad enough to think myself mad without other people thinking it too.

Our guests stayed the night that night, meaning we had a fun morning too, rising late, attempting the crossword, eating a fry up, sipping endless coffees in the courtyard out back.

Then not long after they had gone on their way, I got a phone call, oh grim weapon of torture, the telephone. It was my sister Grace (you'll meet her soon). She said she was calling about Luke. She could hardly speak. I grabbed a cigarette.

Grace said with choking voice, "Luke jumped from a bridge last night," and then could go no further.

The pause was excruciating.

I asked, "So? What? Is he all right?"

"No he's not all right."

"Is he … dead?"

"No. He's not dead."

"Oh thank god. He didn't drown."

"Drown?"

"From falling from the bridge."

"Not a water bridge."

"What?"

"A rail bridge. He jumped head first from a rail bridge onto the road."

We both began to cry.

"He's got massive head injuries," she said.

"Head injuries."

"He was found by two men just after he did it."

"When?"

"What?"

"When? When did he do it?"

"Just after 6:00 p.m. Why?" she asked.

"Oh God, oh God."

"The two men who were driving and found him called an ambulance, and he was air lifted to the city."

"So he's here? He's here? So we can go and see him?"

"Not yet."

"Why not?"

"Because Mum and Dad have to identify him first."

"What do you mean identify him? He isn't dead."

"No but he had no ID on him when he fell … jumped … so he's a sort of John Doe. The police need him to be identified before we can go in."

"Oh God, oh God."

"They're on their way now."

"Who, the police?'

"No, Mum and Dad! They're driving down now. We're all going into the hospital later. Debbie and Peter are coming too, but they won't be here until late."

We each sat quietly for a minute, hearing by then only ragged breathing.

I asked, "So what do we do now?"

"Nothing yet. There's nothing we can do yet. Come over when you're ready and we'll all go in together."

We hung up. A ten-minute phone call. A lifetime.

Dear Luke had jumped a few minutes past six, and I had felt him falling. As I sat at the kitchen table strewn with the dishes of good living, I could hardly breathe. How could we have connected like that over space and time? Had he been thinking of me, sending his last despairing thoughts towards me, his treacherous friend? Did he blame me?

It is a thought I can still hardly bear to contemplate. I had even felt myself to be physically falling, had ended up all folded up, as if broken with my head upon the carpet. And it was over in minutes, over I think when he too lost consciousness, for as I later learned, he had lain bleeding on that dark country road, still aware, when he was found but not for long—thank God not for long.

My idiotic half-baked psychic ability had given me a bridge, but I had added the water. The water was my illogical leap; I had not seen it. I had only seen the bridge. It never occurred to me that it could be a bridge over a road.

Head injuries I had not for a minute foreseen, and I felt like banging my head upon that kitchen table until nothing could enter it ever again.

# Chapter 10

# Thomas

Dark days in that glaring light, they surely were.

How I wished I could spirit her away, my little charge, or improve the situation for them all.

For them all.

But there was not much I could do out there on the veranda.

The youngest child was learning to adapt to her environment by distancing herself from it, becoming cold, observant, shrewd. A shrewd toddler. Really, it beggars belief.

By then all the little ones were growing so awry, each little person, or rather personality, uniquely damaged as they struggled to grow, to find the light in the increasing darkness of their family home.

All were harmed, each one, but each one was isolated in the suffocating secrecy of the cult of Faith, meaning they could never discover a pattern, a coherent framework around which to build their ideas of love, kindness, responsibility, their personal strengths, group solidarity.

As time passed and Faith found herself with child again, at her wit's end, almost you could say, demented, it became clear something must be done.

She needed more money. She needed more space. She needed to get away from that hellish place, which had only ever been intended as a stepping stone but which had become more like a swamp. She was filled by now with a passive but mighty rage against him, her husband, at them, her children.

Late at night she raised the subject outside, out of the hearing of little ears, knowing there would likely be raised voices.

She said, "We can't stay here.

He said, "This was your idea."

She said, "We need more money with the new baby."

He said, "That was your idea."

She said, "Don't you hate it here?"

He said, "Oh yes. I hate it here. I really hate it here."

It was (apart from Claire) about all they agreed on.

But still he did not act. He did not look for another job, and when Faith brought advertisements to his attention, he did not apply. He did nothing.

And this is why: pride. Joseph had absolutely no intention of putting himself forward to be chosen or rejected by anyone. Not anyone. Who were they to decide?

Knowing (or believing) himself to be the smartest man in the district, well-read and articulate, meant that the idea of presenting himself for selection was simply not to be borne.

What would they know? What would any of them know? What if they said no?

So he did nothing.

Do you know people like this? Do you know people whose pride is so absurd, so crippling, that comes at such an enormous cost to them and others that it simply seems too hard to comprehend?

Surely you do. The world is full of people like this.

These are the people who only have as friends (if any) others who are less intelligent than they are, fatter, poorer, more ignorant, more vulnerable, or less fortunate. These are the people who watch asinine television for the pleasure of being able to look down upon all they see. These are the people who talk over others, know more than others, who simply feel they have a greater right to be than others. These are the people who take a difference of opinion as a personal insult, as if to say, "But you've made a mistake. It's my opinion. Mine. There can't be another."

You must know at least one or two.

You can recognise them by such phrases as, "My house, my husband, my child, my car, my career, my, my, my." They are now in such numbers in your Western world, really, as to have reached almost biblical plague proportions, and I should know. I also know why. The rise of the egotist is a direct consequence of the age of the individual and the supposed death of God yet again—sigh.

Surely you saw it coming.

The cult of celebrity, the banality of reality TV, of the Facebook pages of the people who don't do anything of note, think anything of substance, surely you saw that such developments could only lead to the rise and rise of the smaller and smallest? Didn't you? Didn't you expect it?

We all saw it coming, not least because human nature, perverse as it is, is consistently perverse.

Always, throughout time, you show such a love of conformity that whatever is held up as worthy (no matter by whom, no matter the agenda) you believe it to be worthy. Those of us like me, who have seen ages come and go, have seen whole societies bow down to thugs in a brutal age, whole communities agog at magicians and charlatans in a credulous age, and whole cities glorify lechers in a lecherous age (the Sun King anyone?).

Not that it has been all a misery in every age and stage; don't get me wrong. There have been some bright spots—thinkers in an enlightened age, doers in a dynamic age, explorers in a curious age, all feted, all honoured and raised most high.

But I've got to say, really, that this age of the egotist is very hard going, incredibly dull. Even the brutes had to have, by necessity, a degree of courage, even the lechers a certain louche appeal, even the charlatans a trick or two up their sleeves. At least they felt obliged to do something to merit some attention.

But now? Why now you need to do nothing and you need no one. No heroes, no good, no bad, no meaning just me, me, me. It's ugly, I must say, incoherent and disturbing. Really you couldn't be further removed from God's original conception. He created wonders for you and you have created *Wife Swap*.

(Really, though we hate bloodshed, and even just the sight of blood, the Mongol wars were more rewarding viewing.)

I should feel compassion. I should. But I don't. I should think of you like the Israelites wandering lost and aimless in the desert for forty years, but I don't.

You know how wondrous, how glorious is the universe—from the genome to the galaxies—and still you insist on dumbing it down. Really, you have no excuse.

Anyway, you could say (fly back in time with me now) that Faith and Joseph, tucked away though they were in that noxious little corner of the world, were also in the 1960s in the very vanguard of the movement, pioneers, you could say, of the age of the ego.

Not that they knew, of course, or would have cared if they had. They only cared about that tiny drop of society that was them, that belonged to them, that was theirs. That was their alpha and omega, the family, a closed circuit, a very private world.

Now let me make one more observation before we return to the story. The most crippling aspect of such egotism, this me-ism, is that people like Faith and Joseph do not like smart, smarter, smartest, big, bigger, biggest. Of course they don't. How can they feel superior to that?

This means that no matter what they say, they do not love anything bigger than themselves, no, not one thing, no matter what they say.

A question: How then can such people learn, change, grow? Answer: They cannot.

Of course they can't, and in your world where stasis does not exist, they must, but necessity, by the laws of earthly nature, shrink.

They would rather shrink. They choose to grow smaller than risk what—a showing up, the need to feel respect for another? Such self-defeating self-regard, of course you know, has also been known to history as hubris.

Which brings us to the Greeks (what wonderful storytellers they were, what astute observers). Is a name coming to mind?

Yes? Of course, Narcissus, the beautiful youth who fell in love with his own reflection. It is a good story, an appropriate term to use in your modern psychology, yet once again you seem to have missed the point that this self-love was a punishment, a curse placed upon him. He died.

It was not, people, a good result. It is meant to be read as a tragedy, a warning, not something to be aspired to, not something to build a society upon.

(Do you remember Echo? The nymph who pined away for love of him until only her voice was left? Poor Echo. I know how she felt.)

So let us say that Faith and Joseph were narcissists. Yes, why not? They were. Both of them were, for how else could the marriage survive?

It was as if, without ever needing to say the words out loud, they had made a pact to protect the other's self-view, to enhance their public perception, no matter what. Really, it was as if their wedding vows should have read, "I promise to protect your ego, keep your secrets, hide your weaknesses, support your lies until death do us part." Both exactly the same and really it could be no other way, or it would have been as mad as a marriage between a philosopher and an airhead.

"What do you think?" asks the philosopher.

"When?" answers the airhead.

Ha! It has been tried, don't get me wrong. I've seen one such marriage up close and found it hugely entertaining, but you could not say it was successful or sustaining.

(It cheers me just to think of those two in their fusty Irish library so long ago now, trying so hard with such good will to reach each other across a sea of ideas, through a tangle of trivia. You can be so endearing, so funny. Note to self: remember this).

Faith and Joseph, though, were not endearing or amusing, but they were loyal in a perverse sort of way, certainly of one mind. But then, right then, with Joseph refusing to act, Faith felt she had no choice but to act herself regardless of his feelings.

She was desperate—so desperate that she not only confided in her mother (hating Joseph for forcing her to admit that all was not well, not perfect) but also asked her for help.

Her mother, moved by the rare intimacy of the request, her daughter's even rarer show of vulnerability, acted immediately by calling her wide circle of family and friends and came up with a job.

But lo, what a job.

It was offered to Joseph through the good word of Faith's uncle, which, hooray, obviated the need for an application or interview process (and thus the possibility of rejection), which made it perfect for him. It came with a significant wage increase, which made it perfect for her.

It was an immediate start (perfect), it came with a large rent-free house (perfect), free utilities (perfect), a company car, and free petrol. Perfect, perfect, perfect.

Crucially, almost miraculously, it was all to be had at an even more isolated location than their previous horrible habitation. Not a neighbour at all for miles.

Really, could it be more perfect?

All this perfection led Faith to believe she must have moved from God's right hand as to be almost sitting on his lap. All she ever needed to do, she thought, was ask. What incredible celestial power!

How she longed, at times, to tell other people of this, to explain who she was, how beloved she was. But she didn't. She could not very well list the death of her son as proof (though she knew it was) or her last agonising labour (though she knew it was). God's mysterious ways, his clear adoration of her, she thought, might perhaps be a bit too complex for others to understand so she kept all this close to her heart, quietly contemplating the miracle of her, of Faith.

But let me give you a tip about God. Rarely, oh rarely indeed, does he give money, status, or worldly goods of any description. (So really you might as well stop asking.)

God is the one who gives you the lift of spirits, the general larking optimism to feel like buying a lottery ticket. He doesn't fiddle the figures to let you win. (That's chance, got it?)

He is the one who will bless you with determination, not find you a job. He gives the strength and endurance to keep praying for rain; he doesn't gather the clouds. He consoles so pain diminishes; he does not remove the pain. He is the one who grants peace, which makes you thrive, which allows all the good things to come to be.

Do you see? You and him. Always. Together. Really, if you just pray the right prayer, he cannot refuse you anything.

The other one, on the other hand, offers things. Of course he does. What else has he got to offer? Why else do you think he has always commanded such a strong following?

He offers things with the unspoken deceitful promise of happiness.

That is, he says, "I will give you power. Won't *that* make you happy?"

Or, "I will let you slake your lust to the depths of your depravity. Won't *that* make you happy?"

Or, "I will give you money …" You get the picture.

God, on the other hand, offers only happiness, strength and peace.

No church, no cult, no coven that praises or honours or promises worldly gain, money, or status has anything at all to do with God. I tell you this so you will understand that when Faith received, practically, physically, those things she so wanted, I do not believe it was God's work.

Oh no, for while it seemed perfect to her, it was clear to us outside that this new move had the potential instead to take them, all of them, just that much closer to hell, for the new job, their new life, was to be had at a vineyard, yes, a place awash with alcohol. So desperate was Faith, so determined was she to escape, that she raised this petty problem only once and only when the deal had been done and only obliquely, to protect his ego, to save her plans.

Standing on the veranda (within earshot) she said, "What about your drinking?"

Joseph said, "What about it?"

Faith said, "How is it going to be there?"

For an instant I thought Joseph might say, "As bleak, as black, as boring as it is here." But he didn't.

He said, "I don't like wine."

It was as if an icy wind blasted through that warm night air, swirling around the house, the others inside listening, laughing, delighted.

I felt sick. I wanted to shout, "Not there. Don't go there. Wait, something else will come along," but I'd learnt by then to save my breath.

Have any of you known an alcoholic? Have you ever heard them make such a statement? If you have, I bet you have.

Certainly many years later, when Claire heard Mark make the same absurd declaration, she shuddered at the words as if they were a grim echo from the past, which of course they were.

But it was enough for Faith. She knew his reply had about as much substance, meaning, as a soap bubble, the froth on his beer, but what could she do?

The children (she) needed a new home. What happened there could be worked out later. She had not signed up for this low-grade life, this poverty, this dust-bowl, hard-scrabble existence, and God clearly did not want it for her.

How could he? She was loved.

Besides, if Joseph's drinking became a problem, she could just pray, couldn't she? She could just ask.

A week before they moved, Faith and her sisters (kind women, they were, distant but helpful, just the way Faith liked it) and her two oldest daughters (already being made so successfully, almost imperceptibly, into little housemaids) travelled to the new house, about fifty kilometres away, almost in those days a significant journey, a different world, to prepare it for occupation.

At first glance from the outside it looked good. It was big, set in a garden (though neglected), ringed by distant hills, and surrounded by lush green grapevines. (Yes, green! In summer!)

Two large old elm trees in the backyard spread their lovely shade across the grass, dappling the light, their leaves swaying in the gentle breeze and casting shadows on the wide, wide veranda.

(Looking back there is no doubt that my spirits lifted at the natural beauty of the location. I wanted to thank God for it, praise his holy name, but of course I suspected this was not his doing, his work. I felt very strongly that this was not the place he would have chosen for this family. Instead, I looked at that veranda and thought despondently, *That's me. That's my new home.*)

Inside, it was horrible.

Unoccupied for a considerable time, it was filthy; rotting curtains, mouldy benches, grimy floors and walls, old newspapers curling, yellowing in corners, a stinking toilet.

But the big and little women restrained their horror and got to work. When they realised the place was infested with vermin, still they did not stop, or only long enough to wrap their hair in scarves and pull up their skirts. Though heavy with child, Faith marshalled her troops like a domestic general, leading the way by attacking the rats and the bats with a broomstick, driving them out, through windows and doors.

(Really, is there any place on earth as riddled with nature as Australia? Had I known, I might well have objected to this job, this mission. Days like that one I positively pined for Ireland. Note again: God finds this funny.)

What a job!

But they did it, as the womenfolk did then, with no help at all from the men. (No wonder a few became such brooding, resentful despots inside the family home.)

And so they moved in, the children almost exploding with excitement. Claire, in particular, was utterly glad to be there, to be far removed from memories she could not allow herself to remember, so delighted with the distant hills, the green.

Looking back I can see that she fell in love with this patch of earth at first sight; the beautiful light, the teeming night sky, the sound of the frogs in the nearby dam, the glorious colour of the vine leaves in autumn, their green in summer, the melancholy aspect of bare, old, twisted vines in winter, the blinding yellow of the daisies that sprouted between their rows each springtime.

She loved the huge, huge sky, the smell of rain approaching, the breathtaking sunsets, the raucous morning chorus, the storms that came through the valley with almost apocalyptic force but which could be safely, wondrously viewed from the protection of the veranda. (I would stand beside her then, watching the violence of creation, the two of us at peace, at one.)

She loved the green of the sky before hail, the clouds that took the shape of fabulous creatures wafting across the heavens, the lowing of cattle that reached her from a distance in the limpid evening air, the creak of an old windmill behind the house.

She loved, will love forever, the outside of that place. And that delight in place, her attachment to it, helped me to understand this country too. (Though we exist outside your understanding of time, still, when here, we travel the journey with you.)

No wonder, I thought, that the indigenes here, the first people of this place have such a deep and abiding sense of country. If a little girl, all alone, could fall in love with a patch of earth and miss it when she left and dream of it forever, imagine the connection between a people and a place built up over millennia. No wonder their spirits were so injured by the dispossession forced upon them. How do you heal a wound like that? (So much pain down here, really, so much heartache.)

It's not just land to them for these peoples saw God in the waters and the earth and the creatures of the waters and the earth, felt his mystic presence everywhere. How can you take the spirituality from a people and expect them to flourish?

Yet still they are so advanced compared to the rest of you, for to see him everywhere is a far more accurate cosmology than to see him nowhere. (As Einstein once remarked, you can either see everything as a miracle or nothing, but everything is much more fun, don't you think? And really, what have you got to lose?)

I thought then, as I trailed around with Claire as she carried out her outdoor explorations, her reconnaissance, that her love for this place might make all the difference, might save her somehow, soothe her spirit from the ugliness inside, and I was right. Besides, it meant she was outside often and that meant being with me, and that was good, for her and for me.

But inside? Well, inside was not good.

After moving in (with all the others fluttering, agitated, gleeful in their wake), it took Joseph about a month to change his mind as to the various merits of wine, about six to establish the habit of starting his drinking on Friday night and finishing on Sunday. Every weekend he was morose, enraged, black-hearted, but not a drop from Monday to Thursday to show he was in control.

Without a word having been spoken, a new secret was also added to the family history, another one to add to Faith and Joseph's hidden, bulging cache.

The secret related to how they came to be there. None of the children were ever to know, at least ever meant to know, that Joseph was helped by her uncle. It was embarrassing to him, so hurtful to his pride. He could have done it on his own, of course. It just didn't work out that way, and no one must know.

Later, in several of his many dinner table demagogic alcoholic rants, Joseph made a point of denouncing nepotism in all its forms and guises as the tool of the rich and the privileged, a conspiracy of the old-school tie and the old boy's network.

Glaring at his children, he'd say, "No one ever helped me. No one would. I wouldn't allow it. Nepotism is designed to oppress the working class."

Faith couldn't help but smirk at this while the children couldn't help but steal glances at each other, wondering what the hell nepotism was.

On and on he'd go. "None of you had better expect a leg up, a helping hand, because it ain't going to happen. You work for what you want or you'd better get used to wanting."

Really, Joseph seemed in those days to be almost entirely composed of bile. Consider the list of those he hated.

Talk about a demonised line up. By then he hated all women (except obedient Catholic wives and mothers), but along with that significant proportion of the human race were rich men, powerful men, well-travelled men, university-educated men, men of any other culture or country, cultured men, dreamy artistic men, farmers, fools, land owners, conservatives, communists, and men from the city.

It didn't leave much.

It didn't leave many.

My goodness he liked to sneer, even with no one else available he liked to simply look around the table and despise all he saw, making the evening meal an exercise in trauma.

("Shut up," I wanted to shout from outside looking in. "They're just children." But I knew it useless for he'd learnt at least one thing from Faith by then, and that was the power of propaganda. She was the saint; he was the working-class hero who had done it All By Himself. Honestly, what lies they peddled, the two of them, day in, day out.)

And as the alcoholic fumes of misery began to fill every corner and crevice of the house, still the babies kept on coming. I adore babies—we all do—but these innocent arrivals filled me with anguish as I gazed in upon them from the veranda.

I haven't named the last one yet, have I? Let us think. What about Ruth? Yes, we'll call her Ruth. It sounds close enough to wrath, and she was angry even then, the poor little thing, breathing it in with the coldness that was all she ever knew.

Throughout all my time here so far with Claire, always one question has plagued me, torments me even now and gives me no rest.

It is this: How different would their lives have been if they, these little souls, had been given to other parents?

How different would it all have been if their weaknesses had been pruned, contained, and their strengths supported, treasured, nurtured instead of the reverse; if they had been taught to love each other rather than compete against each other; if harmony had been the goal instead of conflict?

God knows.

I don't know.

So there was Ruth who even then understood that Claire was available for hating, who even then knew she came into the world to sit at a higher place than another. What poisonous food to feed a child.

Then came another little girl, my favourite really (apart, of course, from Claire, but Claire came with so much care!), a sunny little spirit, gentle, good, and cheerful.

Let's call her Grace. Yes. Why not? She was filled with it.

Really sweet Grace was so loveable, so innocent that she was spared much brutality. Thank heavens. For even there, in that house, even then, going after Grace felt, well, almost evil, like torturing a kitten.

This is not to say little Grace was not fed upon, not manipulated by Faith. Of course she was. But she was not attacked so to say, bullied or brutalised, and that was a great blessing for her and for all of us outside.

Actually, while I'm here, using this word, let me explain grace because it seems to cause so much confusion down here.

Grace is what happens when you and God meet. Think of it as a subatomic particle reaction that happens somewhere in the atmosphere between you and him. If you could see it, as we can, you would see a tiny shower of sparks made up of all the colours in the spectrum, gorgeous and bright, with those sparks cascading back to earth, back down to you.

Every time you show strength, kindness, humility, love, a microscopic rainbow of cosmic fireworks rains down upon your shoulders and seeps into your soul, giving you more strength, more love, more peace. It is like rain for the soul garden, and it is quite beautiful to see.

Think of it this way: imagine the well-known image of Adam and God in the Sistine Chapel by God's great and amusing friend Michelangelo. Picture the hands reaching for each other. The optimists among you think: "So close!" while the pessimists moan, "So far!" but in that space, that sublime space, is grace. You and God. Always. Together.

So little Grace entered the earth as a sparkling little soul.

Two years later, finally there came another son. At last.

You've met him, of course, at his agonised end, but at his beginning he was beautiful, perfect, almost girl-like, and what an easy birth, before time, quick and relatively painless.

Joseph (so long waiting between two moments) took one look at him as he lay in his crib beside Faith, compared him to Peter (so masculine, such a perfect son), and hated the child. Just like that.

Once again. The second daughter, the second son. An ugly girl, he thought, and a beautiful son. What kind of a joke was God playing? It was preposterous, ludicrous, against all an upright man could reasonably expect. He washed his hands of the child then and there and forever.

Faith was delighted by the child and by Joseph's reaction to the child.

"Really," she whispered when her husband had fled the scene, "could I be more blessed? One of each, to do with as I will."

He, Luke, would be the very making of her, she thought, the key to the kingdom, her most wondrous creation.

Oh my. My heart broke to meet him.

And so they all grew in that pulsing, menacing home, surrounded by the usual weird melange of religious iconography placed, as was Faith's way, on every available wall. And every evening the members of that little tribe would be forced upon their knees for the rosary.

Joseph, who still refused to cross this line, would take his paper (Monday to Thursday) or his wine (Friday to Sunday) into another room, trying to block out the monotone chanting as best he could.

Yet always he heard Faith say in her most strident tones of piety, "And now we will dedicate this decade to your father."

Sometimes he felt like killing her. Sometimes he felt like killing himself. Sometimes he felt like grabbing Peter and Debbie and making a run for it.

More often, he just felt like walking out into the night and never coming back.

# Chapter 11

# Claire

"Police appeal for clues to bloody railway mystery."

That was the headline of the Page 3 newspaper story that greeted rural readers on the Saturday morning following the Friday night that marked the start of Luke's destruction.

I have the article in front of me as I write. I keep it in my "book of the dead," which may sound a bit Egyptian, a bit ghoulish, but I was collecting so many funeral items, I didn't know what else to do. Here I keep the photos of Jess and her funeral mass booklet, here the notices of the two other dear friends of mine you haven't met yet, here, even, a card sent to me by a dead person (I kid you not), and here also the items relating to Luke.

It may sound macabre to create a scrapbook or photo album about dead people, but at least they are not photos of dead people. I'm not that weird.

Strangely enough, I made it as a healing exercise, and in a way it worked. To put them all together, to know where all the dead stuff was—the memorial cards, the service booklets, the thankyou notes and pleas for prayers—helped contain the loss in a way, contain death, so I could visit it instead of it visiting me. I did it also to reduce the chances of coming across an image unexpectedly or being knocked sideways with the thought that I was failing them still if I found their memorial mementos lying at the bottom of a dusty drawer.

I bought a fine bottle of French champagne to drink as I did it, I put on sweeping melancholy strains rather than slit-your-wrists misery music, lit some candles, smoked some smokes, and it proved to be a good thing to do.

The tears were cool not burning, and they were a choice, not a necessity. I did it not long after leaving Mark and that crazy house and moving into my little hermitage flat where I forced myself to face that fact that ghosts or no ghosts, still the dead are dead and need to be put in their rightful place.

But back to the newspaper story, and as I read it now, I'm forced to look at a picture of dear Luke lying unconscious and bleeding on the road, a shocking photograph that should never have been taken. My heart does flip flops to see it. It was such a cold, bleak winter's night that night in the country.

You might wonder why I kept it, and in response all I can say is that at the time I had no idea except that it felt important. It felt to me as if it contained a clue of some kind but what kind I did not know, for clearly he was no mystery man to me.

Perhaps Thomas suggested it. It's the type of thing he does—particularly when I'm too distraught to think straight.

The story goes on: "The identity of a man found late yesterday underneath the rail overpass bleeding profusely from massive injures remains a mystery.

"The man was found shortly after 6:00 p.m. by passing motorists, who alerted ambulance and police. The cause of his injuries remains unknown. Acting Inspector (Jones) said it was not known whether the man had fallen from the overpass, jumped or been pushed from a train, or was the victim of a hit-and-run accident.

"Also unknown were whether the man had any possessions with him that could help with his identification and whether he was conscious and talking when found. Inspector (Jones) said the two middle-aged men who found the injured man were at first too distressed by the incident to talk to detectives.

"The man was administered first aid at the scene for several minutes before he could be placed in the ambulance while the road was sealed off for more than four hours as detectives examined the site. A large amount of blood covered the road, and late last night city forensic detectives were due to inspect the scene."

It makes for difficult reading, this story, tragic and graphic as it is: the blood on the road, the question as to whether he was conscious and talking, his last words unknown and un-noted.

Yet it does provide a small measure of comfort in that at the very least his personal calamity was taken seriously by the local police, the ambulance team, the hospital, the air-lift crew.

Luke had been a nonperson for so long, a solitary member of that drifting underclass of the sorrowful and sick, the neglected and the ostracised, that to read this now, to know that the front-line emergency crews cared about him then in that dark and terrible hour, seems to me to at least partly redeem us all.

We, the comfortable people, are so afraid of the outsider, aren't we? We wrinkle up our noses at how they smell, we turn our eyes from the way they look, from the dishevelment and chaos. We deafen our ears to their muttered truths, so terrified of contagion, of the possible spread of affliction, as if the sad and mad could crumble our defences.

I imagine that's why historically they have mostly been locked away out of sight and hearing, to save the sound and fortunate from the contamination of bad luck and misery. I should know. I've lived on both sides of that metaphorical wall.

Yet while being shunned as a threatening outsider caused me great pain, it has always been my actions as an insider that have caused me the most shame, and it is on that note that I bring you to the doors of the city hospital on that wintry Saturday evening. Grace, Ruth, and I were standing on the street at the foot of the main stairs awaiting the arrival of my mother and father.

It seemed to take forever though it was only about ten minutes by the time they parked their car, and then there they were. I think I expected us all to weep or to embrace, to acknowledge the moment somehow, but there was none of that. There was nothing. My parents acknowledged us, told us to wait another ten minutes before we went in, and then walked hand-in-hand up the flight of stairs, jaws set, eyes fixed, calm, collected, and … cold.

I'll never forget it. Not only had I never seen them hold hands before, but I also recognised that look in their faces, gazing at them as I was with eyes made huge from shock, but still I could not place it. There was something wrong about that expression, even if only because it was recognisable and surely nothing like this had ever happened to them before to give rise to a look that was familiar, a look that struck as an echo, as a warning.

I know what it meant now, but I didn't then. I couldn't think the thought then, but now I can. They looked, these two upstanding citizens, not broken or heartbroken but angry and humiliated, as if they were thinking, *Look what he's dragged us into now.*

Yet I was having so much difficulty composing myself that I thought their hard, cold expressions a function of shock, as if they too were doing their utmost not to let their sorrow bring them undone. As Thomas says, we all see the world through the prism of our own characters and experience.

Isn't it strange how powerful and long-lasting are those memories where something strikes you as deeply wrong, even when you don't know what it is? Though I no longer see my parents, that image of them ascending those stairs will stay with me forever.

They went in, they recognised their son, and they gave the police the required information. Then we were allowed into the intensive care unit, and I am profoundly ashamed to say that as soon as I was in, as soon as I saw Luke, I wanted to run straight back out again.

Hopefully you have never seen anyone, anyone at all, let alone a loved anyone, with massive head injuries, for it is an unspeakable sight. Where light should be, where life should be, there was instead a darkness I had never seen before, a thick and monstrous matte black band that wrapped around his eyes, an image from a nightmare, a scene from a horror film.

He'd smashed his pelvis and his collarbone, and dark bruises peeped out from all over wherever the sheet left him exposed.

Oh Luke. By then in a deep coma, his head was misshapen from the swelling, swathed in bandages and supported by a neck brace that tilted it back, leaving his eyes slightly opened but showing only red within the black.

I wanted to cover my eyes with my hands. I wanted to hide behind the couch. I wanted to wake up. I was terrified and thought if he moved I could have a heart attack. Am I not small?

I had never imagined a human being could like look this, and as I sat there, I even thought wildly, *This isn't Luke. This can't be Luke. There's been a mistake.* I couldn't even bring myself to touch him, not even to take his perfect hands in mine. I could not do it. I was too horrified, and only later did the meaning of his unblemished hands occur to me—that they were unharmed because he had not raised them to break his fall. Oh my brother.

I only stayed that first night by his bedside for a pathetic fifteen minutes, and there is no escaping then or now the fact that I ran from the ugliness of it.

What a hopeless person I am. I couldn't even talk to anyone to find out what exactly had happened. I rushed out, hailed a cab, and raced home. Then I rushed in, grabbed the crucifixion picture, that strange, neglected gift, and held it tight against my chest, as if it could ease the pain somehow. I sat at the kitchen table in the dark and began to rock and rock and rock.

Have you ever seen people rocking in grief? I had seen it on the TV news, black-clad women usually from another generation, keening, ululating, and swaying back and forth. I thought it to be a cultural phenomenon, a learnt behaviour.

But it's not. It's primal, a reaction to horror and shock born from the depths of the collective unconscious, perhaps passed down in our mitochondrial DNA, from generations of women without number as a way to help bear the unbearable. Certainly it has nothing at all to do with the conscious mind.

I'm not even sure I was aware I was doing it that first night. Later in the week I knew. I was even aware that the motion gave me comfort, though it was a very strange sort of comfort given that by then I was beginning to fear I could not stop.

Then I thought, *Good one, Claire, now you're going to spend the rest of your life as some sort of bizarre animated rocking chair,* which was not a very comforting thought at all.

Talk about making life harder than it has to be.

On the Sunday I was slightly more composed, if only for having seen the worst, for having spent the entire night awake coming to understand, step by step, that Luke's injuries, despite all the technology and medical science in the world, would be—maybe even should be—fatal.

I wanted a miracle, of course. I'd wanted one for years, but I let that wishing go somewhere before dawn or it left me. But it did not leave us all.

Peter, for example, who arrived at my place early on Sunday morning, having just been in to see Luke, walked in with his usual positivist gusto, making me think he must have gone to the wrong hospital.

I looked a wreck. He looked manfully concerned.

Confused, I said, "So you did see him?"

He said, "Yes. I saw him."

I whispered, "Doesn't he look terrible?"

Do you know what he said? He said, "Oh well. You never know, a good knock to the head could make all the difference."

I didn't know whether to laugh or hit Peter over his own head with a frying pan. A good knock to the head? Our brother was likely brain dead, and once again I was forced to pose the internal question: *Who exactly is mad here?*

Yet I knew Peter was upset, and we all say idiotic things when we're under pressure. Honestly I thought as long as he didn't start banging on about how it would all have been different had Luke taken up running, I'd have forgiven him anything. Indeed I felt an overflowing love for our hopeless family unit then, at the beginning of Luke's end, believing that his imminent death, this collective loss, could not do other than bring out our best, bring us together.

I have, I believe, already described myself as a gormless Pollyanna.

At the hospital that Sunday, I found out the following information: that few brain function tests could be done until the swelling had subsided, possibly late Monday at the earliest; that there were no positive signs; that Luke was not responding to any stimulation; that he could not breathe unaided; that there were no indications of neurological activity; and that while he was unlikely to die now he had been stabilised, we should prepare for the worst.

The hospital provided us with a private room and a family liaison officer to navigate us through the foreign landscape of tests and experts that stretched before us.

But the real information I was seeking could only be had from Faith, like how anyone knew the mystery man was Luke. Like how anyone knew it was suicide and not an accident.

This is what she said.

Faith said that on that Saturday morning she went on a whim (?) over to Luke's flat to clean it for him. She said the door was open. She said that God gave her a miracle (?) by allowing her eyes to alight, amid all the mess, papers, and chaos of a schizophrenic's living quarters, upon a tiny piece of paper that read, "Dear family, I can't take the pain anymore. Forgive me. I hope we meet again. Luke."

Faith said she then began to drive back home when she miraculously (?) came upon some police officers along the way, to whom she showed the note. They then told her of the mystery man of local newspaper fame, the man found under the bridge, of which she claimed to have no knowledge.

They asked her to describe Luke. She did. They asked, as you know, for her and my father to identify him, which they duly did. The city detectives went back to the city, the mystery was solved, the case closed.

I had so many questions, but it was not the time or place to ask them. Besides, I was trying not to rock or cry, the collective will of the group making it profoundly, staggeringly clear that I was not to make a fuss, that the situation was bad enough without me making it worse. Even then they made it apparent that I was somehow the weak link, a threat of some kind, but they had so often made me feel that way I'm not sure it even registered.

And it was, as it had always been, so powerful, that I, as I always did, shrank before its wordless might, meekly submitting to the wishes of the majority.

I wanted to scream, "Our beloved brother has gone mad, lost hope, and tried to kill himself! Isn't that worthy of fuss, of anguish, any emotion at all?" But I didn't. I just sat silently waiting, terrified, for my allocated time by his bedside and broken body, hoping I'd do better this time while Ruth and Grace flipped through trash mags, while Debbie ducked out to do some shopping, while Faith said a rosary, while Joseph did the crossword and Peter paced.

When I couldn't bear to watch them, I went to the chapel to sit silently weeping (it was allowed in there as long as it was not fussy) and to give God an absolute hammering, which I can only assume he took in his usual celestial stride.

I said, "Luke only ever wanted to love you. That's all he wanted. He wanted to dedicate his life to you. To you! And now look. How could you treat someone who loved you like this? How could you not have given him comfort in his affliction, hope in his despair? Isn't that what you're meant to do? Isn't that your job?"

Ah yes. I certainly told God a thing or two, that's for sure (Thomas is laughing), but all I got back was, "And where, pray tell, were you?"

Don't you hate it when he does that?

So I shut up and went back to rocking. And I did do better that day, could look upon Luke without fear of fainting and by Monday even heard myself ask the nurse, "Would it be all right to touch him?"

That poor woman. What an idiotic question.

She was probably tempted to say, "He doesn't feel anything dear—not the needles, not the pins we're putting in his feet to test his responses, not heat or cold, not anything. Whether you touch him or not won't matter to him."

But she didn't.

She said, "Of course," and gently moved his arm from under the sheet and placed his hand in mine, and I almost collapsed not only for the skin contact but for the kindness of her gesture.

Then, of course, I never wanted to let go.

Those days, those nights were so long. I couldn't sleep. I couldn't eat. I couldn't talk—not the excruciating chitchat required of me by the family, not even to Luke. Mark did his best to offer what comfort he could, but he represented light-hearted love then and I could find nowhere to place such a feeling that week. It had been hard enough isolating such a chamber of my heart in the wake of Jess's death. That week all was flooded, and I wondered if I would ever be able to reclaim it.

Every night I spent rocking, clutching the photo, for no religious purpose but only because I had nothing else of Luke's to hold onto, unable to think anything more than, *How did it come to this? How could this have happened? How did it come to this?* for hour after hour in the darkness.

On Tuesday we had the anticipated conference with the medical team. In our private room we sat while the head of neurology and trauma told us there was no hope, no brain activity, no sign of life. They said we had two choices. We could wait to conduct more tests—which we were told were almost certain to show the same results—or we could turn off the machines and let Luke die.

We asked how he would actually die and were told he'd slowly stop breathing. We asked if he would be in any pain or distress and were told no. We asked how long it would take, and no one knew the answer to that. It could take hours or it could take days.

Then they left us to decide his fate, a jury of seven, an execution party, with one supposed weak link, one feared refusnik, which, I guess, was me.

I didn't know that then, of course, the story of my life. Then I thought I knew them, but while I have been wrong time without number, while I have laboured under illusions both many and various, never have I been more wrong than I was in that half hour. For I thought we were all thinking, *What's best for Luke?*

I was even afraid Faith could choose to keep him in a vegetative state rather than allow him to commit the sin of suicide, believing, as I did then, that she believed what she said she believed in.

I thought none of us wanted to let him go.

Wrong, wronger, wrongest.

Have you ever had the experience of being totally mistaken about something, totally misunderstanding a person or situation and still doing the right thing, better even perhaps than what you could have done had you known what was afoot, as if guided in your ignorance or led by subconscious wisdom?

It's happened to me a few times, which is fortunate given how often I am clueless. This was one of them.

Though later I understood myself to be singing from a completely different hymn sheet from everyone else in that suffocating room, still good prevailed. As we sat in silence with me not understanding the meaning of it at all (that they were anxious about me), I thought: one, Luke had suffered enough; two, even if he came out of the coma he'd still be sick and sad (despite the lauded benefits of a good knock to the head); three, that we should respect his wish for his life to be over; four, that no parent should ever have to say the words, "We choose that our child should die"; and five, though I think this was more Thomas talking, that whoever should say it first should say it only from love.

It was and is the hardest sentence I have ever uttered in my life, for while inside I was moaning, *He can't go, I don't want him to go, oh don't leave me here, Luke,* I cleared my throat and broke the silence by saying, "We have to let him go."

I said it for him, I said it for them, my parents, but I did not say it for me. I would have had him stay.

That sentence was the last true and uncorrupted gift I could give him.

As soon as the words were spoken, the family came to life, nodding solemnly, agreeing heavily, and I stupidly thought the lift in the atmosphere was caused by a collective determination to do the best by Luke, a willingness to put our sorrow aside to set him free.

Not for a long time did it occur to me they were relieved. Not for a long time did I understand that they'd wanted this outcome all along. Not for ages did I realise they were ashamed of Luke, that they considered him an embarrassment, a blight, a blot on the family brand.

Perhaps not Grace and Debbie so much, to be fair, but they could easily be worked on, easily convinced it was all for the best. And Faith and Joseph were delighted that I had handed down the sentence first, had fired the first shot, so to say, for being first, I could never recant. To them it became a fact, a weapon they could keep in their hearts forever just in case they ever needed to remind me. I wonder now, given all the time they spent together in those first few days when I was absent from shock, whether Faith had even orchestrated the silence so I would be first. I wouldn't be surprised. What is surprising is that, if so, none of them had any idea of the power of love.

And yet even though I had no idea of such horrible undercurrents, I have no regrets on this at least. It felt like it almost killed me to say those words, to set his death in motion, yet I'm so glad he was released by love and not removed by shame.

It was, as I said, as if I was guided that day given that I get very few things as right as that. Stranger still, once I'd said those words, I found that I could at last talk to Luke, as if I'd atoned somehow. I asked to sit with him alone, held his hand on the Wednesday, the day before his last day, and this is what I said.

I said, "I know I failed you, Luke. I was afraid we'd both sink if I tried to keep you afloat. I thought if I tried to help you they'd abandon us both. I was a coward and a fool, a poor friend. But I never stopped loving you, though it must have seemed like it. Please don't leave me here though I know you have to go. What am I going to do without you?"

It went longer than this, of course, but still it is amazing how little there is to say at the very end, at the extreme and desperate moments. Oddly, I had to keep reminding myself to actually speak, to say the words aloud, because I felt like we didn't need words then, which is a crazy notion I know, not only talking to someone in a profound coma and hoping to be heard but not speaking to a person in a coma and feeling that you are.

Life, it seems to me, is a most glorious mystery.

# Chapter 12

# Thomas

So much hate, misery, and confusion was building up in that house that really if it had been in the form of a noxious gas, the tiniest spark could have blown the whole place sky high. You could almost smell it, a sulphur smell, bitter and acrid.

Peter beat up Debbie, who flopped like a little rag doll, powerless, utterly defenceless against aggression, the girl trying so hard to be perfect for her father, which meant being perfectly passive.

Claire could not stand it. First she'd scream at Peter to stop as he laid into Debbie with his fists as she lay curled foetus-like on the ground. Then she would scream at Debbie to get up and fight. Finally, desperately, more often than not, she would feel obliged to step in and take the blows herself. Then, when Peter had run out of anger and gone on about his business, the two little girls would turn on each other.

"You've got to fight," Claire would shout at her wailing older sister. "You can't just let him do that to you. He will never stop if you don't stand up."

But Debbie would not stand up, could not, and it made Claire crazy. She was by then starting to fill with a slow-burning but diffuse rage at the bullying, the injustice, really starting to believe survival might literally depend on fighting for her life. Surely, she thought, life was not meant to be so violently incoherent, yet it was.

Why didn't Faith act to stop it? How could Joseph find it funny? Why were boys more important than girls? Why were doll-girls praised, really, warmly accepted when it came at the cost of regular beatings, physical abuse? And the biggest question of all: how could they as a family claim to love Jesus, the prince of peace, when violence, discord, and injustice were not just accepted but encouraged?

Really, it made her crazy—well, all of them crazy now I think upon it: Ruth and Claire, Peter and Ruth, Debbie and Peter, Peter and Claire, everyone at each other's throats, barbaric, lawless, abandoned.

By now both Debbie and Claire were regularly sleep walking, and already sweet Grace was waking screaming in the dark. It was so traumatic to hear her in the dead of night. She was too little to be so terrified. (The children could sense the others, I think, fluttering, restless, malevolent.)

And all the while Faith looked on and was glad with what she saw. And this is why: control.

All this conflict gave her enormous power. She was dividing and conquering while floating above the maelstrom, saintly and virtuous, drying some tears but not others, pulling some close and pushing others out into the cold, the bitter cold, of maternal disregard.

It was random but deliberate, and it was profoundly effective. It meant no child felt secure in her affections, which made them desperate. It set up a hierarchy (boys, then girls, then Claire), which made them hate each other. And it set Faith above it all, really rather godlike, really, omnipotent.

How I despised her for it as I watched her sitting in her garden in the shade of a tree, reading the Bible while she listened to that music of misery, the screaming and wailing that was so sweet to her ears.

How happy were the others inside, for they didn't need to do anything—no goading, no incitement, no pushing—to keep the pulse of anguish beating.

All they needed to do was enjoy the show, and they did and more kept coming.

By then the house was becoming ever darker, with room lights necessary even in the bright of day, despite the large windows, the clear blue skies outside.

And all those children harmed within. But none more so than Claire, for by now Joseph's loathing for her was floating to the surface on a storm surge of wine.

He'd tell her to shut up at the dinner table, to not eat so much ("aren't you fat enough already?") or eat more ("show your mother some respect for her efforts"). He'd say how pretty his girls were and then slide his eyes over Claire (revolted, they said, appalled). He would rant or laugh about chatterbox girls, windbag women, frivolous females who made so much racket for so little purpose and stare and glare at Claire.

"Name me one brilliant woman?" he asked one night at the dinner table before the children had had a chance to escape. "Go on. Just one. You, Claire, name one, you think you know so much. And don't even think of listing any idiotic novelists. Women can't write. So go on, I'm waiting."

On and on he'd go, round and round, and night upon night Claire would sit there and take it and then run outside to me. How I ached to hold her, to scoop her up and give her warm, physical comfort. Of course I couldn't, but I could talk to her (an abiding gift to us both, give or take a few communication breakdowns along the way).

The two of us would head out through the gate in the early twilight and wander together around that place she so loved—lying and staring up at the evening clouds or simply walking to let the rage subside.

She would weep at times and ask me why she was so hated, what she had ever done to be so hated. Looking back I fear I failed her then, but I didn't know what to do, what was for the best.

I didn't want her to become filled with bitterness by that poison being daily dripped into her heart, for that seemed to me to be the worst possible outcome. I wanted to keep her little heart open for the good things I hoped so desperately would one day come. So I didn't tell her all I knew but offered only comfort.

I would tell her that she was loved, I would tell her to be strong, and I would tell her not to hate them back.

And as the tears and rage subsided, she did listen. She would say, "But why do they treat me like this?"

And I would reply, "They're just unhappy" (which was true, you must agree, but not the whole truth).

Then, more often than not, she would feel pity for them all, decide to try harder, to love them more. (*Oh Claire*, I thought. *Don't go that far!*)

Do you think I did the right thing? Don't get me wrong. We never counsel hatred, but we are of the truth. We tell the truth. Question: Can too much truth be a bad thing? It felt like it at the time.

It felt like it could cripple her, that knowing she was the chosen sacrifice could help actually to make her one by sending her crazy, and crazy people are perhaps the very easiest to hate, to blame, to sacrifice.

In hindsight, I think I decided that if there was only a tiny portion of justice I could win for her, then it was this: I would at least help her to make it harder for them to hate her. So I counselled strength, but I thought to myself, *Fight them, Claire. Fight the injustice. Man the barricades!*

By then Claire was about ten (I'm not so good on earth years), and this is what she looked like. She had flyaway blonde angel hair. She was small and sweetly plump. She had clear grey eyes that looked enormous behind her spectacle lenses, and she had the rosiest cheeks you ever saw, which for many years she saw as a terrible affliction. Later, a few years after this, she would look at them in the mirror and bemoan to Debbie, "They make me look like an alpine dairy maid, like Heidi, when I want to be pale and wild and interesting like Catherine Earnshaw."

Debbie, so pretty, taller, looking over Claire's shoulder, would reply (it was a standing joke between them), "Dead or alive?"

And Claire on cue: "I don't mind," and the two would collapse with the giggles.

But you know who she reminded me of, the story she brought most to my mind? Can you guess? Yes? Cinderella. Of course. Princes and pumpkins and fairy godmothers aside (I know we are considered a very poor second), I can't think of a better scape-goating story.

She was Cinders, and feel free to laugh; Claire is as she's writing. Not the best of developments, is it? But fear not. She never sold matchsticks. She never played the pipe or danced in red shoes. Yet when I think of her and Luke together, I must admit Hansel and Gretel do come to mind.

I know you scoff, but you'll just have to forgive me, for fairy tales have become part of the fabric of my being having heard them read upon my re-entry for centuries. Don't you find them strange? Don't you find it interesting that parents for generations have felt the need to warn their young of the malice, danger, deceit, and cruelty found on planet earth from their earliest days upon it?

But those were the days before evil was tossed out as irrational and antiquated, before it became an aberration, not a constant. You're wrong, you know.

So Claire was Cinders – without the step-mother.

Note: Very few stories tell of mothers who deliberately prey upon their own children—well, except those told by those wonderful Greeks. There is Medea, of course, but she annihilated her brood swiftly, to make a point. She didn't torment them or relish their pain.

Question: Is it because such women are rare or too unnatural to be understood or is it that the children affected have been so affected they cannot tell the tale? God knows. I don't know.

By this time it had become clear that Faith had a plan for Claire, but what that was, was not yet clear. Not yet. But certainly it involved forcing the child to understand she came second, that she must sacrifice herself, that she must be obedient.

It first played out when Faith found a way to destroy what little peace and happiness Claire could find for herself in that family war zone. She loved doing that because Faith hated to see the child happy—really, I could see it in her face, as if Claire's happiness was vaguely threatening, as if she was somehow undone by it.

Indeed, sometimes I think the thought may have flitted across Faith's mind that if the day came in which Claire did find a measure of peace and happiness, the calm to think, then on that day, she might find herself in very big trouble (and she was right). So if Faith saw Claire quiet and contented, she searched her mind for something with which to destroy it.

She'd call out, "Claire, bring in the washing."

Claire's joy was mostly to be found in the pages of books by then, where life was rational, where characters made sense, where love, romance, justice, and freedom were all to be found, just waiting for her to find them and I love her love of literature. Over the years we have spent countless happy hours together, me reading over her shoulder.

Sometimes then, so absorbed was she, that the girl did not hear that raucous call.

Faith would ask, "Claire, did you hear me?"

Claire (big eyes looking up) would reply, "What?"

"You are a useless child. I said bring in the washing."

"I'll just finish this chapter."

"Now."

"It'll only take a minute …"

"I said now."

So Claire would put down her book, trudge outside, and more often than not pass two or three idle siblings along the way.

Claire would ask, "Why didn't you ask them?"

Faith would reply, "They're busy."

"No they're not," Claire would respond, maddened by Faith's lying that could not be Faith lying.

"Just do it."

"But why? Why me?"

"Oh for God's sake Claire, do you always have to be so difficult!"

And Claire would say for the thousandth time, "But it is not fair," when what she actually meant was, "It is not honest. It is not reasonable."

Faith would say, "Not one more word."

And the little Greek chorus of children and others looked on and laughed.

It never stopped. Claire, feed the baby. Claire, peel the potatoes. Claire, watch the young ones in the bath, put the vegetables on, hang up, take down, fold the washing, vacuum the lounge room, set the table, pack up the toys, sweep the veranda, water the plants.

It never stopped. But neither did Claire's protests until she felt her whole life to be one enormous fight.

But Faith persisted, driven on by a burgeoning jealousy towards this child who refused to play the role assigned to her at birth, this spirit that refused to be broken. Question: Could we have made a difference then if we outside, eight of us by then, had been able to go in? Could we have nullified the poison, or was it already too late?

God knows. I don't know.

Claire knew her mother held her in a special place but didn't know it too. She began to suffer a recurring nightmare then, which she called the good-mother/bad-mother dream.

In it, all would be ordinary. It was Claire in that house with her mother. Yet, without an iota of physical alternation, dream Faith would morph from kind and benevolent to cruel and malevolent in the blink of an eye, a change only seen in her mother's eyes.

It affected Claire's waking life profoundly, this dream, because she simply could not untangle the knot of her mother. Rather she thought perhaps it meant she was a disloyal daughter, that perhaps she was bad and ungrateful, perhaps she was difficult, impossible to please. I knew the truth and so did Claire's subconscious, but her conscious mind was stuck at the sticking point of religion.

By then (remember the cult) Faith had demonised all other faiths, every single denomination, then Catholics who were not Catholic enough, pagans, atheists, agnostics—well, everyone really. Only Faith knew God, only she had the answers, and only she loved him truly, purely, perfectly.

Priests and nuns were honoured mightily, the only visitors outside the extended family to be welcomed in, given high tea, and permitted to inspect the children, who would sit, docile, afraid, perched in their Sunday best in a row on the couch like little ducks in a shooting gallery.

The daily rosary, the mass, the midweek devotions, the travelling missions, it was unrelenting. No one was allowed to disturb Faith in the early morning or at dusk as she sat in prayer (very comfortably), sighing in mystic ecstasy whenever someone was within earshot.

How, thought Claire, could her mother be bad?

We feel prayer, you know, like a warm breeze, but there was no warmth emanating from Faith. I used to watch her during her contemplations and wonder what she was reading because really you cannot read the New Testament, her favourite, without understanding love, kindness, gentleness.

But then it came to me. She was not thinking, *God is love.* She was not thinking, *I love God.* She was thinking, *God loves **me*** (with the ecstatic feeling, the sighing, and the wonder all resting on the "me"). I think she had completely conflated the idea of God's will with her own by then thinking that hers was his, which is, of course, a very dangerous idea.

She was thinking, even, *God loves me and not others, only me,* and that in turn meant she could righteously avoid feeling compassion for anyone ever, certainly for anyone outside the zone of fundamentalist Catholicism. Really, if they were afflicted, what could they expect? (Note: Narcissists do not feel compassion. Why should they?)

Life to Faith, then, was really quite perfect if she kept Joseph out of the picture, which she did as much as possible. But for Claire it more and more resembled a ceaseless, reasonless fight for survival. She was well aware of Joseph's antipathy but not for years and years did she understand it to be locked in stone. She understood, too, the huge gap that lay between what Faith said she believed in (love and harmony) and what she actually believed in (upset and discord).

She thought the discrepancy must be caused by unhappiness, perhaps the misery caused by Joseph's drinking, but really, she just thought and thought, running it all over and back in her tired mind, unable to sleep, unable to stop biting her fingernails, pulling at her hair. Then one day, to her immense disgust, her woes were made manifest when she began to sprout warts like tiny mushrooms, first on her right knee, then her left elbow, and then on both her little hands. The two of us wept for this, really, not just for the ugliness but for the vast new territory it opened for cruelty.

"Mum, Claire touched me."

"Mum, make her wear gloves. She's so revolting."

"Mum, don't let her touch the food. It's just disgusting."

And it was, and Claire felt it in the depths of her spirit, keeping her hands in her pockets as much as possible, hiding the worst with Band-Aids at school, trying so hard not to touch another living creature that she'd wrap her hands in cloths before holding little Luke or Grace.

Everyone was appalled. But although various mixtures were purchased and painted on each little eruption, nothing worked. Each failed attempt hit Claire like a crushing blow, which, in the way of the mind-body-spirit nexus, caused more to sprout.

How I wished I could have held her hands, shown her that I for one was not repulsed, afraid of contagion (ha!), horrified.

Joseph, on the other hand, given such a green light, such reasonable cause for his disgust, could not contain himself, raced to add his measure of misery. Really, he thought the child was going out of her way to give him reasons to hate her. How right he had been to take a stand against her upon first sight.

"Oh for God's sake, Claire, why do you have to be so … so … bizarre," he'd say, proud of his restraint. "Why isn't anything working, all that money spent at the chemists? What is it with you?"

And Faith would tell her, "Pray harder" or "Offer up your suffering to the souls in purgatory" or "You must deserve it or it would not be happening to you."

And Claire would leave the room, the table, or the garden as a veritable walking waterfall of sorrow. *What indeed?* she asked herself. *What is it with me?*

Faith, at her wit's end with the child, the very sight of her, finally packed Claire off to her parents on the farm at the first opportunity, the first school holidays.

"Let Claire's beloved Nan and Pop deal with her for a while," Faith whispered. "See how they like it."

And do you know, they did like it and they did deal with it, and this is how. When Claire was alone, Faith having escaped in a cloud of dust as she drove so relieved down the dirt road to the highway, Nan sat the child down in the early evening light and asked to have a look. Tiny, silent tears rolled down Claire's cheeks as she hid her gloved hands behind her.

"No, Nan," she said. "They're horrible."

"Just show me, love," said Nan.

"I don't want to," the little one wailed. "If you see them, you'll hate me too."

"No I won't," said Nan. "They're just warts, hardly worth hating someone for. Let's start with your knee, love, and then we'll work our way up. How about that? You can't be afraid to show me your knee."

So Claire lifted the leg of her jeans, and Nan took a look. Then she raised one sleeve of her shirt and Nan took a look.

Minutes passed and minutes passed while Claire found the courage, the trust, to remove the gloves, slowly, finger by finger, hand by hand, shutting her eyes as she held them out, naked, for inspection.

Nan sighed. There were so many, more than thirty she guessed, on knuckles, on finger pads, above the nails, running in a line down the side of one hand. But she held them. She held them until Claire understood that she held them. She held them until Claire found the courage to open her eyes. Nan gazed straight into them.

She said, "Well, Claire, it's bad but not so bad."

Claire said, "It's very bad."

"But I know how to fix it."

"You do?"

"Of course I do. Everyone knows how to get rid of warts."

"No they don't, Nan. Nothing has worked. No one knows."

Nan, always amused by this child's stern straightforwardness, her clumsy honesty, gave a little amused grunt of acknowledgment. "Well," she said, "they're not Nan, are they?

121

Because I know what to do and we will do it and they'll be gone. What do you think of that, Claire?"

Claire thought: one, she would love her Nan forever for even trying; two, that if anyone could do it, it would be Nan; and three, is this what love feels like?

And that was such a big idea she gave herself heart and soul to the endeavour, as if it were more important that Nan be known and praised for her loving power to cure the incurable than the cure itself (upon which lay only the weight of the world and her entire future).

So it was agreed. Claire was to stay with Nan and Pop for ten precious days. During the first two, this is what Nan did. First, she told Claire to remove the gloves. She told the child she had no reason to be ashamed in front of Nan and Pop and that they'd soon be gone anyway. Then she telephoned a daughter in the city and asked to stay, just her and Claire, for one night.

She explained the plan to Pop who laconically, characteristically, nodded his approval, eyes sparkling, pleased to participate. Then she prayed, humbly, simply, as was her way.

During the next three days, this is what Nan said. She said (as the two of them collected the eggs, baked cakes, prepared dinner, watered the roses): "I know the cure, Claire. It's very old, an old, old cure for warts that never ever fails. It's sea water. Yes. Does that surprise you? Plain old sea water, but it has to be the sea. It can't be salt water. It can't be any old, what do you call it? Saline solution. No, it has to be sea water in the sea, not in a bottle, but in the sea itself."

Claire listened in amazement.

Nan said, "Haven't you read in some of your books about people going to the seaside for a cure? Well, the sea is amazing. It can cure any number of diseases or disorders, including warts. It never fails."

Claire, remember, was born and raised in the baking interior of that huge land, a daughter of the wide brown plains. She had never seen the sea. Consequently, it had always seemed magical, incredible, to her.

(*Bravo, Nan*, I cheered at the time. *You smart, smart cookie!*)

And Pop said, "You've got warts then, mate, a few lumps and bumps, nothing to get bothered about, hey?"

Claire almost melted with gratitude at this comment, gazed at him with those huge eyes, for he made them seem so ordinary, as if they were of absolutely no consequence.

"Ah well, the sea's the thing," he said.

*Yes*, thought Claire, *the sea may be the thing, but it's a million miles away. I'll never get there, not now, not until I'm old, old.* (She was thinking, of course, of eighteen. Ha!) Those eyes of hers then almost popped right out of their sockets when Nan told her to pack her little case and be ready to leave the next morning to catch the train to go to the city to see the sea.

Her mouth gaped open. She hopped from foot to foot, and Nan and Pop had to work very hard indeed to retain the serious demeanour appropriate to people arranging a visit to the seaside for a cure.

When Pop dropped them at the station the next day, he took Claire's hands in his and said, "They'll all be gone tomorrow, mate. You won't even remember what all the fuss was about."

Claire said, "I hope so."

"Hope?" said Pop. "You don't need hope. You've got Nan."

He gave Claire a delighted wink, and chuckling to himself, he strolled across to the old farm truck and drove off, not even staying to wave them off, as if to make it clear that it was no big deal, that it was a guaranteed solution, that it was already almost done.

(How I loved the two of them. How wonderful they were, I thought, which always gave rise to the next—how did Faith come to be from them? God knows. I don't know.)

It was such fun. (I hadn't been on a train for ages, Claire never.)

We had our own little compartment. Nan talked about the sea, about perhaps painting Claire's fingernails a pale and modest shade of pink when all the warts had gone, told her how much her aunty and uncle were looking forward to seeing her, crooning, almost hypnotising the child.

She was so smart, Nan. She had not let Claire talk to Faith on the phone before the trip (and although she could not admit that she feared Faith's nasty interference, she did fear it), and she had arranged for the two of them to go straight to the beach upon their arrival and only to be collected later by her daughter, after it was done.

As the train entered the outskirts of the city, Claire pressed her nose to the window, completely awed. The concept of suburbs thrilled her (like small towns within a huge town!), the tall buildings made her giddy, the trams, the people, street after street after endless street.

She loved it.

They got off at the central station, Nan hailed a cab (which impressed Claire no end), and the two of them were driven down to an inner city beach upon a bay.

Oh that funny day. It was a haven in those days for small-time criminals, the hurt, the lonely, some of God's favourites. Let me just say there was not much oceanic or primal about that strip of urbanised, polluted seashore—being to the idea of the sea as a tap to a waterfall—but to Claire it was simply incredible.

A child of dams, of creeks, of rivers, she could not see the other side of the water. It could, for all she knew, go on forever.

It had waves and tidal markers rather than currents and eddies, sand instead of mud underfoot, and it was gloriously blue, not brown. It was, she thought, the most beautiful thing she had ever seen. (How the locals would have laughed had they known a child was gazing upon that water with wide-eyed wonderment.)

"Right," said Nan. "You know what to do."

And Claire did.

As Nan made herself comfortable on a bench looking down over the water, with their bags spread at her feet, Claire took off her sandals and picked her way down to the shore, marvelling at the softness of the sand.

Gingerly, she stepped into the shallows.

First she sunk down on her right knee, and then she immersed her left elbow and then finally both hands, plonking them in, waving them gently through the magical water, letting the healing happen.

(I sat beside Nan, feeling delighted, really delighted.)

And do you know, Claire prayed one tiny prayer. It wasn't about the warts, for she felt that was already covered. No. She prayed, "Thanks for Nan, God."

Simple, beautiful, powerful.

The child had no idea how long this cure was supposed to take but was, nonetheless, surprised when Nan called her back after only about fifteen minutes.

"Shouldn't I stay longer?" Claire called back.

"What for?" called Nan. "It only takes a minute."

"Does it?"

"Of course."

Oh, thought Claire, another amazing fact in a totally amazing day. Not much later, they were picked up by Nan's beautiful daughter, who was aware of the cure. They drove home (to a suburb!) and had pizza for dinner (home delivered!).

Now what do you think happened next? You know and I know that the sea doesn't cure warts, don't we?

What do we know, I wonder, for the next morning when Claire woke up they were gone, every single one, gone from her knee, her elbow, from fingertip and near the nails and all those that ran in a line down the side of her hand.

She couldn't believe it. She walked out in her nightgown, hands held out before her like a mad somnambulist, like a little Lady Macbeth. She showed her Nan, she showed her auntie and uncle, all of whom simply said, "Good."

They said, "Of course."

They said, "It always works, the sea, with warts."

They made it no big deal and only to be expected. They all disappeared over one quiet night while Claire slept secure in her grandmother's love, and they never came back.

(I know this is a quirky little story—I'll get to the point in a minute—but I've got to say, that moment, those good people, their kindness and good will moves me still. I called down blessings upon them all, and I think I was heard.)

But to the point. Yes, of course, the power of the mind, the power of love, the power of trust. Was that a miracle, or was it to be expected given all Nan's clever effort? Was Nan's clever effort, her gentle love, the miracle?

You are the miracle makers. You are the means. Love is the force behind all the miracles in the universe. Get going. Make them happen.

You have the power to kill (Luke) or cure (Claire), using nothing but the force of your spirit.

You humans have such power.

# Chapter 13

# Claire

When I dragged myself awake on the Thursday morning, the likely last morning of Luke's life, I couldn't move. I tried to stand, but my legs gave way. I tried to pull myself up, but my arms would not obey my instructions. I could not even compose a normal facial expression mainly because I could feel every nerve in it, and each one seemed to have a mind of its own.

It's a boggling experience to feel what we don't normally feel, to be forced to think about something always taken for granted, but it isn't very pleasant. Imagine if we always had to concentrate on making a usual face, let alone a pretty one. We'd never get out the front door.

I felt like I was made of some weird, twitchy plastic, like I was a malfunctioning electronic doll, and it was only through sheer concentration that I coordinated my various bits and pieces, as my body felt itself to be, to get myself into the shower and back again without incident.

Back on the bed all I could then think was, *What do you wear to a death?* Funerals are easy—we all have the hang of them—but to a death?

I would have chosen a full burka complete with eye grill if I'd wanted to reflect my mood and hide my unruly face, but not only do I not possess such a garment, I also still had just enough wit to understand that would not have been appreciated by the family and would definitely have been seen as making a certain fuss.

Should I wear all black? Would that be too fussy? Should I wear some colour to reflect that we were doing the right thing? Were we doing the right thing? Should I look groomed, as if it were any other day, or go with crazy sticking-up hair to show my state of mind? Should I put on cosmetics that would only be washed off by tears?

The questions must sound shallow, but in my defence, I think they say more about them, the clan, than me, for if I'd been with normal people, it wouldn't have mattered a jot. The pressure to do what they wanted me to do, to behave as they wanted me to behave then in that most public moment, was profound, but as it was all I'd ever known, I had no resistance.

I'd already been asked not to make a fuss. I'd already been told to stop crying, to think of other people, to stop asking questions at such a difficult time. I'd even been asked to put on a dinner for them all for the first time ever, on the Tuesday night, which I now know to be a classic Faith control manoeuvre, forcing me to manage, to behave, to meet everyone's needs, even though she'd never deigned to dine at my house before.

She made it sound like she was bestowing an honour upon me, as if the Queen and all her entourage were gifting me with their presence. Now it feels more like the visit was used, as royalty once used it centuries ago, to bankrupt the host, to render them powerless.

But I did it (two barbeque chickens, a few bags of chips, a couple of sides, and one near nervous breakdown). I did it all as I always did, and looking back now, now that I have escaped their clutches, I'm so embarrassed, for I behaved then and for most of my life much like a pre-programmed automaton but one so delusional as to be manipulated by a word or two while feeling fiercely proud of its independence.

Faith needed merely to say, "Claire dear," in a certain tone and I'd be ready to launch into any mad action.

"Claire dear, jump off that cliff so the others can see it's dangerous, would you? Claire dear, try this poison so we can see how toxic it is, would you?"

I'm joking of course, but it was not funny. Why on earth did my rational mind shut up shop and roll down the shutters merely at those two words?

And when, upon the rare occasions she used "Claire darling," a spasm of fear shot through me, yet still I was willing to obey. How creepy I was.

The day before the dying day she'd used "Claire darling" as the two of us sat on opposite sides of dear Luke, and even now, after all this time, I still don't understand the meaning of what came next.

Faith, wearing an expression only seen on icons of the sorrowing Madonna, said, "Claire darling."

"Yes, Mum?"

"I'm very worried about your father."

"What?" I said, utterly bewildered given where we were, who we were watching over. "Dad?"

"Yes. He's feeling bad."

"*He's* feeling bad?"

"Yes. He thinks everyone will think him a bad father."

At a complete loss, I asked, "Why?"

"You know why."

"No I don't."

"Because Luke didn't like him at the end."

"But Luke didn't like a lot of people …"

"Yes but your father is taking it badly."

"But Dad didn't like him much either …"

"Your father loved him dearly."

"No he didn't."

"Just as he loves you all dearly."

"No he doesn't."

"And I want you to say something to him."

"Say something to him?"

"Yes."

"What? Say what? Why?"

"Just tell him you think he's a fine father and that you love him."

"Me? Why me? Wouldn't it be better coming from Peter or Debbie or Ruth …" (Or anyone at all, I wanted to say but didn't.)

"I'd like you to do it. I'm asking you."

"But won't he think it's weird if I just bowl up and …"

"Oh Claire, really. I'm about to lose my son. Could you not just do as I ask this once without argument? Could you not just do it for me, a mother losing her son?"

What could I do?

I released Luke's cool hand. I stood and walked out of the intensive care unit. I found out that Joseph was downstairs getting a coffee, so I got in the elevator, made my way down, and found him. I went up to him and said in a tremulous, breathy voice: "Mum says you're feeling bad about Luke, that you think people will think you're a bad father. I just want you to know that no one thinks that, that we love you, that you've been a good father. I love you, Dad."

Then I moved towards him awkwardly to sort of hug him, but he stepped back as if burnt, staring at me in silence with a look of absolute loathing on his face, as if he thought I was mocking him, as if he thought me grotesque. Then he turned and walked away without a word, leaving me to feel as if I had been shattered into fragments.

I did say it sincerely. I did mean it. I'd forgiven him his unkindness to me as a child years before, had put it down to his drinking, to too many kids and not enough love. It was a bit of a stretch to say he'd always been a good father to all of us, but he had been to most and I thought that should count. That week I wanted us at last to be kind to each other and felt it was way too late at that eleventh hour for recrimination and blame. I thought the least we could do was learn from Luke to love each other.

But I was the only one, it seemed, in search of that particular holy grail. Certainly Joseph felt otherwise. That look of withering scorn he cast me was the very last thing I expected.

Why did Faith have me do it, do you think? Was it to show Joseph that she was in control of me and therefore in control of the situation, and if so, why the need to exert such control? Did she set us up to hurt him or me?

To quote Thomas, God knows. I don't know. I only know I felt like vomiting there in the hospital concourse and that Joseph did not speak to me again until it was all over, until Luke was safely dead and buried—oh except once, which almost brought me completely undone.

Later I told Faith that the moment she had engineered had been ugly and painful and Dad had seemed embarrassed and angry. While she looked at me with a strange sort of satisfaction, all she said was, "Oh well. I thought I was helping. I don't know." No amount of further questioning could get her to say more.

The story of my life—actions without meaning, questions with answers …

Yet now, at least I can answer the question: How does one dress for death? One should dress comfortably. I went for mostly black (to hide the tears), flat shoes (in case I needed to run for it), and my big comfort coat to hide in even though the hospital was very, very hot.

Thought by thought that Thursday morning I got my body and myself together, called a cab, waited outside my house like a breathing statue, and stuffed myself in upon its arrival with about as much physical grace as that possessed by a tossed-about marionette.

It's a very odd experience to forget how to get into a car, but it isn't very pleasant. Legs first? Bum first? Head first? How do you do this again? But I did get in eventually and told the cabbie my destination.

Perhaps he'd seen me struggling to manage my gross motor skills. Perhaps he was just chatty or bored, but upon hearing the name of the hospital, he asked, "Have you got someone in there?"

I could have just nodded, but I didn't. I could have let him know that I was not for talking but I didn't. Perhaps I wanted the world to know—perhaps just one person. I said, "Yes. My brother is in intensive care."

The cabbie and I made eye contact through the rear-vision mirror. He said: "I'm sorry to hear that. I hope he'll be okay."

I could have let that it go at that, but I found I could not. I said, "No. He's dying today."

Of all the replies, the empty banter and chat that cabbies hear, this answer clearly came as a certain surprise. He did an about-face, taking his eyes off the road to physically turn behind him to look at me. "Today?" he said. "How do you know?"

"We're turning off the machines this afternoon," I said with a stately gravity that took me aback, for it felt like it was going to come out as more of a shriek.

We made actual eye contact then, and he said, "I'm very sorry to hear it," before turning back to watch the road. "That is a terrible thing to happen. May I ask how he was injured?"

I could have come up with something, but somehow having looked into this stranger's eye, I felt like I wanted him to know. "Suicide," I said. "He jumped from a bridge onto the road. Massive head injuries."

"Young?" asked the stranger.

"Only twenty-nine," I wailed in reply. He shook his head from side to side.

"That's dreadful," he said, sighing. "What's happening to our young men? Why are so many of them giving up? What makes them feel so sad, so hopeless?"

I gazed out the window. "I don't know," I said softly.

"I'm very sorry for you, miss," he said. "I can't imagine losing my brother like that."

I wonder to this day if that man recalls that day when two strangers met to ponder such imponderables. What moments we sometimes share with people we don't know and will never meet again. I sometimes think we have more impact upon each other than we will ever know, for that man's kindness made a difference on that dreadful day.

It was peaceful there in that cab, and I wished I could have had him drive me around for hours, drive me anywhere. But then the spell was broken when he pulled up outside the hospital but on the opposite side of the furiously busy road.

When it finally dawned on me that I was meant to get out, I wailed, "Oh no. You can't leave me here. My legs aren't working. I'll never get across the street."

"Of course," he said. "I'm sorry. I should have thought," before deftly moving through and around the traffic and pulling up right outside.

As I went to shut the door behind me, he said, "I hope it's peaceful for your brother and for you."

I had no words to give in reply, so I just bowed my head in recognition and walked into the death chamber.

After some last-minute tests (no improvement) they turned Luke off at 1:00 p.m. in a procedure that I feared at the time would haunt me for the rest of my life. When they took out his breathing tube, dear Luke jerked forward and groaned, his eyelids rolling up, showing only bloody whites, his limbs flailing, and only Peter catching me stopped me from dropping like a stone.

Grace, a nurse, said later that we should never have been there for the extubation, but it was a bit late to tell us then.

Blinded by tears, I rushed from Peter's grip and tried to escape the ICU (which is where the flat shoes came in handy) but could not get through the door because I'd forgotten the difference between push and pull, a sure sign of a troubled mind.

But here's something I also learned about the mind that day. Of all the things I remember, the showering, the dressing, the cab ride, I do not remember how Luke looked when he reared up in final protest. I know it happened. I know it was shocking, but I cannot picture it. I cannot bring it to mind.

What extraordinary mental machinery we have at our disposal, to have internal mechanisms to protect us without even having to wish it, to have such brains that can decide, *No. You don't need that. There is no point keeping that,* and wiping it from the hard-drive.

What a piece of work is (wo)man.

It seems a miraculous survival tool to me. I think I remembered that image for about one month and then it was gone, to be replaced with memories I once thought long forgotten of lovely Luke, happy Luke, as if there is always a gift given if only we can bring ourselves to see it.

★★★

During that long, long afternoon we took turns by Luke's bedside with Faith and the priest in constant attendance with their oils, chants, and rosary beads while I stood around hoping Luke found their ministrations more comforting than I did and while his breathing slowed and slowed.

When not in there, when it was not my turn, I sat in a little courtyard I had found outside and smoked a million cigarettes. I thought of Luke as a baby, toddling around the garden with the family dog. I remembered the day I'd been inside reading when I heard squawks of protest coming from outside, only to find, upon investigating, little Luke dangling from a branch of a tree, caught up by his suspenders. Since I was his older sister, he had the right to expect some assistance of me, but I couldn't give it for laughing. I even called out to the other sisters to come see. But dear Luke, while any other boy would have been tempted to crack it, being the focus of such female hilarity, just bounced around some more with a deliberately vacant look of nonchalance upon his little face, which made us laugh all the more, as he had intended.

I remember the time he'd fallen backwards into a ditch at night for gazing with such rapture at the stars like the Greek genius Thales and thought that most symbolic.

I thought of the two of us camping, of fishing, of making up songs, of sitting under the glorious skies of our childhood home on Christmas nights when he seemed to have spirit enough to bring out the good in us all. Those nights, those starry nights, with our laughter blending in with the crickets and the frogs, made the two of us believe that all was well, that all would be well, even there, even in that place, for he such magic about him.

I remembered the stories of his travels around the country, shooting crocodiles at night in the outback in a tiny old boat with a tiny old woman, of driving through forest fires, of getting the sack from a carnival sideshow because he told the punters that the gun barrels were bent.

Most of all I just remembered his goodness—that apart from the odd crocodile he had not harmed one living creature in all his time upon the earth—well, none except himself.

It shouldn't be so rare, such gentleness and honour, but it is. It also shouldn't be so hard to describe goodness, but it is. Explaining bad is easy, it seems to me, but true goodness is ineffable, like trying to grasp a bubble. Perhaps goodness is similar to beautiful music or a sublime painting. You can't describe it, you can only experience it.

During that afternoon Luke's friends from high school, university, and even from his boyhood dropped into the hospital to say good-bye, to show him he was loved despite the madness, despite the sadness, by everyone—well, everyone but us.

It was almost unbearable, and by five o'clock I found myself begging God to take him, to let him fly with the angels where perhaps he'd always belonged. That feels horrible to me now, to think I was trying to hurry him off, and I have no excuse. I simply couldn't stand it.

Not long later, at about 5:45, we were all rounded up upon the advice of the nurses to gather by his side, for Luke's breathing had developed the ominous, laborious rattle that often marks the end.

We stood there, Grace and I, Ruth, Peter, and Debbie while Faith and Joseph sat, Faith praying to the end, to the bitter end. At least she did it softly so we could hear what we needed to hear or not hear in this case, and each time Luke took a ragged breath, the rest of us waited in hushed suspense to see if there would be another.

At a few minutes past six o'clock—six days exactly after he jumped from that lonely, bleak bridge—there wasn't. We waited, watched and quietly wept until Grace, who had seen death many times, said, "He's gone. He's gone now." I felt her words to be absolutely accurate, absolutely perfect, for she didn't say he's dead or that it was over. She said, "He's gone," and the departure of his spirit, even from that comatose, brain-dead body, felt tangible, truly as if he had just left the room.

Luke's death remains one of the most spellbinding experiences of my life. I had expected merely a cessation, but it felt more like a beginning. I had expected it to be a dull and miserable nothing, but it felt more like a glorious something. It made me consider that perhaps no matter how marvellous the human body may be, it may be as nothing to the human spirit.

(Thomas is laughing, and if I hear him correctly, he is saying something that sounds an awful lot like, "No shit, Sherlock.")

Ha. Though I didn't ever appreciate the extended visit, still at that moment, just after six on a cold July evening, I thought the angel of death might be the most beautiful one of all. Yet in our world as always the beauty lasts only an instant, leaving only wisps and shadows for us to cling onto.

In less than five minutes it was just a body we were looking at, a broken machine we were standing around, so we all filed out, some of us teary, some of us not, to get on with life without Luke, which felt to me then, as it still does on some days, a long and dreary prospect.

Yet—surprise, surprise—he was not quite finished with me.

That night, that night of the harrowing day, I'm not ashamed to say I got stupendously drunk.

Not being able to bear the sober, stoic, sanctimonious clan, I refused the invitation to go with them all to Grace's house to talk of other things and chose instead to go with Mark to our local pub to drown in fine wine, to live and die it all over again. Mark got me home somehow (see, he must have loved me once), and I collapsed into blissful unconsciousness for the first time in a week.

I don't think I'd even been rocking, and in the morning, I could even eat. I felt famished and scoffed a huge breakfast, which sounds terrible, I know, but still, it felt like the first morning in years that I could let go of my fear for Luke, my guilt and useless, impotent worry. I knew enough from my grief over Jess that you take those moments when you can.

I didn't do much that day—returned phone calls, I think, explained that it was done and lay on the couch in a sort of post-traumatic stupor. Then later I went out with Mark for a more moderate evening out.

We arrived home at about 10:00 p.m. and were sitting in the kitchen in candlelight surrounded by condolence cards, by flowers, by the signs and symbols of the kindness of my friends, all of which I had arranged around the Jesus photo I had clutched so frantically for what felt like an age.

The two of us talked softly and wept quietly together over all that had come to pass. I got up to go to the loo, but as I walked back into the room, with Mark still sitting at the table, a puff of wind from out of nowhere, which moved nothing else, launched the crucifixion picture into the air in a slow-motion arc of a type that defied the senses as much as the laws of physics, carrying it through the air about three metres and dropping it at my feet, right way up, the glass shattering and lying like glittering tears in the candlelight all around me.

Note: The candles had not been extinguished. The paper cards had not fallen. The flowers had not shivered.

Nothing had moved except that crazy photo, and Mark and I simply stared at each other, at it, at the glass, and I was terrified. I thought my heart would surely cease to beat; I thought my limbs to be permanently frozen. Even Mark, that great cynic, had turned a whiter shade of pale.

I think I stood there for five minutes before my breath came back, and even then all I could do was a sort of hopping motion, saying, "Oh God, oh God, oh God, what does that mean?"

For it was violent. It smashed, after all, at my feet. Was it just a freak incident? Was it Luke? If so, was he angry with me or simply letting me know he still was?

I cleaned up the glass. Then I poured an enormous glass of wine and sat down at the table before my quaking legs had me fall down.

Mark said, "What the hell was that?"

"I have no idea."

"Do you think it was Luke?"

"I don't know. Do you?"

"I don't know, but if it was, do you think he's angry?"

"I don't know, I don't know …"

We did some more staring at each other, and then I said to the atmosphere: "If that was you, Luke, please don't be upset with me. I know I let you down, and I'm so sorry. But if it was a sign that you're okay then I'm sort of grateful, but please don't ever do that again or I'll be with you before you know it."

And just to duck back to the very start of this story, sharing this with Mark, and the week of Luke's departure, even the life and death of Jess, all played a part in why I found it so hard to leave him. It felt like we had shared some amazing moments, but I suppose we all feel like that at the end of the affair.

# *Chapter 4*

# *Thomas*

When Claire arrived home from the sea and the farm, she held out her hands shyly, delightedly for inspection, believing that at last, at long last, a development had occurred in her life that could only be met with approval.

Instead, she was met with silent astonishment. As the story of the train, the city, the sea, and the suburbs bubbled out to fill that silence, the bewilderment grew.

Joseph knew it was ridiculous and scorned the child for her wide-eyed credulity. Faith knew it was ridiculous and simmered at her mother's intervention, her ability to fix the unfixable.

But for once, just this once, they kept their malice to themselves, their mouths shut, because really the warts were revolting and their fear of contagion and public shame were in play as always, just under the surface.

But note, they did know that if they burst her bubble, the warts could return. They did know the power of psychology, the power of their influence.

So they said, "Thank God. They certainly were disgusting."

Then they pretended that nothing at all had happened. Faith put her to work, Joseph went back to his newspaper, and only sweet Debbie took her hands and said she was glad.

By then Claire was so used to such disappointments that that was enough. Someone was glad, and Claire loved her for it, putting Debbie up there in her small select pantheon alongside Nan and Pop.

The experience of their kindness, however, made life harder, more confusing upon her return home, so at my suggestion, the two of us made ourselves scarce as often as possible. We began to spend time after school, after the vineyard workers had retired for the day, on the long, long summer evenings and on weekends on the other side of the property, hidden away in Joseph's empty office.

And this is why—Claire loved to write. She loved to write but could find no peace at home, was never left alone in contented endeavour. Until then, she had been banned from using the office typewriter. ("Dad's secretary doesn't want your warty fingers all over her keyboard. Don't you ever think of other people, Claire?") But when they had disappeared, there was really no excuse and being the focus of so much friction, the farther away she was, the better most of them felt.

So off we'd go, walking past the vines, the creaking windmill, listening to the birds chirping their evening or morning calls, the frogs croaking out their amorous longings. Really it was beautiful there. Outside.

Little Claire would set herself up on the grown-up chair at the grown-up desk and spin her little stores. Oh they were so funny and so sad. (I looked over her shoulder as she tapped out the words, slowly with such stern concentration, and never knew whether to laugh or cry.)

The only independent women she knew then were nuns, for not one word about the feminist revolution had ever been let filter into that house. (Such a closed and censored world had Faith and Joseph made for them all.)

This meant that if she wanted a female hero (which she very much did), the protagonist had to be a nun. But she knew the only adventures available to nuns came in the form of foreign missionary work.

Result? All her heroes were nuns of various orders (mercy nurses, presentation teachers, Carmelite contemplatives) on various associated missions to save the pagans in the jungles, search for lost children in the frozen wastes of Siberia, or pray for the dying in disease-ravaged outposts.

All of them, every single heroine, was sadly, madly called Deborah, and all of them died despite their courage, their derring-do, their best never being quite good enough to save the day. Could she have made her pain clearer? I didn't think so, but all they represented to Faith, when she finally agreed to read one or two, was that her hour had come—that it was time to push on with the plan.

I wonder as Claire takes all this down (what an amazing experience this is for me after so long of silent witness) whether I have painted too dark a portrait of Faith and Joseph (yes, clearly I am biased), for they could be charming. Yes. They could be, really they had to be, consumed as they were by how they were seen, tireless in their determination to present a perfect picture to the outside world.

So Joseph could be a wag, a joker with the men on the vineyard, courteous to his secretary, deferential to his boss while all the time keeping his contempt for them all only for home, for contemplation when in his cups and in his private kingdom. He became secretary of the local golf club as an avenue of escape on Friday nights and Saturday mornings.

Faith became a tireless volunteer at school (reading and tuck-shop), at the church (cleaning and flowers), and for the Catholic Women's Association (baking and catering). What assets to the district they both were, how highly regarded yet, still, they had no friends. No one rang them for a chat on the phone, no one popped in for a visit, and no arrangements were made to spend time with anyone, anyone at all. They had no need for friends, for narcissists rarely have friends. True friends are challenging, and true friendship requires the truth.

No place for that there, in that house, with those two. Though again I wonder what on earth Faith read as she read the New Testament, the greatest story of friendship ever told. Really, did nothing go in?

Yet still to be fair, it is an aspect of the story often overlooked. Don't ask me how given that friendship is the predominant relationship that ties everything together: Jesus and his disciples; Jesus and Mary and Martha; Jesus and Lazarus; men and women; rich and poor. It is not a story of a man and his family, a man and his tribe. No, it is a story about a man and his friends.

But friendship no longer seems valued in your world now for in your rush for riches, for material comforts, you've chosen to squash the notion of love to fit into the small box labelled "family." You can love up (parents), down (children), or across (partners) but less and less do you love out in the glorious, free-flowing waves of friendship because you have no time, because you work too hard, because there are only so many hours in the day.

But really you are missing out for there is no greater love than the love born of friendship for the simple fact that it is free. It comes without the mutual obligation of marriage, the responsibility of parenthood, the duties of clan.

Laughter and friendship are quintessentially human—the first a matter of consciousness, the second a matter of choice. It is what makes you human. Friendship is pure, it is free, and it is big, and if it isn't, it isn't friendship.

So Faith and Joseph had no friends. They let no one near who might look inside their hearts, their house, and see the shadows hiding there.

But Claire did. She was loved at school and consequently loved it back, for it was a place where life made sense, where life was fair. In a calm environment, Claire made so many friends that Faith had to limit the invitations that flowed in to her upon a gentle stream of good will and good humour.

One, she could not be more popular than her sisters (Cinderella, anyone?); two, she could not be exposed to too much fair family dealing; and three, she was needed at home, for at last, at last, it was time to start the plan, which would take time.

And Faith had been waiting a long time.

So Faith could be warm, attentive, generous, and considerate—if she felt the need to be, if it suited her purpose, her design. At any instant she could emit a soft glow that anyone could find appealing if they did not know it most closely resembled the light spilling out from an open refrigerator. Or perhaps it was more like a torch, quickly turned on and off, useful, practical, illuminating only what she wished.

Anyway, I mention this because when Faith shone that soft, purposeful light on Claire, the child simply melted. Seemingly overnight, Faith began to treat Claire as if she was special, deserving of special consideration.

(I feel the chills now just thinking of this, as I felt then, wondering what she was up to, why there was such fluttering agitation inside the house, which was never a good sign or a sign of good.)

She stopped making Claire do endless chores and drudgery. She would assign them instead to Debbie or Ruth in front of Claire, beaming at her as she did so, ruffling her hair or squeezing her shoulder. All three found this shocking but no one more so than Claire. (*At last,* she thought, *I am loved at last,* but I thought differently. *Oh Claire,* I thought, *don't go that far.*)

Faith would dole out the tasks, make sure little Luke was being suitably supervised, and then invite Claire to join her for a walk, to sit in the garden, to go for a drive. It was creepy, so I followed them closely, and this is a taste of what she said.

She said, "Don't you just love God, Claire? Don't you think he's just wonderful? You know I do. You know how much I love God. And Jesus. And Mary."

Through the glorious evening light the two would walk around the garden or down the dirt road that wound its way between the vines.

Faith would say, "I sometimes wish I had given my life to God, Claire. I wish I'd become a nun, but then of course I wouldn't have all my lovely children."

(Poor Claire would gaze up at her mother at this thinking, *Lovely? Lovely?*)

"So I know God called me to be a mother, but I think it would be a beautiful life, the life of a nun. Don't you think so, Claire? Don't you think it would be beautiful to be a Bride of Christ, to marry Jesus?

"I can see from your stories that you would like to be a nun, have adventures, to be free of a husband. Why Claire, you're so smart"—Claire's mouth dropped open at this one—"you could study, you could go to Rome. Well, you could go anywhere and you'd live in beautiful convents and it would be just like living here with your sisters. You wouldn't have the drudgery of babies, all that mess. You wouldn't have a husband telling you what to do. You'd have the time and the peace to think and read. Wouldn't that be lovely, Claire? Don't you think that would be lovely?"

On and on for weeks and weeks, and really Claire did not know what to think.

It did sound lovely. It did sound lovely to be spoken to like this. It felt warm and safe, and Faith's gentle attention, never even imagined, made the child feel so lightheaded, so light it was as if she were floating, buoyant at last in her mother's love. And Claire was so naive and innocent, so unworldly, so dependent on her parents for an understanding of the world that she was ripe for exploitation.

Example one: She had been told time without number that it was a very serious sin, a cardinal sin, to sleep with boys, but for the life of her she could not figure out why or follow God's logic.

She said to Faith, "But what if a girl had travelled all night on a terrible and difficult journey"—thinking, God love her, of gothic coach rides in gothic storms—"and finally made it to her destination and was made warm and comfortable and given something to eat and fell asleep on the couch with a man there, on the couch too. How could that be a sin, Mum? Why would God be angry about that?"

And Faith looked at the child, saw the choice before her, and chose. "He just does, so don't do it."

Was God a bit mad, Claire wondered for the millionth time, and why was it always the girl's fault? You can imagine her horror when not long later she awoke one morning to find little Luke curled up asleep at the foot of her bed. She'd slept with a boy, committed a huge sin that came with terrible unknown consequences.

Crying, she woke Debbie (I heard the weeping and lamentations even above the morning birdsong and wondered what on earth had happened so early in the day), who explained as best she could without going into detail that the sin involved more than sleeping, but more she could not say.

Example two: From her reading, Claire understood the power and the timeless cosmic pull of romance, of attraction, but had no idea about the mechanics of sex. She'd been given a book describing the process, which was of course a Catholic text and so really, next to useless. It showed pictures in outline of a naked man (on one page) and a naked woman (on the other just so they didn't get too close, not even on paper), yet while the words explained penetration, they did not explain male tumescence, so when Claire looked at the figure of the male with flaccid member and read the text and looked again, she became more confused than ever.

She turned the book upside down, she pictured the man upside down on the woman, she pictured having to squash the penis into the vagina, and frankly, she was appalled. Trust the Catholics to remove desire, the effects of love, attraction, beauty. Note: God does not require or honour ignorance. How could he? It took billions of years to create your brains. Why on earth would he not want you to use them?

So when Faith gently bamboozled her, Claire could say that yes, she loved God (now that the madness of the sleeping thing had been sort of sorted out), that being married to Jesus did sound romantic, that having the time and peace to read would be pleasant.

But Faith did not stop there.

She said, "Just between you and me, Claire, sex is very unpleasant, and women are much better off without it."

"Is it?" asked Claire, still unsure despite the disturbing diagrams.

"Oh yes. Men need it, but women don't. We just have to put up with it, do it as a duty."

"Do we?"

"Oh yes. It's disgusting really, but that's marriage for you. Now Claire, don't take this the wrong way because I love you—you know I do—but you're not very pretty. You're not like Debbie, so the chances of you finding a nice husband aren't very big."

"Aren't they?" asked Claire.

"Oh no. Not very big, and men don't like clever girls much so that doesn't help either."

"Don't they? Doesn't it?"

"Oh no. Really you could be a spinster the way you look, I'm afraid, and no one wants to be a spinster."

"No," said Claire. "No one wants to be that."

"So you see being a nun could just be perfect …"

It was toxic and confusing, for Claire would have signed up for anything if it kept Faith warm.

And Faith knew it, had been busily creating the need for love, happily creating the absence of love for more than twelve years, just waiting for this time, this second stage in which she offered it to the child (much like a poisoned apple), as if to say, "Here is my heart, my sweet daughter. Here is my love, just here, so close, and all you have to do is make this one little choice, this simple decision …"

Though thank God a thousand times I have never been asked to witness paedophilia (though I know some of us who have and who are never the same again; exposure to too much evil can shatter us too), I think the grooming process, as you call it now, would be much like this.

Don't you want to make me happy? Don't you want me to love you specially? Don't you trust me to know what's best for us both?

It was horrible, but even now, all these years later, Faith would never and could never see this base manipulation as being wrong or psychologically scarring.

Of course not. She wanted Claire to be a nun and to do God's work. How could that be wrong? Lairs lie to themselves first, for otherwise they might feel shame, and egotistical liars do not do shame.

For none of this was about God. It was only and ever about Faith, the glorification of Faith. She wanted to offer the church a child, this child, with an almost violent determination really. In another age and stage, she would have gladly thrown Claire into the volcano just to be the faithful, sacrificing mother of the sacrifice and to be held most high.

She thought it crucial, for how else, in that fecund parish, was she to rise to the top, to prove her piety beyond all others? With a fierce desire, she wanted to shine in the radiance of the absolute religious perfection of offering a child to the church, to replicate on earth the glory of the Madonna. And if it was her will, it must perforce be God's will.

Yet still, I would point out that Faith was never alone in her egotistical manipulation of her child. She had it perfected, but she was not alone. Don't you all know parents who want their children to follow in their footsteps, to take the family name on into medicine, law, architecture, music, trade? And don't you know such people whose hearts snap freeze when they are met with a no?

You must. They are everywhere in this age of the ego, the people who see their children as mere extensions of themselves—pretty, vain mothers wanting pretty, vain daughters, sporting fathers wanting sporting sons. Really, how you lost the understanding of children as a gift, a wonderful surprise, giving more than they could ever take, is simply beyond me.

Now, more than at any time before, you are turning your children into achievement machines, racing them from school, to music, to dance, to sport, to maths, to chess, to language class.

I really hate to see it. Children need childhood. It's what it's for, yet you seem determined to diminish it, cut it short, fill it up with worry.

Haven't you noticed that you notice us most, see us most clearly, as children before your heads snap shut? Really, haven't you noticed? If you take away that glorious, aimless time of childhood, you separate us, and really you don't have the right. The prattling, the chat, the dreamy play, the luminous innocence—really we belong together, and if not then, when?

And here's a warning. Beware the future. If you have made it clear to your children that it is only their achievements, their abilities, their successes that count, you will have no right to complain when you are old and without apparent purpose or use and being useless, abandoned.

Children are gifts. Could you imagine your world without children? Doesn't it make your blood run cold?

Faith's blood never ran cold, though. How could it?

In those days of which I write, it felt like she walked Claire, talked Claire into exhaustion, into submission, as if the physical movement gave her the absolute belief that she could literally steer the child towards her desired destination.

And there was another reason why Faith crooned of God outside, conducted her mystical exercises out in the light of day. Have you guessed? Yes, the shadows. Inside, the rosary worked all right because the beaten sound of the children's voices, the mind-numbing chanting, the dull resentment all fitted inside perfectly, being, as it had become, such a parody of prayer. But anything else, anything with meaning did not work inside. Inside, too often Faith seemed to hear the word *hypocrite* echo inside her head as a sort of laughing shriek she could neither explain nor abide.

(I heard it often. Often. For once and only once we outside and those inside seemed to be in complete agreement.)

So she too was forced outside but like everyone else felt better for it.

And for Claire life was better too even inside that ever-darkening house as Faith at last defended her from bullying and protected her from Joseph. And he, by then aware the game was afoot, backed off both because of Faith's obvious determination in the matter as well as a certain acceptance of the entire idea, as if to say, "So there may be a use for the creature after all."

You could not say that he admired Faith for her machinations, the creepy, crooning voice she used was verging on the sickly, but being of a more volatile, passionate disposition, it would be true to say as he watched them strolling down the road at twilight that he felt a certain discomforting awe towards this wife of his, for her patience, her control, her capacity to play the long, long game. He left her to it.

But someone else was watching (apart from me) who did not like this new twist one little bit. Dark-haired, dark-eyed Ruth, the only child who could sleep peacefully in that house, who until then had watched with steady gaze the victimisation and low-level brutality of family life, was not best pleased.

She was beloved of her mother—not Claire. She understood her mother—not Claire.

(Even now I can't entirely blame the child given that this reaction, this jealousy and discord, had been deliberately cultivated. Still it reeked of future woe.)

And it was right then, with Joseph looking out one window and Ruth out another, that another lifetime's hatred was born. Although only eight, Ruth was so cold, so calculating. As I watched her, standing at the bedroom window with the shadows gathering behind her, the look in her eyes made me think of a miniature Iago. She might as well have howled into the gloom, "I hate the Moor!"

Really she might as well, that's what her eyes said, and as I watched, a cold blast of air shot out the window into the balmy evening air, and I was afraid.

# Chapter 15

# Claire

Can you imagine how much loathing would be launched in my direction if Faith and Joseph discovered I was writing this?

I sometimes imagine it as a great black shadow sweeping across the drought-stricken landscape that stretches unbroken across hundreds of kilometres between their house and mine, like a swarm of locusts, an emanation of bad intent.

And it makes me fearful just to think of, for they would wish me harm in a heartbeat if they thought me to be betraying the secrets of the cult. Their lives have been dedicated to the creation of an illusion, to the establishment of their own deification, and apostates like Luke and I can only be seen as a threat.

I'm a coward, don't forget, and the two of them, that holy pair give me the shivers. So I tell no one of what I write. I keep it a most close secret, for if they knew, their rage at being exposed now, when they are old, as they near the end, when they thought they'd almost carried it off, would, I suspect, be quite spectacular.

For they have worked so hard to cover their traces. They have wiped out every piece of evidence that does not conform with the myth of them as holy, devout, pure, extraordinary. And all of us, the offspring of their dark coupling, have been forced to live our adult lives as if we came fully formed into the world at the time of our maturity. That is, when we were responsible, not them.

Having moved into town upon Joseph's retirement, the two of them set up their new house—no longer our home—exactly as they wished. Up went all the icons, and out went all the evidence.

No photos of us as ragamuffin, vaguely neglected children can be seen on walls or upon cabinets in the house of Faith and Joseph. There is no memorabilia, no signs that we were ever young and vulnerable. No stories are ever told of the way we were, no explanations given to fill in the gaps or confusion that besets our understanding of our youth, and if we ask, all Faith ever says (no one would dare ask Joseph) is "I don't know" or "I don't remember."

Not for decades have we spoken of Joseph's drunkenness, not for decades of the ambient violence, the emotional abandonment, of being let set upon each other like savages, of the coldness, bullying, and lies. How could we? Faith is a saint and Joseph her faithful consort, and no further discussion will be entered into, amen.

The last time I tried, quite innocently, to reminisce a few years ago, Faith completely boggled me by suggesting we were all so happy then that nothing in the daily bliss of family life occurred for memory to latch onto.

She said, "Claire I don't remember anything about you when you were young. I'm sorry. I think it must be because we were all so happy, one day just rolled into the next."

And then she walked out of the room.

But still I could not see it, such amnesia as a technique or even as a lie. So I persisted. Before I exiled myself, before I became such a peculiar self-made orphan I tried twice more to bring some reason into our relations, but the blast of contempt my attempts were met with blew me right out of the family and into future freedom, which came as a shock, to say the least.

Not wanting to take such a drastic step as self-exclusion without trying everything within my power to allow for forgiveness and understanding, I wrote a six-page letter to Faith explaining how she made me feel and asking why she treated me so, asking at last for answers. Did she blame me for something of which I was unaware? Did she treat me with little interest because I was childless? Was that why she gave so much to the others, the daughters in the mother's club, and so little to me?

I told her how close I had come to suicide, how long I had thought upon it but that in the end, I felt I could not do that to them again. At the time I thought that might have made them glad, but now I am not at all sure.

It was not an angry, vengeful missive. I just wanted answers at last, at the very last.

I received in reply a six-line missive that began with, "I do not feel the need to justify myself to you" and ended with, "Lots of love, Mum."

So that was that.

Later I wrote another to say good-bye, but to have that final letter read, to have my reasons known and understood by them both, I knew I could not send it to Faith for I knew she would burn it before even completing her own perusal. I knew because I'd asked her to show Joseph the first one, and when I asked her if she had during our last meaningful, though most unpleasant, phone call, she had told me no.

I asked why not.

She said, "Because he didn't want to read it."

"Why not?"

"He thought it was too personal."

"Too personal? He thinks a letter from a daughter too personal to read?"

"Yes."

"Like he thinks we're a corporation then and not a family?"

"I don't know, Claire! That's all I know."

It made no sense, of course, because it was not true. She hadn't shown him because she did not want even him to know she was being held to account by anyone, let alone the lowest of the low.

To have the final letter read, then, I had to both acknowledge their cunning and get around it, so I wrote the letter to Faith but addressed it to Joseph. And lo how they hated that and me for doing that. I know for only a few weeks later—oh wretched timing—my beloved Pop died.

I tried to convince myself I did not need to attend his funeral but I did. I tried to convince myself I could show my respects in private, but I couldn't. I tried to convince myself I was no longer afraid of my parents, but I was.

Yet in the end love won out. I took a train into the country, and upon disembarking, I stood waiting patiently at a deserted train station outside a tiny, dusty tumbleweed town waiting for Grace, the only one who was then willing to offer me such assistance, to meet me and take me to the church. As I stood there under an enormous blue sky all alone but for the birds, I felt like a character in a mournful Tex-Mex song.

As I took my place alone at the back of the church, I felt like the black sheep returning in a Victorian melodrama, for Faith and Joseph both saw me before we all filed in and gave not even a sign of recognition.

No one in the immediate family spoke to me before going in, and no one spoke to me after. Later, at the cemetery, in a twist on Jess' funeral, instead of feeling inclined to throw myself into the yawning grave, I felt a strong desire building behind my back to push me in. Ha!

Later still at the church hall when I accidentally found myself close to my father at the coffeepot, I could feel the waves of his loathing washing towards me. Honestly he was stooped with it, and I backed away feeling vaguely nauseated and very, very hurt.

But I did not run, and I did not hide. I spoke warmly to aunts and uncles, cousins, nieces, and nephews, and I think, in hindsight, this might have added to my myriad offences, for clearly I had failed to understand I should have been ashamed to show my face.

Would I never play my role as it was written?

This too I think must have gnawed at Joseph mightily, for only a few weeks later I received my first-ever written communication from my father, who chose in his seventy-fourth year to finally put some of his thoughts on paper for my particular attention. And what thoughts they were.

He wrote to say he felt sad that I thought they held me in such low esteem. He wrote that nothing could be further from the truth. Then, without bothering to explain what that truth consisted of, he went on to infer I was a monumental idiot.

He wrote that I had hurt Faith greatly but that I should know nothing that someone such as I could say could ever possibly hurt one such as her. Do you like that twisted logic?

He wrote (I could almost see the sneer), "You must be the only person on the planet who thinks your mother has ever done a mean-spirited thing in her life. We can only pray that you see the foolishness of this attitude sooner rather than later."

Honestly. What claptrap. Not even Faith would go that far. And I noted with interest his use of the phrase that I was the only person on the planet to hold such views for Luke had known, but as Joseph so rightly pointed out, Luke was no longer on planet Earth.

Still, though poisonous and the last communication between us, at least it proved one thing I had not known. That is, that they were up to their necks in deceit together because for some time I had wondered if she had conned him too.

But no. Not one mean-spirited act had Faith committed over her long life, no error of judgement, no mistake, no offence, and though I didn't reply to this rubbish, if I had, I would have written, "Dear Dad. If that is so, perhaps you should alert the municipal authorities to expect and prepare for a host of angels to descend upon your fair town to take her bodily into heaven at the appointed hour. Just think of the tourism!"

But I didn't. I resisted that sweet temptation for I thought it might give him a heart attack brought on by incandescent indignation. I've been blamed for enough already, so I let it go.

Still it would have been fun. The whole family freak show would be funny if it hadn't proved fatal to Luke, if it had not almost pitched me into madness, and if it didn't even now sting quite so much, for all I ever wanted (oh Pollyanna) was for us to be normal and treat each other well. Yet it took more than forty years to realise that they do in their own way.

It was only ever Luke and I who stood outside the huddle, the scrum, the circle of family feeling.

Being an idiot then for most of my life, when I signalled my impending departure from the field of combat, I thought they'd be sorry. Honestly I did. I thought it could still all be put right, right up to midnight. I thought if I could calmly list the issues we could then discuss them, understand them, and resolve them, leaving me free to forgive them.

They thought, *How dare she!*

Then I believed—having got that wrong—they'd be glad to see the back of me being such a difficult daughter, but no, wrong again. All they felt was fury.

And perhaps, if I understand them at all now, at last, a smidge of fear, for Faith knows I am writing something and will not let me go. She sends little meaningless notes ("I love you. I have always loved you. I will always love you."). She leaves little meaningless messages on my answering machine. ("Just to say I'm thinking of you.") She passes cheap and meaningless gifts (a bag of oranges, a teacup) to me via the siblings, which allows her to both play her favourite role of the suffering Madonna while implanting the suggestion that I am a wicked, ungrateful daughter.

One of her best efforts, though, was handing over a hand-knitted jumper to Grace (surrounded by the siblings) for eventual delivery to me. Even I had to give her a bow for that one, for who on God's sweet earth could wish to reject a hand-knitted jumper from their mother, seeing both the object and the objective as sinister, suspicious, alarming?

Only a paranoid psychotic, don't you think? Or me.

When Grace handed me the package, the lacy pink jumper inside beautifully wrapped in tissue paper, I wanted to refuse it, to keep my hands behind my back or play pass-the-parcel, but sometimes even I get sick of looking like a head-case, so I took it. I even tried to leave it behind me as I was going, but that didn't work either when Grace handed it back to me again.

I took it home, shoved it in a cupboard, shook my head over the motherly manipulation of it, and put it out of my mind.

I suppose you're wondering why I'm telling you this woolly tale but there is a point, and it is this. Over the following two weeks after bringing it into my pretty, peaceful perch, my little flat, I began to experience a personality change of sorts. Every day I awoke feeling angrier than the day before, furious and most hard-done-by, an emotion I had not felt for quite some time given that it had been years since I'd been the screaming banshee of the Mark-and-me fiasco. I'd find myself sitting with clenched fists. I'd find myself stewing irrationally on past grievances I had not thought of for an age. I found myself getting short and scornful with the people I loved.

And day by day the anger grew until it became a white-hot rage, and the rage was centred exclusively on injured pride, which, in my defence, despite all my other failings, I can say had rarely, if ever, shown up on my emotional radar.

I was needy, not proud, foolish, not arrogant, weak, not wilful.

It felt horrible. It felt like all my hard-won peace, acceptance, and contentment was being sucked out of me, leaving a dark and bitterly cold absence in its place that was rapidly filling with prideful, vengeful misery. I, of course, had no idea what to do about it or what to make of it, and I still don't. But Thomas did. Thomas stepped in.

It felt like he began shouting from a distance (in my head), trying to make himself heard over the dissonant clamour of my furious thoughts. He said, "Claire, get rid of the jumper."

Can you believe it?

I replied (in my head), "You have to be fucking joking," which is not the way I ever speak to Thomas—well, not these days.

He said, "Claire, it's got badness attached to it. It's brought darkness with it. You must get rid of it."

I shouted (in my head), "It's just a freaking jumper!"

But Thomas would not give up or give in. "Do you like feeling this way?"

No.

"Don't you miss the peace?"

Yes.

"Haven't we come far enough now for you to trust me?"

Well …

(Perhaps I should point out that this incident occurred before we embarked on this literary adventure, so I was not quite as accepting of his presence as I am now.)

Anyway, while all of this was going on at various times of the day and night as I went about my angry business, finally one night I gave in, for the hateful rage felt truly hateful.

I said (in my head), "What do you want me to do?" His answer came as such a surprise my initial response was, once again, "You have got to be joking."

But he wasn't, and while it took about half an hour of frantic internal disputation, I finally conceded.

He said, "Get the jumper and put it in a plastic bag. Then pour wine on it while you say you love God or choose peace. Then tie it up and put it in the bin outside. You must take it outside, Claire, and you must make your choice clear."

I rolled my eyes in utter consternation but then said, "What choice?"

Thomas said, "Light over darkness, Claire. You've got to choose."

"And the wine?"

"Just do it, Claire. Don't think about it, or if you have to, then think it's just to make sure you don't change your mind, to ruin it so there's no point keeping it."

Crazy, huh? Crazy Claire. But I did it. I felt like a complete and utter idiot, but I did it.

I wined it, I tied it, and I binned it, and lo, within a day or two calm had been restored. My mind returned to its more quiet contemplations, and all the anger and wounded pride evaporated like fog in the sunshine. I still don't know what to make of this.

Thomas says it partly relates to all the rage and thwarted ownership Faith knitted into every single stitch, the tangled manipulation that went into its creation. But I don't know. It was just a jumper. Yet he says I should think of it as a mystical take on superstring theory, which I think quite hilarious. He says if physicists can postulate there might be up to ten dimensions to reality created and connected by miniscule oscillating strings within subatomic particles then why can't I? And why, if so, couldn't emotional resonance be one of those dimensions?

He says the jumper—worked on by Faith night after night for month after month—was positively vibrating with negative energy. He also said it came with very dark strings attached, but more on that he will not say.

He's a crazy cat is Thomas.

Still his plan worked, and thankfully Grace has never asked me if I wear the damned thing. Yet the look upon her face if I told her this story would be priceless to behold. Perhaps one day …

So Faith gives with one hand and stabs me in the back with another. She tells other people she has tried to talk to me but that I will not listen (lie), she tells them that she does not know why I have left (lie) and that she would do anything to make all well (lie).

And she's so good at this false dealing now that much of her mischief no longer requires any detailed explanation. Any slander, so easily believed after so many years, fits what she has always said of me and makes me more reviled than ever, yet still she has no problem writing, "I love you, Claire."

And she will not stop. Every second week she's up to something, as if she simply cannot comprehend that soft-minded Claire could ever stand up, as if she thinks the brittle bravado I have shown in the past is my only form of courage and cannot last. It's as if she thinks, like the hundreds of times before when I have shown some measure of resistance, she can wear down my opposition through her historically successful strategy of private protestations of love and public slander.

She does all this, but she will not say, "I'm sorry." To quote Thomas, she will not bend, she will not stoop, but she will not let go of me either.

At one point I even contemplated the notion of harassment, of going to the police to see what could be done, but I knew any attempt to explain Faith would only leave me looking like the freak. I can see the expression on the police officer's face even as I think of it.

I would say, "Good day, Officer. I wish to take out a restraining order on my mother."

"Your mother?"

"Yes. She's harassing me, and I'd like her to stop it."

"Your mum is harassing you?"

"Yes."

"And, um, how is she doing that?"

"By sending me little notes and gifts and knitting me a jumper and leaving messages on my answering machine."

"Saying what?"

"That she loves me."

"That she loves you?"

"Yes. I want it to stop."

"So, let me make sure I've got this right. Your aged mother writes you notes and says she loves you and you think that's harassment, a problem of some kind?"

"That's it. I know it sounds strange …"

"You don't think it's normal then? You don't think it's rather sweet?"

"No … well …I know it sounds sweet …"

"You think it's what? Offensive? Menacing? Threatening?"

"Yes … well … no … you don't know my mother."

"No I don't, but I feel sorry for her already."

You see? Impossible though hilarious. The power of the mother, as if once impregnated, forever impregnable. Yet really it is harassment. It is the behaviour of a jilted lover, don't you think?

For what does she want of me? Not forgiveness clearly for she thinks herself perfect. Not understanding because she will not talk about it, not any of it. Not love, for she continues to blacken my name whenever such a moment presents itself.

So it can only be control and domination. Faith wants what she sees as hers, and that, frighteningly, is me. Besides, my absence from the family no doubt raises certain questions she does not want raised and presents an irritating gap in the two-dimensional family facade.

To paraphrase my hero Mr Wilde, to lose one child might be seen to be unfortunate, to lose two careless.

Like an enraged lover, she also seems to think if she can't have me then no one can. Creepy, oh most creepy. I know this because even sweet Grace has had enough poison dripped into her ear to now see me as an incorrigible liar, a delusional fool, an unmitigated attention-seeker, or a most delightful combination of all three, which hurts actually, for I loved her and her children and her good husband.

It hurts and disappoints and raises the question of why people with so much feel content to give so little in Grace's case, not even the benefit of the doubt, not even a fair hearing. I thought my love for her and hers might be enough to stand against the vilification, but surprise, I was wrong. We have all been too corrupted now, too bent out of shape by Faith and Joseph, for justice ever to take root in our family plot.

I'd resisted saying anything about my leaving for more than a year, either to justify myself or condemn them, out of respect for her, not wanting to bleak her with reality, destroy her illusions, and also because I knew her treatment at their hands had been much better than mine. I wanted her to understand that I had no problem with them having a love-in from now until doomsday; I just wanted to stop pretending I was a part of it or that Luke had been either.

I didn't need Grace to stand up for me, by me, with me, but I did want her to stand up for reason.

I wanted her to bring some logic to bear on the question of how I could be evil incarnate while also being a doting aunt, a generous godmother, and a helpful sister, willing to babysit, making her laugh, buying them gifts. You'd think them somewhat incompatible, wouldn't you? But she didn't. She couldn't, I see now, for it has always been incomparably easier to condemn me (and Luke) than to doubt Faith.

I should have known that, but still, when Grace finally raised the issue of my departure, I took it (oh sigh) as a good sign, a sign of trust and fair-mindedness.

She and I were sitting on the deck of her new beach house one evening, the children blissfully asleep, when she raised the matter over a glass of wine, giving me a huge surprise. She had invited me there, my first visit, and I was delighted to go. I felt warm and safe and appreciated. I should have known.

She said, "What's going on between you and Mum?"

I replied, "I got sick of the rubbish. I couldn't find a way forward, so I left."

"What rubbish?"

"The lies, saying one thing to one person and another to another."

She didn't contradict me. "Dad says you've hurt her very deeply."

"She's hurt me very deeply."

"But they'd do anything for us."

"Like what?"

In my case, she could think of not one thing, so she changed that line of questioning. "But you know our childhoods are a blur to them."

"This hasn't got anything to do with childhood."

"So you refuse to forgive them?"

"Forgive them for what?"

"For whatever it is you hate them for."

"I don't hate them. I just want them to let me be. Anyway, they aren't sorry. I can hardly forgive them if they're not sorry."

"They shouldn't have to be sorry.

"Why not?"

"You've made them very upset. Don't you care about that?"

"They've had over a year, Grace, and they refuse to even talk about it. They can't be too upset."

"Mum says she's called you."

"Yes, for a little chat, to play the let's-pretend-nothing's-happened game."

"What's wrong with that?"

"I'm not pretending anymore. I shouldn't have to. It's dysfunctional."

"So what do you want her to do? Get down on her knees and beg your forgiveness?"

"I don't want anything of her anymore. I said that. I just want her to leave me alone."

Both of us, by then, despite the soft night air, the gentle rustling of restless night creatures, the children stirring in their sleep, the soothing sound of the wind in the trees, and the pounding of the surf in the distance, were in a state of extreme anxiety. Our hands were shaking as we held our wine glasses, our voices low but impassioned, both of us shocked at our misunderstanding of each other—her that she could not talk me around to the consensus view (that I was dreadful), me that she clearly thought me dreadful. And notice not one detail had been mentioned, not one fact; the two of us were drowning in euphemisms and nonspeak.

She broke the silence first. "Well. Have you thought about how you're going to feel when they die?"

With appropriate sad face, I replied, "Yes."

"It could be soon."

"Yes."

Becoming hysterical, she said, "But it could be tomorrow!"

"Yes. I take full responsibility for my decision."

"You can't mean that."

"Of course I can. Don't you think I've thought this through? Don't you think having to leave caused me pain? I tried to sort it out. They wouldn't have it."

"But they love you."

"No they don't."

"Well I refuse to believe one word you say about Mum."

"I haven't said anything yet."

"No parents can be expected to love all their children the same …"

"But fair though, surely you believe parents should be fair?"

"You can't give one good reason."

"Hang on. I can if you'll listen …"

"You just love being difficult."

"But you brought this up."

"I'm going to bed."

All of which meant that while I thought we had been loving each other, she was just being charitable to the barren woman by allowing me to love her and her children. Kind to the barren woman, Oxfam cards at Christmas, what more could be asked?

So there was I, wiped off the board yet again.

Did Faith set her up, do you think? Did she ask Grace to talk some sense into me? Did she consider it a win-win situation in that even if it failed, then if she, Faith, was no longer on the receiving end of my devotion, then neither would Grace be? Or did she just want to show me that she could and would take Grace and her children away from me too just because she could?

God knows, I don't know, but it has broken our delicate bond, that I do know. When her dear children ask why Claire is no longer around, I wonder what she'll say. The thought of another generation growing up despising me is a difficult one to bear.

# Chapter 16

# Thomas

The greatest plans of mice and mothers are, as you know, as nothing against the vagaries of fate, God's marvellous mischief, or that which is written.

As nothing.

For as Faith developed her plan, her courtship, her weird wooing of the child, the detente it necessitated at home gave rise to a twist that left her stunned, irritated beyond measure, temporarily at a loss.

And this was it.

Given that Faith had made it clear that Claire was no longer to be treated as the whipping girl—that she had a use and was therefore now under her patronage—the girl, no longer constantly tormented, felt it was safe to linger at the table after dinner and listen to Joseph. (Note I did not say talk to Joseph. This is a twist, not a miracle. Ha!)

Claire would listen to his lectures, delivered sober or drunk, and was amazed at the breadth of his knowledge and no longer under attack, worshipped at his feet. While her sisters cleared the table and washed the dishes, and before Faith called her out for her evening indoctrination stroll, Claire sat and listened and listened, sometimes shyly offering a theme, other times simply taking whatever he randomly presented.

Given that by then Joseph could picture her safely locked up and away in a convent, he could see no harm in it. Besides, she was the only one interested. (How he would have loved it had it been Peter. What fun they would have had, father and son, but Peter was by then, by design, incapable of listening to any voice but his own.)

Joseph had so little opportunity for intellectual grandstanding—not there amid the field workers, the farmers, the simple country folk, the *women* - he could not resist. He spoke of politics, of history, of geography, culture, literature, and religion. Having an almost photographic memory, a mind as sharp as a dagger, Joseph had read voraciously in his youth and remarkably retained most of it despite his efforts to drown it all.

Although it was a monologue, a lecture, on Saturday nights an outright rant, Claire listened, rapt and attentive, basking in the light of knowledge that was so profoundly scarce in that house and in her small Catholic rural school.

And as Joseph gazed over her head, past her and out the window and through me into the night, pretending he was talking to someone else, someone who mattered, expounding his views, and exercising his intellect, he quite liked it too.

He wandered through the Greeks and the Romans, revolutions from the French to the Russian, movements from the enlightenment to the Cold War, the great explorers, the philosophers, kings and dynasties, the great discoveries, the wars, the Jews, and the writers, Shakespeare, Tolstoy, and Dickens.

Oh my little friend just loved it, I know. I could see her eyes grow huge with it all as I watched in upon them from the veranda.

But what Joseph didn't realise, could not have imagined, was that his showing off was queering Faith's pitch. Indeed, it was creating the most monumental metaphorical spanner to throw into her works because as he talked on, musing, philosophising, pontificating, Claire sat quietly developing a passion for knowledge, for intellectual enquiry, for finding out rather than being told.

At one particular moment, on one particular night, I saw the joy in her face (Joseph was looking elsewhere), and for the first time seemingly in a long, long time, I laughed and laughed and laughed. I could see she felt this new love to be bigger than her need for her mother's love, bigger than her fear of her mother's God, bigger than the joy of her father's more benign attention, and I sent my praises heavenward in a tinkling rush of delight.

God can be so funny.

Almost it seems instantaneously, Claire knew she could not, would not be a nun, could not, would not have her mind squeezed dry in the wine press of catholic dogma, could not hide within convent walls—could not, would not. If only Joseph had seen the effect his grandstanding was having, but he could not see past himself, and later (how it makes me laugh still) he went even further, even so far as to lay out for her a bright alternative future.

For while Claire became determined to refuse her mother's tenderly presented veiled offering, she needed an alternative plan, a dream of her own if she was to have any hope of resisting that particular siren song. Lo and behold, Joseph gave it to her.

One cold, sparkling night after another droning rosary, after dinner and amid the bustle of bath and bed and the ever-present fluttering, Joseph sat back in his chair, bottle of wine at his elbow, glass of wine in his hand, and said to Claire as if to no one, "Really, life here is so small, so rural, so dull. Sometimes I feel wasted here or at least that my brain is wasting here."

He took a deep drink of the wine, refilled his glass, and looking almost directly at me through the window, said, "Yes, if I had had my time again, I would have been a journalist."

That's it. That's all he said.

Not much, but it was as if the earth stopped moving just for an instant, the fluttering stopped for one beat of the heart, and the land around them lay silent, as if waiting. The word hung between them, glittering with possibilities previously unimagined. Dearest Claire felt her little world click into place. Writing, finding the truth (a growing obsession), travel, adventure, courage.

Hadn't Joseph always claimed as a central plank of his socialist manifesto that knowledge was power? Couldn't she empower the working class, defend the weak, give voice to the sick, the sad, the suffering? Couldn't it all be God's work?

Oh that child of mine.

If ideas were pure electricity her flyaway hair would have been sticking straight up out of that busy little head, shinning like a halo, and I loved her for it. I wonder if you find her high-blown, idealistic vision of a life in newspapers somewhat amusing. I do, for it does seem rather quaint now.

But it didn't seem silly then, only a few decades ago now, but this was long before the once-proud industry of Dickens and Twain chose to sink into a morass of mediocrity, a perhaps-inevitable outcome in an age without heroes.

Really when I think of the modern media, I imagine a butler sinking up to his knees in muck but still holding out a tray, serving up a sickly meringue of puff and nonsense, poisonous teacup storms, malicious titbits all presented in a fog of idiotic, henny-penny, self-perpetuating panic.

In affluent nations, you should be ashamed to peddle such clap-trap or buy into it, for you are the most fortunate people even born. You live twice as long as your forebears, with more comfort, more freedom, more opportunity.

Really you should let the whole thing sink into oblivion and go back to the days of the town crier just to hear a more accurate account of the state of affairs. "Four o'clock and all is well. Five o'clock and all is *still* well." It would do your collective spirits so much good.

But neither Claire nor I knew this would happen then. Then we both believed in the dream.

"Fight, Claire, fight against the dying of your light," I whispered to her. Fight she had to and fight she did.

Are you wondering why I did not support the nun proposal? I suppose you think we're all for such otherworldly enterprises, bells and smells, chants and mantras. Well, we're not. We're here to be part of the world (whether we like it or not), not to hide from it, not to limit our exposure to it. What would be the good of that?

So what can I tell you about God and religion? Not much. He doesn't like it much. None of them have worked out as intended, like so much in this experiment. All of them were only meant to offer guidance, to aid and enhance thinking and dialogue, not to shut them down.

They were meant to be inclusive, not exclusive, to draw people towards him, not to push them out, not to claim ownership of a single truth. How God hates that, for there are as many paths to God as there are souls in the universe. He is within, not without. Find your own way.

Really, in some ways the perversion of religion, of spiritual understanding over centuries and centuries, is one of the God's greatest disappointments. After all his effort, each religion then and now still insists on creating a God who bears a most uncanny resemblance to the earthly leadership. Really, do they think no one notices?

Modern Christian mega-churches who see him as a savvy entrepreneur, the mad mullahs who envision a vengeful warrior, the Church of England who like him to resemble some sort of gentleman farmer, a benign landlord, or the curia in Rome, who revere him as some sort of ageless factotum, tirelessly listing sins and penances, crimes and punishments, a cosmic clerk of courts.

Really. Dull, duller, dullest.

(In many ways Buddha is one of his favourites, a friend, but still God yearns not for you to transcend but to transform, a difference of only four letters, but lo what a difference!)

You seem to have such a need to turn life, the universe, everything into a one-note dirge when it is a symphony. All the music is within you. You don't need religion to find God; you need love. God is love. You don't need to be poor to find God; you simply need to be grateful for your good fortune. You don't need to lock yourselves up in monasteries or ashrams, you need to be free. Freedom is the point, remember?

All you ever need to do is love God and thank him and tend your soul garden. Could it be easier? Really, could it?

(Don't get me wrong. I know I need to spell things out—such confusion down here, so many faults in the transmission. God loves those people who honestly, faithfully dedicate their lives to him. Of course he does. How could he not? But such people are rare indeed, and besides, they don't need a church; a church needs them.)

So no, I didn't encourage her—not at all. Really, in the days following her epiphany I was the happiest I think I had been until then down here on this mission.

"See the world, Claire," I said as we lay on the grass in the sun amid the vines on the following sleepy Sunday. "There is so much you don't know. Think for yourself. Think as big as you can."

And I think she heard me. But I also said this: "They won't be happy, Claire. It might get ugly. You will have to be strong."

This the dear child did not appear to hear, for she thought and murmured in the sunshine, "Dad will be so proud."

She thought she could at least make one of them happy. *Oh Claire*, I thought, *don't go that far.*

Having said that, I think now that perhaps she did hear me because she did not rush to tell them, not wishing to break the spell of her mother's kindness—not quite yet. Really it was such a huge idea it took some time to absorb. It took some time for her just to get her breath back.

By then Claire was in secondary school, but oh what a school it was. Located (in space) on the outskirts of a small regional town and (in time) in the mid-1970s, it was run by ageing nuns and floated upon a sea of ignorance. It was a ladies' college designed to emit only Catholic mothers, nurses, teachers, perhaps a nun at best, a secular secretary at worst.

Even then, in those blistering summers, the girls had to wear hats and stockings and petticoats. They learnt to cook, to sew, and to type and were taught various musical skills (to bring credit to future husbands) and a European language in case they married into money.

(Really I was shocked. I'd had a close involvement with a similar school in Italy, but that had been in a previous century.)

Still Claire didn't know anything different, and any knowledge was better than none. She had made a friend there, Sally. It was a friendship that was destined to last a long time but sadly not nearly long enough, and it was to Sally that Claire made her first confession.

Sally was shocked, then thrilled, really in that environment, that small world, feeling as if Claire had said she planned to become an astronaut and fly to the moon.

Could girls be journalists? Did they know of any women journalists?

The two of them worried over the questions before school and over lunch, and after much discussion, they really could find no rational impediment to the idea. It was just writing and listening. Women could wield pens like men, couldn't they?

There, in that school then, the two girls didn't even have a library within which to search, no Internet, really no access to the outside world, so they finally took the matter to the one worldly teacher there, a young woman, newly arrived, a maths teacher who was single, attractive, and city-bred.

Miss Mahoney liked Claire, liked her curiosity and spirit, and was happy to give her some time as she strolled the school grounds on lunchtime supervision.

Unable to find a subtle way in, Claire blurted, "Miss Mahoney, can girls be journalists?"

*Well*, thought the young teacher, *what a question. So there is some life in this place.* (At least that's what her eyes suggested, lit as they were with warm surprise as she looked down at Claire.)

"Of course they can be, Claire. Why do you ask?" she said.

"Because that's what I want to be."

"Really? How exciting. Yes, why not? There are a lot of women working in newspapers now."

"Really?" asked Claire.

"Really. Wait here," she said and walked over and ducked into the staff room, bringing back with her the daily paper.

The two sat on a bench, Sally and I watching from a discrete distance, and Miss Mahoney told Claire to flick through the pages and count the by-lines of the women while she kept a supervisory eye on the other students.

The female names weren't in the majority—of course they weren't—but they were there, and that was enough for Claire.

As they sat there, the teacher, as all great teachers do when caught off guard by a student's enquiry, ransacked the cupboards of her mind to bring forth all and any information she had stowed away that might be of use.

*Bless her*, I said to God, and I hope I was heard.

Miss Mahoney explained about cadetships or that Claire would not need to go to university (a possibility the child knew to be out of the question given the family finances and fecundity and her gender). She said some newspapers held exams to choose cadets but that she didn't have to worry about that yet, that was years away still.

But there was a way, Miss Mahoney said. Indeed it could be done, and certainly, why not, done by a girl. That was a good day, a very good day. Claire and little Sally were positively throbbing, bobbing with the bigness of it, the city-ness, the worldliness, the secularity of it.

Of course, as soon as she announced her decision, one night over dinner (having sneaked a peak at Joseph's paper beforehand just to check yes, there they were, the names of women)—well, what can I say? It did not go down at all well.

# Chapter 17

# Claire

Luke was laid to rest—or should I say sent upon his way—as cheaply, anonymously, and efficiently as possible, as a problem solved, a difficult matter dealt with.

As we all began to arrive at the house of Faith and Joseph, the word went out that any signs of overt distress would not be favourably looked upon. We had to be strong, and we were not to make matters worse. All of this, I now realise, was aimed directly at me.

And although I did try to keep my sorrow in check, it was a bit hard. First it was hard because Faith asked me to construct the mass—that is to choose the readings, to select the hymns, to write prayers and responses, which I think now to be rather cruel, for no one was more distressed than I was. Any of the others could have done it with far, far fewer tears than it cost me.

But Faith said, "Claire dear," so what choice did I have?

I sat in the study at the computer for an entire day, crying and writing, occasionally emerging for a glass of water, a cup of coffee, to be met with scorn from Ruth, who was most unimpressed by my tear-stained face, and I felt duly ashamed that I could not keep it together at this most difficult time for the good of the family.

What madness it was, for I did think myself inadequate. I thought all our hearts were breaking, that we all felt enormous grief but that I was the only one too weak for stoic endurance. Ha! And if my periodic teary emergences from the study weren't bad enough, good lord, you should have seen the scene I made at the funeral parlour.

I didn't want to go, but Faith said, "Claire darling." I didn't entirely want to see Luke either but was talked into it by the undertaker. Tall and lean and grave, just exactly as you'd expect, the man addressed me, Faith, and Joseph (the others having been excused this most difficult rite of passage).

In solemn voice he said, "I understand you might feel a little anxious viewing Luke, but I can honestly say I think we have done very good work. I think you'll be pleased. I think seeing him might give you some peace and comfort, but of course it is entirely up to you."

Dear God he seemed so serious, so trustworthy and upstanding, so knowledgeable in this grave new world that my brains completely failed. I thought he was going to give us a glimpse of old Luke, Luke before the bridge, even Luke before the madness, golden Luke. I kid you not, for he said we'd be pleased, and to me, that was the only image that could possibly have been pleasing, so what else was I to think?

Yet, what he actually meant was pleasing in the face of having to work with a corpse that had a smashed-in head, that had been cut apart for autopsy, and that was by then almost two weeks old. We were speaking the same language, but I had no idea, no notion at all, of what he was saying.

I went into the viewing room thinking that one last look at Luke, without the bandages and the blackness, would indeed give me some comfort. When I looked into the coffin, though, I burst into burning tears and fled, not only because he looked as dead as dead could be but also because they'd shaved his wild-man hair and covered him in a shroud, with only his grey, cold face poking out the top.

I had expected him to be dressed and even now I don't know why he wasn't, though I can only assume it would have cost more. Faith and Joseph would have had to purchase a suit given that Luke by then had nothing appropriate to wear into the afterlife, which they must have decided was a complete waste of money. Perhaps I'm wrong. I never asked, I must admit, given that talking about Luke, let alone asking questions, even then, was considered the grossest of bad taste and manners. Then and forever.

I might be wrong, but I doubt it, for Faith complained more than once about the cost of his funeral, the "rigmarole" involved in tying up his affairs. When she did I wanted to say, taking the most lenient of positions, "But you've given everyone else their wedding money, so how on earth could you begrudge him the cost of his funeral?" But I didn't of course. I just blocked out the hideous coldness of it as I had always done.

Yet if this shroud decision had been theirs, they could have warned me, for he looked macabre, his poor skin collapsed in around the bones of that dear face, ghoulish and unrecognisable, and I thought the horrors would never cease as I battled with another door in my hurry to escape.

"That's not Luke!" I wanted to shout. "That's nothing like him. How could you possibly think we'd be pleased with that?"

That poor undertaker. He must have felt so hurt and unappreciated by my reaction. He must have thought, *What in the hell were you expecting, lady? I'm a mortician, not a miracle worker!* What a job they have. They must think us death virgins a most lily-livered lot, and I wonder if they prefer dealing with older people who have seen it all before.

Faith and Joseph were not upset, though, their expectations clearly having been more realistic than mine. As I sat in the crying garden out in the back, they emerged, solemn and stoic, and yes, just as the man had said, pleased.

Faith said, "He looks very peaceful, don't you think, Claire?"

"Well no … yes … I don't know. It doesn't even look like him."

Then Joseph spoke to me for the first and only time between the miserable encounter in the hospital and the burial of Luke in a strange aggressive tone, quite inappropriate for such a place and time. "Of course he does. Your mother and I even commented on how much he looks like Peter."

And I must say that right then, right there, I wanted to tackle that old man to the ground and smash his head into the lawn and shout, "Could you not, just this once, stop comparing him to Peter, to your beloved firstborn son? Do you not think that may be one of the reasons we find ourselves here, you horrible, vicious old bigot?"

But I didn't. Of course I didn't. We were, after all, dignified, decent people.

When we got back to their house and I had a moment to think, without the mass or corpses to confront, I suddenly remembered something I could not believe I had forgotten. I found Faith sitting quietly in the garden in her usual early-evening contemplations and said, "What's happening with the flat?"

She looked up at me from her comfortable garden chair with a look of bafflement upon her face. "What flat, darling?"

"What? Luke's flat, of course."

"What do you mean what's happening with it?"

"Who's going to sort it out, go through his things, clean it up?"

"Oh Claire, it's already been done."

"When? Who did it?"

Faith answered with a big sigh, "I told you."

"No you didn't."

"Oh well. I thought I did." She closed her eyes. I waited. For nothing.

"Well? Tell me."

"One of the parish women that Luke was close to did it."

"When?"

"I don't know."

"What do you mean you don't know?"

"Well when we were in the city then I suppose, at the hospital."

"What? Before he died?"

"Of course not."

"Well when?"

"I don't know. It was done when your father and I got back."

"Where is his stuff then?"

Faith answered with another heavy sigh, "What stuff?"

"Luke's things. His possessions. Where are they?"

"There isn't anything."

Silence.

"Nothing?"

"There was nothing worth keeping."

"How do you know?"

"Because I'd been there, Claire. I know. You don't."

"But who was this woman? How would she know what to keep? What right did she have?"

"I don't know. I don't know. She took it upon herself, Claire. I suppose given the state it was in, she thought it an act of kindness to me at this difficult time."

"So what? You didn't know?"

"No."

"She didn't even ask your permission?"

"Oh, Claire. Please. Do you have to make everything so hard?"

"But how would she know what he might have treasured, what we might want to keep?"

"Trust me, darling, there was nothing we might want to keep."

"It's outrageous."

"It was kindness."

"So there's nothing? This nameless woman destroyed everything?"

"Claire, it was a tip in there. There was nothing to keep, only papers and books …"

"I wanted his papers and books."

"Don't be ridiculous, Claire. They were just the focus of his illness. It wouldn't do anyone any benefit at all to read his papers, let alone keep them."

"But—"

"No more, Claire. I've told you what happened. I'm very sorry if it's not to your liking, but given that it would have been left for me to deal with, I'm grateful to her. Now no more. Please go. Luke needs my prayers."

And that was that. That was all she ever said on this ever, and I walked off more confused and traumatised than ever, far too befuddled to think the following: that no middle-aged country Catholic woman would ever presume to do such a thing without the permission of a fellow local Catholic mother, particularly the mother of a suicide victim; that Faith must have at least been told after the event, so she must have known the identity of the mystery woman; and that there must have been a reason for wanting all Luke's affects, his papers in particular, utterly destroyed and lost forever.

The story was bizarre if it were true and sinister if not.

Either way it was, quite simply, destruction of evidence, but it took me years to think these thoughts because of the logical logjam created by that one big idea I could not think: Faith lies. Until I could think that thought, I never knew what to think.

Dear Luke. Dead and buried but not forgotten, at least not by me.

That night—the night before the funeral—I could not sleep. Every time I closed my eyes, I saw Luke flailing with bloody eyes in the hospital bed. I saw Luke's dead face emerging from the shroud, his blackened head, his broken body, and I feared such images could get even worse if I were to lose consciousness.

Also, having asked Faith twice about the eulogy and having only been told a priest would do it, I felt sick with worry that Luke would not be spoken of with love and respect. I was afraid he would be sent upon his way in anonymity and shame and that I should offer, despite my great aversion to public speaking, to stand up for him then, at last. I felt I must speak of him and for him to explain his journey, his triumphs, and his tragedy to ensure he was known at last, even at the last.

By 3:00 a.m. I was determined.

By 5:00 a.m. I had it written in my head.

By 7:00 a.m. the idea was dead in the water, Faith quashing the notion utterly when I told her at dawn.

She said it was not done in Catholic funerals and it would not be done in this one. She said it was for the officiating priest to speak, not a member of the congregation. She said that while she did not know what the priest intended to say, she had complete faith in him and the Holy Spirit to find words both suitable and worthy.

I said, "But the priest didn't know him. Lots of Catholic funerals have other people speaking. Don't you think it's the least we could do, for one of us to do?"

But she said, "No, no, no. Don't make this day harder than it has to be, Claire, for God's sake."

I should have put up more of a fight, for when the priest began to speak of him, almost from his first word, I wanted to stand up and shout my protest. I stared wild-eyed at Mark sitting beside me, who grabbed my hand in a vicelike grip to prevent me, I think, from leaping over the front pew, tearing up to the altar, and tackling the vestmented viper to the ground.

For this is what the holy man said: "This is a very solemn and sorrowful occasion as we lay young Luke to rest. However, it is not a surprising one for this young man—this son, brother, and friend—did not take his own life from suffering, even from the effects of mental illness, but because he abused drugs. You might find it hard to hear but it must be said, and I do not believe any good is served by pretending otherwise. Tragedies such as this don't happen without cause. Luke came from a wonderful, loving family. He was intelligent and fortunate, but despite these blessings, he experimented with drugs. He removed himself from the embrace of the holy Catholic Church, and now we find ourselves here."

How vomit didn't shoot out my mouth and spray his sacramental skirts, I do not know. I looked at Grace, who looked back in bewildered horror. I looked at Debbie, who'd gone a pale green colour. I turned to look at Ruth, who was already looking at me, as if waiting for my reaction, as if she knew.

And he went on and on, declaiming he was no longer able to stay silent in the face of the twin scourges of drugs and atheism while I thought, *Who the fuck are you talking about? Luke loved the church. The church rejected him.*

And what drugs? Was he talking about the one-off LSD trip? That had been years ago, years and years ago. And if so, how did he know? Later it hit me, of course. Faith had told him. Faith had used the information I'd given her in loving trust to place the blame as far from her and Joseph as she could. And she had lied. She knew what the priest had intended to say. She'd furnished him with the misinformation, but she'd lied because she knew I'd object, that we would all object. Well, everyone but Ruth, for she clearly knew; I could see it in her eyes.

It was slander. It was treacherous, vicious character assassination of their own son, yet Faith and Joseph flinched not at all, stayed sitting stately and sad at the front of the bursting crowd filling the church, the innocent victims of a wayward child, a godless world, broken-hearted but taking comfort, as they always did, in the warm and protective bosom of the church.

For fifteen minutes the priest droned on without speaking one word about the gentle soul hundreds of people had come to say farewell to, some from overseas, some from across the continent, some who had not seen him for years and years but who loved him still. No. Not one word, and when the service came to an end, when it was time for us, the remaining siblings, to escort his coffin down the aisle, I could hardly see for tears.

*I'm so sorry, Luke,* I said in my head. *I'm so profoundly sorry.*

Still even then, though I knew Faith must have lied, I could not think her such an arch deceiver, for really what kind of mother would do that to her son? What mother would slander her child at his funeral after his suicide?

Perhaps, I thought, she had confided in the priest years ago, when I'd first told her, when Luke first became sick. Perhaps she didn't know what else to do.

My mother.

For if Luke had been spoken of truly, the thoughts that would have occurred to everyone there that sad day would have been: *What happened to this young man? What happened to beautiful Luke? How did this come to be?*

And Faith was clearly prepared to use anything (the information I'd so naively given) and anyone (a zealous priest) to make sure no one asked those questions. Yet it beggared belief, so I did not believe it. Not then.

Ruth knew, and Ruth told. Outside the church I wailed, "How could he say such lies?"

Ruth replied, "Well they weren't lies."

I said, "All Luke wanted was to be a priest, and that priest says he abandoned the church?"

"Yes. That's a point, but the rest of it wasn't a lie."

"What are you talking about?"

"The drugs."

"They were a one-off, Ruth, and it was years ago."

"Yes, but look what happened."

"But we don't even know if that had anything to do with Luke getting sick."

"Of course they did."

"But how did that priest even know about that? He didn't even know Luke."

"Mum must have told him."

"When? Years ago?"

"No. When they spoke on the phone the other night, when they were going through the mass and the eulogy together." She gave me a hard, hard stare.

"But she said she didn't know what he was going to say."

"Oh well. It's done. Let it be."

Wailing through tears, I said, "But it's a lie."

But off she walked to join the others who were socialising calmly, catching up with old acquaintances and relations, getting through that very difficult time in a way to make their parents proud while I made a sorrowful spectacle of myself.

Would you have been outraged? I wasn't. I was too confused, too stunned to think straight and instead could only think my betrayals of Luke were stacking up so high and heavy as to be a crushing lifelong burden. Later we watched his coffin descend into the ground, just us, just the family, Faith and Joseph having asked the people who loved him to stay away, to let us dispose of the body in dignified privacy. And that was that. No talk of him then, no talk of him later, no wake, no grief, but there was laughter and food and wine like we were celebrating our successful navigation through tricky waters.

I thought I'd go mad if I stayed, so I left Mark there to get drunk with the brothers-in-law and went in search of someone sane, my dear friend Sally. We had met at a local bar, and I was so glad to look upon her dear face. Much like Jess, I'd fallen for Sally in minutes so many years before as the two of us stood, scared and unsure, at assembly on the first day of the first year of high school.

Or I was scared and unsure. Sally seemed rarely rattled then, when we were young, and never as we aged. An only child, she was the ruler of her domain in those early years of our acquaintance, a child adored, a princess, a resident, it seemed to me then, of a glorious foreign country, the land of the loving family.

Although I stayed at her house frequently through those school years, her life never ceased to cause me astonishment, and at times when Joseph was being particularly vicious, I'd pray and pray and pray, begging God to let me live with her in her house, where I was welcome.

Did he hear me? Who knows? I suppose it would have required the obliteration of quite a considerable portion of my family to be free, and while I can't remember now, it wouldn't surprise me if I thought that a pretty fair deal at the time. God may have thought it somewhat extreme, though.

Over the years, while I became more anxious and fractured, my steps metaphorically cautious and shaky, Sally stepped into adulthood like the world had been waiting for her. She took her lovers when and where she felt like it, and she moved around the country and the world as the mood and the money took her. She bought and sold properties, she traded in shares, she gained degree after degree in biology, anatomy, and science. While I was accumulating a fine array of phobias (heights, depths, enclosed spaces, crowds, and flying), she was being fearless and accumulating skills (scuba-diving, parachuting, white-water rafting, mountain climbing, and skiing).

While I was mad for commitment in my relationships, or just mad, she married and then left him within months ("He was a bit dull, Claire") and took off for Arabia, where the status of women and her inability to treat female patients except through layers upon layers of shrouding drove her to desperation.

I fear I've made her seem shallow or flighty, but that's not true—not at all. She made deep friends wherever she found herself. She cared for her patients truly and she laughed so readily, so easily, and so often she made everyone she came into contact with feel like they had the power to bring out the sun on an overcast day.

She was tall and angular, with flowing dark hair and while I was often stuck and stunned, she was restless and driven. What a fabulous friendship. She thought me deep and sensitive. I thought her thrilling and wonderful.

I'd asked Sally, who for the first time in years was living in my general geographical zone, not to come to Luke's funeral. I didn't want distraction. I didn't want to feel responsible for anyone else but him (fat lot of good that did). I also knew it wasn't her thing, and she was glad I knew.

She said she hated funerals, had barely been able to survive her father's and did not want to revisit the experience, so as usual we were in complete accord. But she said she'd love to see me afterwards if I needed to talk, and oh I did. Not of Luke, though, but them.

I told her about his flat being cleared out by a stranger, of all his possessions being destroyed. I told her of trusting Faith with the information about drugs and how that had been used and abused. She was horrified by it, which eased my weary mind.

Sally said, "I'd be furious—particularly about the flat. He could have written something important, something explaining his desire to die."

I replied, "I know."

She asked, "But why aren't you furious?"

"I don't know. I don't know. I don't know what to feel or think. There's something so strange going on. Every step of Luke's death has been weird, but I'm so tired now I can't think straight."

"They've always been odd though, haven't they?"

"Who?"

"Your parents. They're so hard, don't you think? So holy. Did they want him gone?"

"Oh no, Sall. They're heart-broken."

"How can you tell?"

"What?"

"How can you tell? I could hear them laughing when we spoke on the phone."

"Relief I suppose."

"That's not grief then."

We stared at each other.

Sally said, "Something freaky is afoot my friend."

We stared some more.

Sally asked, "Did Mark come up for the funeral?'

"Yes. Just."

"What does that mean?"

"It means he went out the night before and got hammered and almost missed the train because of the hangover. He claimed it was grief."

"Did he know Luke?"

"No."

"Hard times, my friend."

Not wanting to feel so desperate for a while, I wound up that line of conversation. It all sounded so sad and tangled that I felt I should talk no more about any of it—not Luke, not the family, not Mark—until I'd worked it (whatever it was) out.

The mess was too big to present to anyone, I thought, to mucky for an outsider to go digging through, too dark. I'd been trained extremely well, don't you think? For every critical word I said about any of them then belled in my head like the words of a traitor, even about Mark, for didn't they use the word *love* all the damned time?

So we talked of her—oh, blessed relief—but the talk was not much lighter. It filtered into my addled brains as disturbing and upsetting, for Sally sounded downhearted for perhaps the first time in our long, long acquaintance, and indeed after another wine slurpy, she began to cry.

(Luckily we were sitting in a dark corner of a fairly deserted wine bar on a week night in a country town. In the city we would have been booted out for being drunk and emotional for all our quiet weeping, but the staff there didn't seem too bothered. Perhaps a lot of people cry in country pubs and wine bars. It would not surprise me.)

She cried about her father, his sudden death, and her inability to accept it. She cried about her fiancé's decision to go back to Canada for work when she'd begged him to say— possibly a first. She cried because she did not know if that meant the end for them. She cried about being alone, back home in the town of her birth, with not enough to show for her glorious adventures to weigh against the husbands and the children of everyone she knew there.

I said, "But Sally, you and I were always different from the girls we grew up with here."

"Yes," she said, "but perhaps that's the problem. I thought it would work out well, being different. Didn't you? I never thought I'd end up here. Like this. Alone. In my late thirties. Did you?"

"No, Sall. No. I didn't think life would be like this."

What else was there to do or say but to call for more wine and then drink it? Dear Sally.

As we sat and sipped and laughed and cried and as I gazed upon that beloved face, I heard the sound of distant bells, that ominous internal pealing, and I was afraid, for I knew what they were but not what they meant.

I didn't have a name for them then, but I do now. I call them the doom bells, and they are another useless mode of warning in my array of useless psychic warnings. I took her hand as I took a fearful breath and said, "Don't stay here, Sally. This town is the problem, not you. You don't belong here; you're of the world, not a backwater. Go to Canada, join your man, or come to the city, hang out with me. Please don't stay here."

But she just gave me a wry smile and said, "I've just bought a house here."

I replied, "Sell it."

"Mum likes having me near now that Dad's gone."

"You can visit. She can move."

"She won't move. This is her home."

"But it's not yours, Sall. And your life is not hers."

She said, "I don't know. Maybe it's not that bad. Maybe I'm just sad, just having a bad day."

I felt desperate for no reason. It's the story of my life, the sonorous, ominous tolling sounding, sounding in my head like the bells of a faraway church.

"Please, Sally, listen. I'm so serious. Don't stay here. You and I left here for a reason, remember? It's too small here. You'll forget how to breathe. Go anywhere. Live anywhere, but please don't stay here. It will just make you sad or mad, and that's my role. That's what I do."

But all she did was let out a gentle peal of laughter and said she'd think about it. And I could hardly say I'd heard the bells of doom, could I? I could hardly shout, "Warning, warning, warning," and flap my arms about. So I let it go. I made her promise to visit me often, to stay over at my house often, every weekend if she felt like it, but I let it go.

We left not long later, our tears temporarily spent, she to her pretty new cottage, me to find a mattress made up for me just inside the front door of my parents' darkened house. It was a bizarre location, I must say, for there was room farther inside. I took it to mean that Faith had placed me there to limit disruption when I came in while also putting me as far from Mark as possible, as if she thought to prevent even the suggestion of libidinous premarital activity, even there, even then on such a night.

It wasn't even midnight. Surely a normal family would be crying, reminiscing, talking, drinking into the small hours, I thought, on such a night. We are of Irish extraction, after all. And who could sleep anyway?

Everyone, it seemed, given the silence, so I lay down fully dressed (let them sneer) and lay and lay and lay there in the darkness waiting for time to pass, which is, after all, the quintessential nature of grief.

# Chapter 18

# Thomas

W hen Claire broke the news of her intentions to be a journalist, it was as if hell had finally quite literally, broken loose in the house of Faith and Joseph.

Life became so poisonous, with so much cruelty afoot it is a wonder to me still that the child was not broken by it. First Faith hit the child, once she assessed the strength of Claire's determination, the depth of her rejection, with a veritable blizzard of freezing contempt and righteous fury.

But don't misunderstand me. She was not angry because she felt defeated. Oh no, this is Faith we're talking about, the master of the long game. No, this was punishment, a crashing shut of the gate to her heart, an emotional exile that would not ease or cease until the child changed her mind.

Within days of delivering her happy news, Claire was back to being the drudge, beaten again by Peter, tormented again by Ruth, and absolutely loathed by Joseph. Really, absolutely loathed because whereas poor Claire had thought to win his approval, she could not have been more misguided, for Joseph was totally appalled.

Who did this freakish creature think she was? How dare she think and dream like a boy. He was enraged. It was his dream. How dare she tarnish it, ruin it, make it seem somehow foolish. He would not have it. At every opportunity, he verbally attacked Claire in a bid to crush that irritating spirit.

"Why are you so clumsy? Why are you so hopeless? Why can't you be more like your sisters?"

And on and on, but Claire was, you could say, used to this frontal assault. What really hurt were the sniper attacks she did not understand then, not for decades, and this is why.

There were two aspects to Joseph that he kept well hidden: his immovable dislike of Claire and his bone marrow–deep sexism. Yet to avoid arguments and having no desire to expose his bigotry to the light of day, he lied, he prevaricated, he covered over the traces of these twin prejudices like a criminal hiding evidence because Joseph saw himself as a liberal man, broad minded and just, and no facts were going to stand in the way of this self-view.

So he lied, which meant Claire did not realise for years that no matter what she did, his opinion of her would not change—no matter what—and it was a very bad day when she finally figured this out.

But he did bully, for he was determined to crush her spirit, and in that misogynistic era, before he was forced by changing times to hide his hatred, he vented his spleen with a vengeance.

"Women can't write," Joseph would rant. "Name me one competent woman writer, one woman writer who doesn't write about idiotic romance. I have never read a book written by a woman, and I never will. Never! If you were serious, girl"—so angry he couldn't even use her name—"you'd be writing stories now …"

"I am," Claire tried to say.

"You'd be reading the paper …"

"You won't let us touch it," Claire wanted to say.

"You'd be watching the news …"

*You won't let us watch it*, she thought but didn't even try to say.

"You'd be sending in stories to the local paper …"

"But nothing happens here."

"You're just typical. You mouth off, and you have no idea what you're talking about. You're all the same, full of sound and fury, signifying nothing. Hey, Peter? A woman didn't write that!"

Claire was battered by such a swift reversal of fortune, but she did not buckle.

Never discount the power of a dream. You might laugh at Claire wanting to be a journalist, but it kept her from running away. It kept her at school, and it staved off madness and defeat. I think some of you only measure the power of dreams in terms of achieving the dream but you are wrong, for sometimes the power is not about getting but getting through. Dream on!

Only little Luke, such a heavenly child, himself already familiar with the feeling of Joseph's hatred, sought her out, climbed up upon her lap to put his baby arms around her. And she loved him for it.

Oh my, it was so cold in that house then that I could feel the chill pulsing out through the walls. Only Ruth was happy. Only Ruth thrived and watched and waited.

But all this anguish, as it always does, found physical expression, in this case bringing on Claire's menses, an agonising welcome to womanhood, feverish and unnatural, and after three of the same, it could no longer be ignored by Faith, thus necessitating a humiliating visit to the doctor.

And when Faith gleefully, brutally told her she would have to undergo an internal examination, the child almost collapsed. Claire refused. She said it wasn't so bad, the pain, now that she thought about it. How Faith thrived on that child's anguish, thinking always of how she could put it to use.

"Well," she said, "you're going to have to get used to a lot worse than this if you refuse to be a nun, if you're going to marry and have children, my dear girl. This is nothing. You won't be so precious about your privacy then, I can tell you. But don't listen to me. You know best, don't you, Claire?"

And as they drove into the doctor's clinic, silent tears fell down Claire's cheeks as the constant knot of anxiety gripped tighter in her belly until even Faith had to acknowledge the reaction was extreme.

"Oh stop crying, Claire. It will be over in five minutes. Honestly, you'd think you were going to slaughter."

And it was over in five minutes, but those five minutes set off a chain reaction that blew her right out of the family for the first time.

The good doctor, being as sensitive as possible, took a look, using the speculum as gently as possible on such unused flesh, and found two things he explained to Faith after steering the quiet child out to the waiting room. (I stayed inside, not trusting Faith, wanting to know myself.) One: there was no sign of disease or malformation, no reason for the pain, and thus all they could do was hope she'd grow out of it. Two: her hymen had at some time been ruptured.

Faith sat there stunned, appalled, humiliated.

These days, that doctor would have to report such a thing to the authorities. Then, in that community, Faith and the doctor were the authorities.

Driving back home from the appointment, with Claire gazing out of the window, I felt more rage and hatred emanating from Faith than I had ever felt before. Really, it made me think she might combust, for its focus was utter malevolence given that it was patently clear she was not thinking, *My poor daughter* or *What has happened to my child?*

Oh no. She was thinking, *What will the doctor think of us? Who will he tell? What will he tell? Will he think all is not right in our home—my home, my blessed home?*

175

At least that is what it looked like she was thinking with her jaw clamped tight, her eyes hard set and flintlike, her knuckles white against the steering wheel. In hindsight, I wish Claire had seen that expression, taken a good, long look instead of gazing out dejectedly at the paddocks and hills so she could recognise hatred when she saw it. Note: not once did Faith think Claire had been harmed, for once a person has been made a scapegoat, he or she is always and forever to blame.

Can you imagine the mother of a thirteen-year-old girl blaming the child for the loss of her virginity, a child who never went anywhere, who had so little access to the outside world? Wouldn't you think a mother would ask a few questions? Wouldn't you think she would want to know?

Not that mother. Not in that family.

I often wonder whether Faith leapt straight to blame and hatred as an almost habitual, automatic response or whether she was afraid to ask, to know, to wonder at her husband and son. God knows. I don't know.

I do know, however, and it appals me still, that she could not wait to tell Joseph, as if to say, "That will teach her. Wait till she gets a dose of that medicine."

Could she not protect the child from anything? It was evil. And let me make a point about this. I think this instance, when Faith decided what to do and then did it, was the first truly evil act of Faith's long life.

While much of her previous behaviour could be described as deceitful, self-serving, and cunning, this was pure evil because, driven only by embarrassment—only personal embarrassment—she deliberately lit the fuse, deliberately handed the child over to her enemy. She really could think of no degree of pain she could inflict upon that child that could come anywhere near to assuaging her rage.

Really, if such evil were visible, she would have looked black, black and burning, as if all the good in her had been consumed, leaving only smoking ashes. But take note, if you invite the others in, all you will hear without us are voices of malignant, impotent rage, their only song hypnotic, ceaseless, catastrophic.

By then Faith had such a subliminal dinning in her ears, a sort of spiritual tinnitus, that she could neither find peace enough to locate her better self or imagine life without it. It had become the black noise background of her life, and she had chosen it and welcomed it.

Every move you make, everything you do matters. You matter.

You are not witless victims in a chaotic cosmos; you are the reason for the cosmos.

Remember, Faith could have banished all that dark agitation in a heartbeat if she had only felt in that heartbeat truly sorry, humbly repentant.

Sometimes the cosmic crossroad is a stark and absolute choice between hate and shame, but one is a dead end, for hate leads only to hate. Choose shame, for shame leads to the widest of wide-open roads.

Later that night, when almost all the children were in bed, Faith told Joseph, her eyes still aglitter, of the visit to the doctor. They stared at each other—all the questions of decent people piling up unasked between them—and simply condemned the child in their cold kangaroo court. In hushed tones they said she was wayward, that she was difficult, that she could not be told or controlled. No wonder this had happened. Note: They never, ever articulated what "this" was.

Did they wonder about Peter? His name was certainly never mentioned in my hearing.

But while so much was left unsaid, enough was said to prick the ears of one secret little listener. Ruth heard. Ruth heard that Claire was in very big trouble, and she liked what she heard.

Even now all these years later I cannot tell you whether this conversation propelled her into action or if that action was already planned. I don't know, but I don't believe in coincidence. Everything happens for a reason—some events helped along by us, some by the others. This was definitely one of theirs.

The following day, not wanting to miss the moment, Ruth in a most serious voice asked to speak to Claire in private. Unaware of the storm brewing around her, Claire found her little sister's earnest request amusing. But not for long.

In the girls' bedroom filled with beds, Ruth presented torn-out pages of Claire's private journal, which she kept under her pillow and which, in that house, could only remain private via a sort of gentleman's agreement, their own take on the Chatham House rules. The pages told of Claire and Sally's breathless adventure kissing boys behind the clubhouse one wintry afternoon at the local footy. Just one kiss each, mind you, and then running away.

Ruth said, "You have to give me your pocket money and do my jobs or I'm showing this to Mum and Dad."

Claire was stunned. So many codes had been broken. "But that's blackmail."

Ruth said, "I don't care what you call it."

"But you stole it!"

"No I didn't. It fell out, and I found it."

"You're lying."

"You can't prove it."

Finally Claire said, "But you know how much trouble I'll be in."

(She could not say, "But you know how much Dad hates me." She couldn't, but it's what she meant).

But no argument could move that small child Ruth. Still Claire refused, not out of principle or honour or courage. No. She refused because she did not think for one moment Ruth could go through with such calculated malice. She thought Ruth was bluffing. She had no doubt.

But Ruth was not bluffing. She waited for Joseph to come home from work. She waited until after dinner. She waited until Grace and Luke were tucked up in bed and took the papers, sad and unwilling, to her parents.

She said, "These fell out of Claire's diary. I … I … thought you should see them."

She hung her dark head as if handing them and Claire over gave her no pleasure at all.

Faith and Joseph thanked her, kissed her on the cheek, and dismissed her. Then together they read of the innocent incident—pages that, if written by Debbie, would have been seen as natural, cute, charming—and found exactly what they were looking for: damning incontrovertible evidence of immorality. They were delighted, for it meant that clearly, now having the proof to back up the prejudice, they could in all good conscience consider their daughter sinful and promiscuous.

They called Claire before them into the kitchen and presented her with the evidence. She was shocked and unable to defend herself. How could Ruth have done it? She said it was just a kiss, but they looked at her as if she had used the word *orgy*. She said Ruth had tried to blackmail her, and she was told to stop shifting the blame. She said her journal was hers, that she had the right to privacy, and they told her she had no rights at all. She was beyond rights, beyond respect, beyond the pale. She was grounded. She was told she could no longer stay over at Sally's house and would get no pocket money, that she could not be trusted, that she was sinful, dreadful, shocking.

Did Faith and Joseph feel any shame? I don't think so. Instead they seemed relieved to have successfully dealt with a matter that could have been awkward if questions had ever been asked.

Yet soon after this Peter was sent off to boarding school, without explanation. Joseph's drinking became worse, the wine pitching him into a black and bitter mood so rapidly that everyone fled his doleful presence at the first possible opportunity, leaving him sitting morose and alone at the dining table, staring out into the night, the wine fuelling his rage, his rage fuelling his thirst.

Yet while Claire tried to stay out of his way, it was impossible to disappear, no matter how hard she tried to shrink into herself and away from harm.

He'd sneer and when really drunk, he'd leer, mutter, and shout.

Claire in tears would ask her mother, "Why does he hate me so? What have I done?"

And Faith would reply, "Don't cry to me. It wouldn't be like this if you listened to me."

But by then even Faith, I think, was becoming unnerved, unsettled, feeling as if she was losing control of him, of them all.

One quiet evening when Joseph was deep in his cups, he screamed at Claire as she made her way through the dining room and past him on her way to bed that she was a whore. Even I was shocked, and I must say after all this time it takes a lot to shock me.

Claire stopped in her tracks, never having heard the word before, but I shouted frantically through the window, "Keep going, Claire, keep going." She seemed, bless her, to hear me and kept going.

But before she entered the bedroom, she ducked into the study to find a dictionary and was, of course, heart-broken by what she found there.

"He thinks I'm a prostitute?" she whispered. "A prostitute?"

She wept then, but she did not break. Yet her only other option, of course, was to become a flailing, crazy, fighting ball of fury, which she duly did. And that, of course, suited everybody. Hadn't they always said she was difficult?

So she began to fight back, but lo it was hard to watch. Sometimes it felt from the outside that if they were all left alone in that house long enough, all would surely die.

Claire shouted that they were hypocrites, that they were frauds, that they were unjust, played favourites, that there were cold, that they were cowards, that they did not mean one thing they said—from God to socialism and everything in between.

And Joseph would scream in reply, "Get this thing out of my house. Get rid of her. I can't stand the sight of her."

It was spiralling out of control, certainly out of Faith's control, the tension and anguish building an atmosphere so volatile and explosive that everyone felt at risk, in danger, worn down by the threat of imminent violence.

(How the others loved it all, loved it all!)

Watching a rational mind attempting to survive an irrational situation is like watching a slow drowning. And my dear Claire was drowning. Metaphorically speaking, if Joseph had had his way, he would have easily pushed her head under just to get a bit of peace, surely the least a man deserved.

Finally even Faith could take it no longer, convinced herself the discord was bad for her other children, and sent Claire away.

# Chapter 19

# *Claire*

Those Victorians knew a thing or two about death, don't you think?

Not that I'd argue for a return of the horse-drawn hearses led by hired deaf mutes, the open coffins in the front parlour, the shower of black feathers, or the ego-driven, fortune-busting monumentalism of the cemeteries. No, even I would admit that was all a tad over the top. Though on the other hand, who wouldn't prefer moss-stained angels to the windmills, teddy bears, and whiskey bottles of now?

Still it seems to me that behind that high formality and perhaps pomposity there did lie a subtle understanding of human nature that appears to me now to be utterly lost, a social system played out in unspoken codes and symbols that were both universally recognised and quietly understood, like the gracious language of flowers or the fluttering of a femme fatale's fan.

I speak in particular of mourning dress. Full black for one year of deep mourning, half black, muted shades, and perhaps a hopeful ribbon for the year following. It was such a brilliant, wordless, powerful solution for an experience that is mostly beyond words. I wished often in the months and years following Luke's death that it had been made available to me, yet I am an inner urban woman, and we all wear black.

For when you are in grief, you are still in the world but not of it. It is like living in a bubble where the outside world seems mad, unrecognisable, pointless.

For the first weeks after the fall, the death, and the burial, I often had the most overwhelming desire to go up to strangers and say, "How can you be talking about football … or politics … or music … or making chitchat? Don't you know Luke is dead? Haven't you noticed that the earth has shifted on its axis? Can't you tell that nothing will ever be the same again? What planet are you living on?" I didn't, praise be, but I did think of it. All of us who have experienced deep grief should give ourselves a gentle pat on the head for every time we didn't because the urge to knock some sense into the world—when there is so little to be found in our corner of it—can be mightily, madly strong.

To know you have failed someone, to know you could have made a difference if you'd been a better person, and to know you can never fix it, never do better, is a catastrophic feeling, as if your entire future stretches as a flat and blasted landscape of your own hopeless making.

Grief is maddening, but it is not mad. It is the loneliest place, but it is not empty. It is outside time and feels endless, yet of every human emotion, it is most affected by time.

One year of full mourning. One year of waking up the first day of spring without them. The first cool night knowing you'll never sit together again before an open fire and talk into the morning. The first time you smell the approach of dusty rain and know you'll see no more storms in together. The first Christmas, the first birthday, the first of everything, each one a new ache, a new pain when it feels as if there is no room for more.

But then year two, the year of the hopeful ribbon that symbolises, if nothing else, the survival of year one. If all this could be said in dress, how much easier life would be. To be able to put on clothes that said to everyone from the butcher, to the boss, from friend to a stranger on the train, "As you can see, I can't do small talk right now."

Or: "As you see, I don't care to eat or to dance. I can't listen to your stories right now. I'm sorry I can't laugh or charm or add to your society. Perhaps soon but not now. Get back to me when you see me with a ribbon in my hair. For I know you know I am not being rude. I'm simply in grief, and like all human beings, I cannot be in two places at once." All of that with not one word needed.

But now people think you're self-absorbed, or not moving on, or in need of medication, particularly if the grief is for someone outside the picket fence of husband, wife, child.

Just recently a dear friend of mine, let's call him Mick, took me aback somewhat as we sat sipping mulled wine in a delightful centuries-old pub in the wintry midlands of England by saying with surprise in his voice, "You're really good company, Claire!"

We'd known each other for years and years, so that this exclamation left me stammering a reply that consisted of not much more than, "Gee thanks. Thanks a lot."

Mick said, realising how it sounded, "I don't mean that you've ever been bad company. I just mean that … that … you haven't been this much fun for a while."

I stared at him, this much-cherished friend, through the delicious afternoon gloom of the inn, and felt like boxing his ears. "When?" I asked. "When I was in mourning?"

"What?"

"When my friends were dead and dying?"

"Um."

"When I was living the dream with Mark?"

(I know I made it all sound highly dramatic, a touch gothic, but I couldn't help myself. Put it down to the atmosphere of an English winter's afternoon. Put it down to the intense, inchoate need in us all to be understood. Put it down to mischief. All would be true.)

"Right," said Mick, looking sheepish. "I hadn't really thought of your life in a list like that. Sorry."

He's a bloke and a scientist, so what can you expect? My stories were also a bit odd, particularly the ones with ghosts in them; even I admit that. Actually, if memory serves, it was during that trip to the UK to see him and his dear wife that I even went so far as to say one late night and one bottle of red too many that I had another voice inside my head—Thomas, so to say—but the look on Mick's dear face, a sort of pained incredulity, was enough to shut me up pretty quick. I've never broached that subject since. His scientific mind has no room in it for that.

Later in the visit, Mick was almost at the point, I think, of suggesting a short stay in a nice sanatorium after I told them I thought their house was haunted because I knew the signs, the oppressive atmosphere, the electric restlessness. But then he saw it. He, Mr Rational Universe himself, saw a ghost, to my great and lasting delight, just a flash of a young man staring in at my old friend through the kitchen window.

Then it was gone, changing his mechanistic worldview forever, in an instant leaving him with a much-reduced capacity for scoffing. Then later, when a picture flew off the wall for no reason, he was rendered virtually speechless. How funny life is.

I understood he meant no offence, and it felt good to be able to explain, to have survived to be able to explain.

I said, "Here's a tip about emotions, my friend. It's a bit hard to be the life of the party when you don't actually want life. Your shout, I do believe, and make mine a fine old cognac."

Yet in a way, I do understand Mick's lack of understanding. My grief for Luke, I know, could seem to others to be disproportionate, but there were reasons for it.

One: Given that we, the family, stopped talking of him, wiped him from the collective memory as soon as he was safely buried in the ground, I felt the need to mourn his passing, to do him honour enough for seven, not just for one.

Two: I had known he would die and even how and had done nothing to prevent it.

Three: I knew as time passed that I was part of a conspiracy—at the very least a conspiracy of silence—but I did not know why, who was behind it, or how far back it went.

Four: I loved him. He was my brother.

And there were more prosaic reasons too, of course, as there are always are, mainly, in this case, a series of new catastrophes that kept knocking me down and deeper into the murk before I ever got the chance to regather my scattered wits or regain the balance needed to stand up on planet earth.

Not long after Luke's funeral, I moved out of the house of the glowing man story and in with Mark, for I knew grieving with my gay pal would be excruciating for us both. Clearly it was not the best time or reason to formalise the relationship, yet still that's what we did. He was virtually homeless and penniless so I thought we could save each other, and perhaps in a way we did. And I was mad for saving people then—really, quite mad for it.

So we moved into a little house, he so grateful that he was kind to me for quite a while, which made me in turn quite grateful too. He gave me the space to conduct my mourning, to go through all the what-ifs and why-didn't-Is until I'd finished that endless, miserable course.

For I made a choice at the outset that I would feel it all based on the experimental hypothesis—or more simply, the hope—that if I allowed myself to experience grief truly then if or when I came out the other side, there would be no more monsters left lurking in my psyche, no more doors of shame and guilt left locked from fear, no more ghosts.

I remember reading a quote then, and I can't remember who wrote it, but it said, "The key to going through grief is to go through." And that helped and my experiment worked, for as Mick noted, I'm quite good company now.

It takes time and courage, but it can be gloriously life changing if you let yourself go through. It makes me feel sometimes that our modern world has blanded us almost out of existence in so many ways, not least by having us believe we can and should medicate for sorrow.

But at its most basic, emotional pain is growing pain.

There is nothing, nothing at all like the dark night of the soul (during which even Thomas abandoned me, an absence he has never adequately explained) to make you appreciate laughter, children, clouds, ribbons, a fine cognac on a winter's afternoon—everything, that is, that makes life not just liveable but wonderful, miraculous. As any artist knows, if you take away the shadows, there is neither depth nor perspective.

One more thing I can say about grief is that it can make you feel like making babies (which came as a bit of a shock, I can say), a desire created not so much by a need to replace the dead as to fight against death with the only thing bigger. Life.

It was a crazy notion, I know, Mark and I hardly being parent material even then in the early years. Still, I had such a war raging inside me between life and death (to be or not to be) that I could not let go of the idea and even developed a love of gardening for the first time ever just to see things, anything, thrive and grow and blossom.

But blooms, though beautiful, are nothing to a baby, and I raised the idea with Mark on quite a few occasions. He hummed and ha'ed and politely prevaricated quite rightly, probably, now in hindsight, gently questioning the wisdom of such a move then. But I was thirty-seven and thought, *If not now, when?* And by then too my menses had become so extremely painful that the idea of nine months off had considerable appeal in and of itself.

I thought up names (Charlotte and Nicholas). We occasionally talked of marriage, and we eased off the contraception as if, while we could not choose, we could at least allow for fate. And fate did intervene. Of course it did, it always does, and like most of us when it does, I was completely blindsided by it.

But that was yet to come.

In the days of which I write, Sally stayed with us often, her presence a warm tonic for my sore heart, her easy laughter music. Yet still I felt uneasy for no reason and never stopped urging her to leave that small town, to join me in the city or her beau across the sea.

But though I knew she suffered there, though I knew her to be the quietest I'd ever known her, I could not move her. Each Sunday of each weekend she stayed, she got back into her car for the three-hour drive home more despondent, more gloomy, more passively resigned than ever, telling me not to worry, that her lover would soon be back, that it would all work out all right in the end. What could I say? What did I know?

I spent a great deal of time weeping over a tiny inner-city flowerbed so was hardly the one to be dishing out advice. Athena I was not. So I dreamt of a baby and she dreamt of her beloved until, to quote TS Elliot, human voices woke us and we drowned.

First, I developed a daggerlike pain in my hip. I went to the doctor, went to the medical imagers, went to the hospital and into theatre. I was told, upon emerging from the haze of anaesthesia, that my womb was growing weeds, that it was a mess, that I could never have children, that it would have to come out.

"Sorry," said the young registrar just before he fled, leaving me thinking: *What? What? What do you mean? It was just a pain in my hip.*

No one else came to talk to me about it for it was such a busy public hospital. A nurse simply arrived not long later and got me up and out of bed, plonked me in a wheelchair, and tipped me into Sally's car, who had driven all that way to help me. (Mark had lost his driver's licence for drunk driving—surprise.)

The nurse said I should ring them back when I was ready to have the operation, as if it were entirely reasonable to expect a childless woman in her thirties to find the courage to phone up and order a hysterectomy.

"Ready?" I screamed silently. "I'll never be ready." But I made not a sound, being too etherised to speak.

I just told Sally, and Mark when he got home, and felt my self-loathing—growing weeds—to have finally reached its zenith. To be barren at thirty-seven. To need a grandmother operation. To have no more hope at all of all that others seemed to find so easy to attain, so readily achieved—marriage, babies, family, future. Normal life, miraculous life.

All gone in a two-minute bedside chat.

I felt like killing myself. Later, I rang Faith.

She said, "Oh, love. That's no good, but you know I always had a feeling you'd never have children."

I asked, "What do you mean?"

"Oh I just always felt that."

"But why? Don't you think I like children?"

"No, it's not that."

"Well why? Don't you think I'd make a good mother?"

"Well I don't know ..." A pause.

"You said this to me when I was just a teenager."

"What?"

"You said this. I remember. You said you thought I'd never be a mother."

"Did I? Well then. There you go. I was right, wasn't I?"

"But why? Why did you say that?"

"Oh for goodness sake, I don't know. Perhaps you were never very maternal. Be honest, love, you're not like the others. You've refused to get married and settle down. And let's face it, dear, you are in your later thirties."

"I haven't refused."

"Oh, I thought you didn't believe in marriage."

"I never said that."

"Oh I must have just assumed it then by the choices that you've made."

"What choices?"

"I don't know ..."

"What choices?"

Faith, hesitated, as if afraid she'd hurt my feelings, ha!) "Your willingness to live in sin then I suppose."

I was, of course, as she had intended, demolished by her view of me, hurt into silence and unable to understand how the conversation had so quickly progressed from my sadness to my badness or to untangle any of it, any of the assumptions, the inferences, the oblique references to my lust and God's justice.

Yet while her motives were murky, her meaning was clear. I had brought it upon myself. Not an ounce of compassion, not a grain of kindness. She knew, had always known. It was only to be expected. I'd been born defective somehow, so what had I expected? Then I felt like killing myself all over again while the weeds grew bigger by the minute.

After the phone call with Faith, I found myself even less capable of making that other call. No. I tried, but I could not. Every time I reached for the phone to ring the hospital, my arm did something else, for I absolutely could not believe it was true. No one lost their womb before they got the chance to use it, and if it did happen, it was the kind of happening that happened to other people. I didn't even feel ill.

"But I've just got around to wanting a baby!" I felt like screaming.

Who am I going to be now? How do I live knowing, absolutely knowing, there is no possibility of it all working out in the end? At the time the answer to the first question was—the bottom of the family food chain, the most hopeless loser, the defective Claire. The answer to the second—I can't. *I'll walk into traffic*, I thought, for I could not find the courage to endure the physical pain of the surgery I needed to live when I did not want to live.

I wanted more and more to join Luke and Jess wherever they were, consumed as I was by hopelessness and horror. But soon I started to swell in a grotesque parody of pregnancy, which proved in the end to be even worse, more monstrous, than my fears. So I made the phone call. I booked myself in. What else could I do?

I'd spare you this tangled, ugly aspect of the story, gentle reader, for no one knows like I do the repugnant yuck factor women's maladies still engender, as if our dark spaces remain vaguely threatening, suspect, but I'm afraid I can't, for though in some ways it represented my darkest hour, it also, as is sometimes the way on planet earth, gave rise to ultimate enlightenment. Certainly the telling of it is not in want of sympathy, for it is done and dusted to me now, and I could have been a most hopeless mother for all I know.

"What's for dinner, Mum?"

"Are you sick of pizza yet?"

"Where are our school uniforms, Mum?"

"No idea."

"Have you packed our lunchboxes, Mum?"

"Just let me finish this chapter."

No. I probably saved some children from a most chaotic childhood.

# Chapter 20

# Thomas

And then Faith and Joseph started on Luke.

So practiced now, so good at it, Faith and Joseph began the ritual of pushing him out, pulling him in, letting him know he was too quiet, too loud, too silly, too serious, too busy, too idle.

By then Luke was at school, and by then too, Joseph had found, as was his wont, a great many reasons to despise this second son well beyond his original and lasting distaste for the child's blond-haired, blue-eyed beauty. Oh no, that was just the tip of the iceberg that was this father's heart.

Much worse were Luke's gentleness and sensitivity, his calm self-sufficiency (always happiest, like Claire had been, out of that house, away from them all, wandering with his little dog), his natural warm good humour, and his most unmanly, most unnatural modesty. All of which Joseph chose to see as laziness, witlessness, weakness.

Really, by then he had to if he was not to spend the rest of his blasted life looking at all he was not. Yet it was another judgement, made without reason and so without the possibility of resolution, which Joseph held onto right up to the bitter end. Besides, Claire's absence had created a vacuum that urgently needed filling, and with only a little encouragement from the others (who were feeling the pinch, you might say), Joseph soon found himself convinced that Luke had been made to measure for the vacancy. Even by then popular, a gifted little sportsman (nothing like Claire there, I can tell you!), a bright student, Luke was already beginning to suffer stress headaches and insomnia.

He was so little for such suffering, and while there are now some very big black questions lurking at the heart of his misery, Claire and I had no conception of them at the time. All we knew was that he had pressing social matters afoot that caused him great anxiety—to whit all his peers, both boys and girls, wanted to be near him, wanted to play on his team, wanted to sit next to him on the bus, in school, at mass. Really everyone wanted to do exactly what Luke was doing even though the little boy quite liked to do some of his doings alone.

But don't get me wrong; Luke was not wrestling with issues of personal space. Oh no. Not at all. He loved people.

He simply hated, really hated, hurting anyone, disappointing anyone, but how can you play a game if everyone wants to be on only one side? His side? It was a headache-inducing conundrum.

Some people really are born with a charismatic light, but for the good hearts so touched, this can be as much a curse as a gift. Luke had charisma. Joseph loathed him for it. Faith was delighted. But Claire and I knew nothing then of their dislike and manipulation, for their treatment of Luke was just another sly secret kept so safely, held so tightly, cherished almost you could say by husband and wife. And I think it was hidden particularly from us, knowing as they did by then that Claire would not lie down and fearing she'd likely find it far easier to defend another rather than herself.

This secret could be kept too because Faith had worked for years—for years!—to make sure her children did not love each other, did not know each other, creating over time, by the judicious use of emotional acid, little pockets of resentment within each for each. She told Claire Luke was hopeless, that he was aimless and dreamy, that he annoyed their father because he was not driven enough, not competitive enough, not masculine enough.

Claire wanted to say, "But he's only eight years old. How driven should he be?"

She wanted to say, "But if Dad finds him so annoying, why does he coach Luke's junior cricket team? Why doesn't he let him be? Why increase the misery?"

The answer was simply because Luke was good at it, so that by coaching the team, Joseph could revel in the twin pleasures of publicly basking in his son's growing glory while tormenting him for it in private.

"Why aren't you out practising your bowling? Why aren't you practising your catching? Do you think you already know everything? Don't you think about the team? Don't you think about anyone but yourself?" Horrible. Horrible. But we could not do much about it, for Claire and I had our own battles to fight.

Do you wonder where they sent us? Where else, of course, but a Catholic boarding school in the city. This, although expensive, had two benefits for Faith. First, it relieved the broiling tension, the menacing escalation in hostilities between Joseph and Claire that she had stoked to a fever pitch. Second, it enabled Faith to send her recalcitrant daughter to the professionals for further sanctioned, sanctified indoctrination.

Yet, while we were at first relieved and grateful to escape that hateful, baleful home, that lift in our spirits did not last long. But that is hardly surprising, really, when I think back because in many ways there was not much to separate the two—the family home, that is, and the religious institution.

As a Catholic girls' school then, this venerable institution was run by the oppressed for the oppressed. How could it be any other way? Only a tiny percentage of the nuns, even by then growing old, sad, and unreplaced, remained happy with their choice, their calling. Only a very few. Most were angry, lost, and resentful to have found themselves members almost of the last generation of unsung religious martyrs, relics of an age swiftly passing into history.

Modernity and secularity felt to many of those veiled women there a wicked trick, a frightful twist. I know. I could feel it. The air was filled with bitter tang. And in that atmosphere, the form of life that flourishes most spectacularly, like fungus in a swamp, is that of the bully.

Claire was so distressed by this realisation that she had arrived at a place much like the one she had left behind that she felt her childhood to be one ceaseless series of shocks and aftershocks. She saw that the bullies were invariably only of average to lower intelligence. She saw that they attracted even dumber, dimmer acolytes. She saw that they only picked on the weak, the isolated, the shy—the little girls who were homesick and heart-broken at finding themselves so far away from all that was safe and familiar. But much worse than this for Claire was understanding that the intelligent, the wiser, the older young women chose not only not to act but also not to see.

Not surprisingly, it did not go well for us there. First, Faith had secretly written to the nuns suggesting that her daughter might with some encouragement and gentle persuasion take up the holy habit. Second, in a final fit of rage before her departure, Joseph had refused permission for Claire to leave the convent grounds at all, with anyone, for any reason whatsoever except to come home. What a horrible combination were these two acts, these two people.

From Faith's sly manoeuvre came countless confusing conversations with some of the nuns about God's mystical power, his glorious ways, the need to listen for him calling, a voice in the night, they said, gentle but persistent. Claire thought them mad. From Joseph's misery came countless weekends of solitary confinement as the scores of boarding girls left for happy visits with friends and family, leaving Claire alone to drift like a ghost down the empty corridors, through the echoing dormitories.

This isolation made her stand out to the bullies (never a good development), it made her accessible to the nuns (even worse), and given the small size of the prison grounds, it made her fat. How pleased her parents were when they saw her at school holidays, for she had become by then perfectly built for ridicule.

Yet by then Claire hated herself more than anyone else ever could, which to haters is good, better, best. Really, then, self-loathing can be quite safely relied upon to do all that could be wished.

But think of this—parents choosing to create a child to hate and never stopping until the job was done, revelling in their biological ability to fulfil their own needs—creating and destroying at home (Luke) and at a distance (Claire), omnipotent, untouchable, godlike. They could always say—and they always did—that whatever they did, they did for the best. Whenever, much later, Faith was ever challenged over anything, anything at all, she would always say as she gazed heavenward, "I know in my heart of hearts I did only what I thought was best."

Right. But best for whom?

It certainly was not best for us, any of it, or for Luke. Only later did it become apparent that their best, as they called it, harmed them all, their entire brood twisted and damaged, which of course affected their own children and the children never born.

★★★

Being a scrapper from way back and being by then in an almost constant state of mild despair, it did not take long for Claire to come to blows with the chief bully boarder. And I mean that literally. Claire punched her in the face, sent her sprawling, undignified, embarrassed, in public, and in front of her followers.

I'd been counselling restraint, but really I was a bit stuck. I could hardly suggest she look the other way when she saw them menacing a tiny, fragile, hopeless child, could I? And to give her credit, Claire had tried to talk to them, reason with them, attempting to call forth their better natures.

But when that didn't work, she belted the bully instead.

Oh my. What a moment! It makes me smile still, for I—even I, the most pacific of creatures—found it good just for that sublime instant, that tiny reordering of the universe. And the looks on their faces! What a tableaux. Even Claire had shocked herself. (Note to self: Sometimes you can be so funny.)

But then of course, in the way of these things, Claire became both the focus of their attention and the outcast scorned. For the rest of our time there, Claire ate in the din of the dining room alone, spent every evening alone, and of course, spent every weekend absolutely alone. Her bed was short-sheeted, threatening notes were delivered, and her schoolwork was stolen, and while she often dreamt of running away, she refused to let go of her other dream, her dream of freedom, that funny dream of journalism. She knew that to bring that to fruition, she had to endure, she had to finish school, and so she did.

As school term followed school term, Claire would not buckle even though, after a time, she realised her persecutors were running out of interest and would accept a humble apology, given in public, to restore the balance and to restore face. Yet she would not give it, which made them crazy.

Didn't she know she was fat? (Yes, she did.) Didn't she care that she was hated? (Yes, she did.) Didn't she want to fit in? (Of course she did).

But by then, as she came towards the end of childhood, of school, of her aching, heart-breaking dependency, my Claire just could not, would not accept any more injustice.

And really, after all she had been through, this was quite literally child's play. Besides, she'd been dying to land just one sweet punch, one knockout blow for as long as she could remember and simply refused to apologise for it. It was an act of defiance against the established order, but it was not her only act. As we whiled away the many lonely hours of her prison sentence, her feeling bereft, me feeling glad to be left in peace, she came up with another. And what an act of will it was.

Looking back to her family life and looking out on the concrete compound that was the teeming urban schoolyard, Claire decided to ignore all the experience she had gained thus far on planet earth and love. Just love. It doesn't sound much, does it, but it's such a huge word, such a very big idea.

Claire made a vow that for the rest of her life she would make sure that no one close, no one in her orbit would ever feel as entirely unloved as she did. If they only had her to love them, well, they would have her to love them.

In that instant, upon making this decision, Claire chose to forgive it all, forgive them all, open that crack in her subconscious that had been fractured during the assault and stuff it all inside, bury it, forget it, and start again with love.

*Oh no, Claire,* I thought, *don't go that far!*

But she did. She thought it was a rational way to approach her future—really the only way she could go forward if she was not to be bent over, crippled by her troubles. And though I was afraid for her, knowing a less-extreme path would be safer and saner, I did really love her for it and prayed for her protection, for it was a good decision.

Mad, yes, but not bad.

It would have been so easy for Claire to harness her chariot to the forces of bitterness and resentment, both of which by then could have taken her a very great distance, but she would not do it. She would love even if it killed her.

And do you know who she reminded me of then? Which character from literature? Yes, she appeared to me then as my very dearest Don Quixote. And that meant I became in an instant a sort of mystical Sancho Panza, a role I found greatly amusing. What a funny pair she and I have always been.

I wonder if Claire's choice sits ill with your notions of genetics, of nature and nurture, of psychological determinism. If it does, it shouldn't. Not all the abused become abusers. Not all the hurt and harmed are broken.

She simply chose to love because it was a choice she had.

# Chapter 21

# Claire

Only a few days after I set in motion my sterilisation, Sally rang in flooding tears to tell that her fiancé was no longer her affianced. He had called off the arrangement. He had said that perhaps the time apart had been too long, that perhaps they didn't belong together if they could not actually manage to be in the same country together.

He did not say it was over, though. He said he still loved her. He just wanted release from his promise, the freedom to reconsider. As all this came out in wailed patches of information, and as I'd never heard her so upset, I found it difficult, most difficult to understand.

I said, "But honeybun, does it mean it's over?"

Sally replied, "No. I don't think so. He says he still loves me."

"Did you have a date set for the wedding?"

"No. We were to set one when he came back."

"Is he still coming over?"

"Yes but not to stay. Just for a holiday."

"So do you still feel like you're together?"

"I think so."

"So what's actually changed? What's making you so upset? If you still love each other, it can still work out, can't it?"

"Do you think?"

To be honest, I didn't know what to think. Her reaction seemed so extreme, and I had so little left in my stockpile of emotional resources that I felt like a floundering fool

193

in the face of such distress. I knew neither how hard to press for answers nor how gently to proceed.

I said, "So if you haven't been dumped, Sally it's okay, isn't it? You'll work it out when he arrives, won't you? He's probably just sick of missing you, like you get the blues being far from him. Could it be that?"

"Yes," she said, sniffing. "It could be like that."

"Or did you hear something in his voice, not just his words?" But that set her off again, making me feel like hitting myself over the head with the nearest saucepan. "Sh, sh," I said. "It will be all right. It will all work out all right. Don't worry."

But to my shame, I could not muster the tone of warm reassurance, of calm confidence and patient optimism such words so clearly need if they are to ring true or cut through. They sounded flat and empty and useless even to me.

When her tears had eased again, she asked about me. I told her about the hospital date, and she invited me to stay in her sweet country cottage to recuperate afterward.

She said, "I'm so sorry, Claire. I shouldn't be talking of my troubles. I'm not even sure what my troubles are."

I replied, "Don't be sorry, Sally. It's okay. I wish I could be of more help. I'm just finding the going a bit tough too. Hard times for us."

"Yes," Sally said with a sigh.

"But we'll get through them, won't we? We'll survive them, won't we? We've just got to hang on and hope for better days. Don't you think, Sally?"

Who was I trying to convince, I wonder? Her or me?

Either way, it was not convincing, for a week later she rang back briefly late one night to tell me her beau had a new woman in his life, that he was not coming over. Instead they were over. He'd tried to tell her in the first phone call but had failed to find the words.

I tried to talk to her, to calm and soothe, to suggest he was just a man, no cause at our age for desolation and despair, but she would not listen.

She said, "I just wanted you to know, Claire, my dear friend. I just wanted you to understand but not to worry. Don't worry. You have enough sorrows. I'll be okay. I'm just upset."

"Of course you are. But you will be okay. You don't have to hang up. I can't sleep these days anyway."

She said she'd be fine once again, that she had to go, that there were things she needed to do. I said I'd call in a day or two.

A day or two. Not long. Not very long. Only a day or two too late, for the following day, a dull, no-account Wednesday as I sat at my desk at home trying to get as much work done pre-op as possible, the phone rang again. I thought it might be Sally, but it was not.

It was her mother, Jean, a woman who had been like a step-mum to me when I was young but to whom I had not spoken for many years. I was taken aback to hear her voice and even more so to hear her ask if Sally was with me. With me? I lived hours away. I thought, *Why on earth would her mother think her to be with me on a work day?*

Oh my, the bells started booming and clanging as Sally's mother explained that she had not gone to work that morning, or called in sick, or answered her phone, or been seen by anyone in that small town of whom she had enquired.

Her mother, in almost a whisper, said, "What should I do, Claire? What do you think I should do?"

Yet while I wanted to scream into the void, "I don't fucking know! I don't know what to do about anything!" I actually did. I did know, God help me.

I said, "You have to go inside her house, Jean."

She said, "She's not there."

How could I say it? How could I say there could be a note? I couldn't. I could hardly breathe.

I said, "She might be there now or she might be home soon or she might have left a message …"

"A message? What kind of message? Why would she leave a message there?"

I thought I was going to vomit. "Do you have a key? Yes? Well go over there now and go in, and I'll call back on your mobile in fifteen minutes, okay?"

"But she's not there. Her car isn't there."

Dear God I felt desperate, for I could have been wrong, of course, and clearly, possibly there could still have been time to be wrong. There still could be time.

I said, "Go now, Jean, and I'll call back. Go now."

She agreed and hung up. I called Faith thinking she could help, for at the very least she and Joseph did live in the same town, and I was miles and miles away, perhaps a lifetime away.

Faith wasn't home. She was at a religious retreat. Instead I spoke to Joseph.

I said with panic in my voice, "I think something terrible has happened to Sally," and told him of Jean's call.

He said, "Don't you think you're both overreacting? She's just taken a day off work, hasn't she?"

"Oh Dad," I said. "I have a very bad feeling."

"Well I hope you haven't upset Jean because of it."

Pause. "What? Um … I suggested she go into Sally's house."

"Why?"

"Why? Because I think she might find a note there."

"What kind of note?"

For the life of me I could neither say the word nor decide if he was being deliberately obtuse. I said I had to go, that I had to ring Jean back, and he told me to call him back too, to let him know all was well, when it proved it be so, as if to say when we, the womenfolk, had regained our senses. So I called and Jean picked up. She was standing in Sally's kitchen, gazing, almost speechless, upon a note placed upon the table.

"Jean, Jean, what is it? What is it? Say something, Jean, please."

"She's written that … that … that she doesn't want to live anymore."

The world lurched. "Okay, Jean. I'm hanging up now. You need to call the police. Can you do that? It might not be too late. Can you do that, or do you want me to do it?"

"Oh my child …" she wailed.

"Can you do it, Jean? You've got to do it now or I'll do it."

Jean gathered herself with a monumental maternal effort. "No, Claire," she said. "I'll do it. My daughter. I'll do it." She hung up, leaving me utterly lost in my own little house, feeling as if, had I turned quickly enough, I'd see death standing, smirking in a corner.

*Not again*, I thought. *This cannot be happening again.* But it was. It was.

Don't ask me why, but I thought I'd best call Joseph back.

I asked, "Do you think I should call the police just in case Jean can't? Do you think I should check?"

Joseph said, "It's not for you to get involved."

Pause. "But I am. Jean rang me and … and … Sally's my dear friend."

"I'm sure it's not what you think."

"It's not about what I think. She left a note!"

"I mean she's probably just sitting in her car somewhere or she's just gone for a drive. Most people don't go through with it, Claire."

*God*, I thought, *that's not been my experience, our experience.* I wondered how on earth he could be so certain after Luke. Hadn't Luke existed at all? Was everyone mad?

"Call me back when you hear anything," said Joseph. I knew I would but not why I should.

For two hours I sat in my godforsaken living room waiting, waiting, one minute contemplating the catastrophe of it, the next listening for a knock at the door that never came. There was not even an answer on Jean's phone, which silenced the bells completely. Finally, late in the afternoon, a man picked up the phone.

I said, "Could I speak to Jean please."

He said, "She can't talk right now. Who's calling?"

"It's Claire. I'm a friend of Sally's."

I could hear the man talking to others, and then Jean came on the line but could only say, "No, Claire, no" before hanging up again.

Glory be, I thought my brains were about to explode out of my ears.

So I had to call back again, as if begging for pain. This time the same man answered, explained he was Jean's nephew, and apologised for the hang up. He said Sally had been found in her car by the lake, dead by both an overdose of pills and the inhalation of exhaust fumes, with music playing on repeat on the stereo and photos of her and her beau lining the dashboard and blanketing the seats.

I had no words, not for ages, but then I said, "How would Sally know how to do the exhaust thing?"

How strangely the mind works in a crisis. That poor man probably thought me horrible and heartless, but surprisingly, shockingly, he did have an answer.

"She got the information from the Internet."

"What?"

"It's here on her desk. She downloaded it from a suicide site last night."

Oh God, oh God. That's what she had meant when she said she had things to do. Oh.

Then he said he had to go because there were many, many people to talk to. I managed only a squeak to say, "Tell Jean I'm so sorry" before we broke the connection.

And I was sorry. Sorry for everything. That in fact was all I could think: I'm sorry, I'm sorry, like a mantra, like a litany of unspecified remorse. I thought I'd failed again. I'd heard the bells, hadn't I? I'd heard doom approaching, and now Sally was gone too.

First I rang Mark, and when I told him he let out a groan of anguish, for her who he'd come to greatly like in recent months and for me too, I think. This was, after all, the third time I'd rung him with news of the dead or dying; such a strange and bitter constant in the course of our romance.

Then I called Joseph if only because I'd said I would but perhaps too in search of comfort, no matter how unlikely the source.

I told him of her death and to his questions answered of the ways and means, the location and the timing.

"I'm very sorry to hear that," Joseph said. "She was always so full of life."

"I know," I whispered.

"Did you know she was upset?" he asked.

"Yes but not this upset. I thought she'd be okay. I only spoke to her last night …" Then I broke down and wailed saying, "I can't believe this is happening again. I can't bear it," only to be completely flummoxed to hear Joseph ask, "What do you mean again?"

"Well … what … Luke, of course, and Jess, my friend."

"Oh," said Joseph. "I see."

Was everyone mad? Luke hadn't even been dead a year. Had Joseph forgotten him completely? No, he hadn't. He and Faith had just done a touch of airbrushing and had, in fact, rewritten the story.

He said, "I just mean that they were all different."

"What do you mean, Dad? They all died by self-destruction," I said through ragged breaths.

"Not really," he replied. "Luke was sick."

"Well … what … yes … but …"

"There you are then. And Jess' death was an accident, wasn't it?'

"Well yes … but …"

"There you see? Not the same at all."

For the life of me I could not understand the point he was making or why he felt the need to make one. As usual, me being me, I mistook it for a strange and awkward attempt at comfort given that this was as close as I ever got with Joseph.

And that misunderstanding brought me quite undone, and I blurted for the first time ever, "Do you love me, Dad?"

Ha! It's impossible to explain the feeling of cold astonishment that seemed to crackle down the telephone wires at that mad enquiry. After seconds of silence, I wondered if he'd not heard or heard and hung up, and I knew I'd never have the courage to ask again.

Finally he said, "Well, Claire. As I've grown older, I've found myself feeling more and more interested in those people who make different choices to the majority of people, who use their time in a way that suits them rather than in ways laid out by society. There is an independence in that that I've grown to quite admire over the years, a form of courage, I suppose."

And then he stopped talking. That was it, and because his answer had been so agonised in both its conception and delivery, I lost the heart to ask for further details. I took it, having little choice, as a yes. I only realised later that was the one word Joseph could not bring himself to use—not even then in that hour of such extremis. He sounded as if he was talking of a character in a novel, a third party most removed.

At the start of the statement, I didn't even know if he was talking about me and thought he'd make the link before he finished. But no. He had grown to admire—to a degree—people who used their time differently than others.

What the hell did that mean? It meant, of course, that the answer was no. Yet I could not think that then. That afternoon I could not think at all.

Two days later when I went out to collect the mail, only to receive a card from Sally, posted the morning of her suicide, repeating her invitation for me to stay after surgery, then I thought I might never think clearly again. I pored over that little card (which I kept, for it is not every day that one gets a letter from the dead), holding it in shaking hands, trying to unravel its mystery, to make any sense of it at all, for when I saw her distinctive handwriting on the envelope, my legs almost buckled, for I thought it must be a good-bye.

She'd posted it at ten that morning, according to the mail stamp, and was dead before noon. Clearly at ten she was still planning to live at least for the next few weeks until my hospital appointment. Yet she had downloaded the suicide information sheet the night before. While I know the desire for self-destruction is not the most rational state of mind, still the mental conflict apparent did give rise to the fear that she had suffered a monumental meltdown within the space of only one morning hour. Just one hour.

Like walking to my hospital past the doors of Luke's hospital, I felt like my life had somehow become stuck on some sort of cosmic repeat cycle as I drove up the highway to attend another funeral. I'll spare you the more morbid details except to say that while I thought Luke's send-off was deceitful and cold, Sally's was bizarre not only because someone read out her suicide note to the grieving congregation (which asked for someone to take in her cat) but also because her former fickle fiancé had flown over from Canada to deliver the eulogy in which he described them—him and Sally—as soul mates forever.

As Thomas says, mad, madder, maddest.

I would have had a nervous breakdown then, I think, if I'd known how to go about it. I felt like I'd spent years trying to shake my most beloveds into a simple will to live only to end up unable to stop shaking myself.

Jess, Luke, and Sally gone forever, and for many, many months, I could not rid myself of the image of all three lying in the dark so deep below the earth, battered by rain, baked by the sun, mouldering slowly to bones. In my imagination I'd fly from gravesite to gravesite to sit with them awhile. Sometimes too if I went to a bar alone to think my thoughts, I'd choose a table for four and picture them with me; crazy, I know, but oddly comforting.

Now do you see what the psychic man meant when he said I'd spent so much time focused on the dead, that the dead had had time to focus on me? Yet he made it sound like a dark and wilful choice, which it most certainly was not. I'd have preferred them to live.

# Chapter 22

# Thomas

Claire was as emotionally bankrupt by the end of her childhood as any of the people I have ever known down here.

She existed in a state of internal emptiness made worse by the fact that she could not allow herself to understand what had happened, the malignant dynamic she had been born into.

That way lay madness, she thought, but she was wrong.

She could not think her parents were bad, deceitful, poisonous people. It was easier to blame herself, to take responsibility for it all, and to find a way to make up to them for her awkwardness, her ugliness, her unruly spirit. Really she felt she had no choice if she was ever to achieve that holy grail of love and acceptance, to reach that glorious day when she was found to be—by them—just right or at least just good enough.

Oh my. She waited and worked for four decades before it finally dawned upon her (on a grim, grey afternoon) that such a day had never been on the agenda. If she'd had a gun nearby on that drear day, she would have used it, I have no doubt. All that misery wiped out in an instant. Who wouldn't be tempted? Yet sometimes a lifetime's endurance hinges on the actions of a second.

All her wasted effort, the years lost to sorrow and depression, the lies she had been fed, the terrible collusion she had been caught up in, the fatal betrayal. And understanding, in an instant, that Faith and Joseph had felt only contempt for her, had found her tireless efforts to please them faintly ridiculous—well, that alone almost finished her off.

That moment of comprehension came not long after she left Mark when, despite all she had lost, she was offered no comfort by her family but rather sniffed in the air that old, familiar scent of danger as if, now alone again, the buzzards were circling, watching for one false step. Then she knew. Then she knew she had always known.

But I'm getting ahead of myself. Come back with me now to then. Claire finished school with high marks, a result met by Joseph with a sneering, "Is that the best you could do?" followed by a hollow laugh to show he was just joking, a routine he later perfected, being perfect as it was. That laugh, if you ever hear it anywhere, is the escape hatch for bigots the world over, used just in case they need to backtrack in a hurry.

Faith, as soon as Claire returned from school, attempted to reintroduce the indoctrination strolls but met—hooray—resistance. (That was one light moment in a sea of dark. Dear God it was dark there then. Really, I could not wait to go.) Yes, Claire resisted. She said, "I told you, Mum, I am not going to be a nun."

Faith was furious—all that money wasted! She had to wound.

"But look at you," she said. "Look at the size of you. I hope you don't think you're going to find a husband."

Claire dropped her head and absorbed the blow. "No, as I've told you, I want to be a journalist."

"But newspapers are godless places, Claire!"

And then my dear girl looked up, looked into Faith's eyes, held her gaze (so rare), and said, "Good."

Faith was speechless at having been met with such defiance: all that effort, all that infernal trouble for nothing. But she had others. She had Luke. She wiped her hands of Claire. And then she got rid of her.

Within a week, Faith presented her—amid all the false excitement she could muster—with a train ticket to the city, a map of the tram system, and an address for a Catholic boarding house for young women. "There you are, Claire. You want your freedom. Here it is. Happy birthday."

Dear Lord, she was poisonous. Two days later she gave Claire sixty dollars to cover two weeks of rent, dropped her at the train station, and left her child to disappear unwitnessed into the future without even waiting for the train. It was so easily done and so timely, for Claire had become an embarrassment again. Questions were being asked as to why such a bright spark was working as a local waitress. Questions were being asked about university. Questions were being asked.

So Faith solved the problem then as I believe she solved a similar problem later (Luke) by removing the source of her discomfort without fuss or fanfare, leaving her the delicious freedom to concoct any story she wished. It suited the purposes of the cult too, of course, for sudden banishment of those who question or defy the leadership is often a measure deemed vital both as a warning to others and as a means to prevent contagion.

Claire was in shock. I was in shock. Faith hadn't even given her time to write out job applications, sit newspaper exams, or compile a resume. She'd just pushed her out and packed her off like so much stinking rubbish.

Claire found the house and then a job (typist). Then she found the house to be more a brothel than a boarding house. Honestly, half the young women there regularly met the navy ships down at the docks. Really, the two of us were innocents abroad in the fullest sense of the phrase.

And there we are with the Catholics again. Anyone would think I had it in for them, but really I'm simply relating all that happened. Besides, it surprises me too as I think about all this now, but don't all these stories, these incidents, personalities give the impression of something horribly rotten, something corrupt and corrupting?

Really from all I've seen down here, you'd be best off to burn them all down, all the organised religions, burn them down and begin again.

And start again with this: God is. God is love. God is in your DNA (a strand now to be found in the list marked "junk"). And tend your soul garden, for when the time comes, you will want to be with him.

Trust me. I know. I've been there.

★★★

I suggested to Claire just recently that she do a little research into the subject of leaving a cult.

And now I can say, of course she heard me. It's like the old days before she felt the understandable need to shut me out, to cut off transmission, mistaking me, like you often do, for one of the others or the voice of madness. Then she was so filled with confusion and self-hatred that she could not trust her mind. How far we've come though, she and I, and let it be known that we never abandon you, no matter what, not ever.

Not that we can't, note, we don't. If we are now the only beings left willing to do God's will, then we will, and we do, so we stay. All you have to do is to keep an open mind and invite us in. Really, could it be easier?

Anyway, as I was saying, we looked it up, and this is what we found. The most common effects listed included depression, guilt, shame, anxiety, panic attacks, self-hatred, and fear. Really, that list could have been written for Claire. She was a human wreck. She was only eighteen years old. But she was not broken. She took up smoking. She took up drinking. She ploughed on, typing in a dark warehouse, sending off applications to newspapers and radio stations, hoping for positive replies that never came.

Finally, this struggle to stay afloat made her sick to her stomach. She went to a doctor, burst into tears, and blurted, apropos of nothing, "My father hates me." (It would take many years for Claire to untangle Faith, but Joseph—well, Joseph wore his hate on his sleeve, you could say.)

The doctor was taken aback and met the statement with silence, at a loss. But can you blame her? Really, if you heard this, would you believe it? Most people don't. Most people think, *You must be wrong.* Or, *You must be too sensitive.* Or, *Your father must simply be one of those men who don't show their emotions.*

But it was the truth, the most unwelcome guest at the party, and why I think scapegoats learn to stay silent—to avoid further blame, to avoid being thought an idiot, hysterical, a liar. Remember, not even Claire's siblings would have backed her on this. Well, only Luke, but the two of them would not know for many years that they shared this dubious distinction, and by then it was too late. No, all the others had been treated better. If Claire thought she had been unfairly dealt with—well, then it just supported her parents' view: she was difficult, impossible to please, awry.

Fortunately, I say ruefully, these were the days before you came up with another of your bright ideas that sadness is a disease best treated with drugs, a chemical condition rather than a rational reaction to life in all its glorious, tragic majesty.

Don't get me wrong—I know sometimes drugs help to calm the agitation, to stop the circular destructive thinking. But I also know at times doping people up can merely prolong the agony by deferring the pain, leaving the problem looming like an ominous monster always lurking on the far side of the fog, in the future. Really, that can be enough to drive anyone mad.

Claire was depressed, no doubt, but she didn't need medicine; she needed hope. The doctor told Claire maybe she needed to see someone, a psychiatrist perhaps. Claire was horrified not just at the thought that she might be mad before she'd even started her life but also for another more deep-seated fear. Yes, even deeper than the fear of madness.

Two types of people had quite specifically, deliberately been singled out by Faith and Joseph for heavy demonization and absolute condemnation. One set comprised psychiatrists and all species of mental health professionals. The other was all those people who blamed their parents, their childhood, for anything, ever. Looking back I see this as another act of evil because Faith and Joseph deliberately targeted their mind-control efforts to ensure those they harmed could not readily get help.

When Claire rejected that advice, the doctor suggested she go home to her family for a rest (really, was she listening?), and then I knew I had to act. I didn't want her going home, and I didn't want her to change her mind, for I feared she couldn't handle psychological probing right then, that she had too many raw wounds. I thought it might be better to let some heal through time. I thought she needed to find her place in the world before it collapsed around her from too much knowledge. Was I right? God knows. I don't know.

So I acted. I had a feeling before we were so unceremoniously seen off the property by Faith that she had perhaps been hoping for this, so expert was she at killing multiple birds with one well-aimed stone. That is, she wanted Claire to be punished. She wanted her to be removed as an influence upon the other children, but if Claire failed in the city, she might well be forced to come back home defeated, humbled, amendable.

Then it was my turn to say I could not, would not let that happen. So this is what I did. On a day left free via the doctor's note giving Claire a medically sanctioned holiday, I convinced her to visit a job agency that I had previously investigated.

I said, "Don't give up, Claire. You might as well just take a look."

So she did, and I steered her towards a pin-up board upon which was posted a notice for the position of editorial assistant at a national magazine. Claire thought it was a miracle, and her eyes grew big with excitement, which in turn lifted my spirits up to heaven, where I put in a little request for help. And I was heard.

When Claire took the card to the man behind the desk, he made a phone call, hung up, and said to her, "I'm sorry. Applications have closed. They closed yesterday."

Oh, Claire. Her bright, hopeful face simply collapsed.

"Yesterday?" she asked.

"Yesterday," he said. "The interviews are being held tomorrow."

"I see," said Claire in a most dejected voice.

We left. We ambled down along the waterfront—the scene of her first great miracle—while Claire thought about walking in and walking in and never walking out.

I had other ideas.

I convinced her to find out where the office of the magazine was located. I reminded her of the name of the man spoken to there. I cajoled her into calling the office and finding out exactly when and where the interviews were to be held. I would not let her rest; her thoughts were becoming dangerous.

I said, "Don't you want to be a journalist?'

Yes.

I said, "Don't they have to show initiative?"

Yes.

I said, "Don't they relish a challenge?"

Um …

Anyway, I got her there and suggested she just pretend her name was on the list.

She thought, *But that's a lie.*

Really, this child of mine!

I said, "Well it's only an experiment in courage, Claire. Just see if you can pull it off. Just use this experience to see what you are made of."

"But it is a lie."

Honestly. I said, "Don't worry. You can atone for it later."

So she did all I suggested. She dressed up, went to the office, bowled confidently up to the receptionist, and evinced great surprise at finding her name missing from the list of candidates.

She said, "But I have travelled a very long way. I don't understand why my name isn't there."

And because it was just an experiment, a game, she was charming, warm, and funny, all in the name of seeing what she was made of. She got the job and not only that job but the promise of the next cadetship.

When life goes well, when it feels that all is falling into place, all is good, even better than you had imagined, chances are we are at work. We can do so much, but we can only do so much without your co-operation.

Claire floated. She beamed, and she was elated, terrified, and as you say beside herself— just like me.

Then she rang home.

Faith said in her sickliest tone, "Well I'm sure that's very nice, dear, but I suppose it just means more prayers for me."

Joseph said, "That's a rag, isn't it? Why would you want to work there?"

Really, I wished them both to hell but thought, even then, it quite unnecessary.

Still, we were free at last, and they could not do one thing about it.

# Chapter 23

# Claire

Although I was quite clearly in pieces during those few days I spent with Faith and Joseph to attend Sally's funeral, not much comfort did I receive, the unspoken message being, as it always was, to pull myself together.

Joseph avoided me as much as possible, leaving a room if I entered, sitting inside if I was outside, talking of banalities if escape proved impossible. Faith blamed Sally for hurting her mother (mothers being sacrosanct, of course, and wilful daughters doomed to a most just punishment). In her most-pious tone she said she feared such wanton self-destruction would leave Sally's soul to languish in purgatory for a very long time—a very long time indeed.

She said, "I wish it wasn't so, Claire, for I know how much you loved her, but I'm afraid it is. But don't worry. I'll add her to my prayer list."

I stared at her, and perhaps because I felt my mind almost full to exploding, I could not confine myself to the family code of conduct and blurted (so frightened of a yes), "So do you think the same of Luke then?"

Faith looked at me in utter astonishment. "Of course not," she said.

"Not?"

"No! Claire, how could you think such a thing? Luke didn't die of suicide; he died of head injuries because he was sick."

"But ..."

"And besides," she went on before I could say another word, "I have good news about Luke, which I meant to tell you before this terrible business with Sally."

I can remember sitting there in their garden (I hated it inside their new post-retirement house, much like I did in the former family home) sipping my cup of tea, thinking, *Oh dear God, what now? How on earth could she have good news about Luke now?*

She waited, smiling, for me to ask. What choice did I have?

"What, Mum? What news?"

"He's in heaven," she trilled, actually clapping.

I almost dropped my teacup. What do you say to that? Where else has he been? How do you know? What fresh hell is this?

I said in a dog-weary voice, "What do you mean, Mum?"

"God told me the other day in mass."

"God told you?"

"Yes, Claire. It was wonderful. I clearly heard God say Luke was with him now. Isn't that amazing? Not even a year in purgatory, but then I've prayed so much for him I shouldn't be surprised but it is such a comfort to me, speaking as a mother. Such a comfort. And God told me I didn't, we don't, none of us have to worry about him anymore. Isn't that marvellous news, Claire? He's with God, so there's no need to grieve him anymore because there's no place better, is there, darling? I feel so blessed. My son is with God, which means we can pray to Luke now, you know. He's in a position to help us now. Isn't that wonderful?"

If I'd had the energy then, I would have stood up, walked across the lawn to the wall of the house, and banged my head into it repeatedly.

Instead I said, "Yes, that is … incredible."

Faith then gave me a searching look, unsure from my tone of voice as to whether I fully believed her version of the good news, but she rose when I said no more to get dinner underway.

But just before she walked off, she placed a hand upon my shoulder, leaned her head down close, and crooned, "You can't do anything for Sally, love, and you don't have to worry about Luke anymore so just think? As soon as you get over your little procedure, you'll have no more troubles. So cheer up, darling, there's a dear. I love you, but sometimes I fear self-pity has always been your big weakness."

She patted my shoulder, kissed me on the cheek, and walked off into the house, leaving me not wordless mad crazy but finally, at last, wordless mad angry, which despite my poor articulation I think of now as a great leap forward. Yet while I was finally furious I was still not past forgiveness, for Faith was Faith and had been so forever.

I did, over the next few days, however, once safely away, decide to tell her how she made me feel, to change the depressing dynamic, to reach across to her before my life changed again forever or as a last cry for justice before walking into traffic.

Still (you can laugh), I thought she didn't know. Still, I thought if I found the right words we could still be put right, for surely to God she wasn't being deliberately cruel. Who had ever heard of a cruel mother, predatory and manipulative, who spent all her time in church? Mothers, of course, can be weak, selfish, unkind, impatient, difficult, demanding, and irrational like all of us can be by inclination or the effects of a bad, bad day—but deliberately, delightedly malicious while hiding behind a passionate devotion to the most gentle Jesus? A pillar of the parish, adored by all who knew her (or so she had us all believe), beloved of God?

No. I thought that she simply, quite often, got it wrong, was clumsy in her attempts at kindness, that she had too limited an imagination to enable her to picture life outside the comfort of her most comfortable life. I thought I could fix it (ha!), and at the next opportunity, when she came to the city for secret Catholic women's business and like a queen requested my attendance at a nearby cafe for afternoon tea to fill a spare hour before her train left the station, I gave it my best shot. I had thought all sleepless night of what to say and how to say it to make her see me at last.

First she talked of herself, of my sisters, of their beautiful children while I listened, distracted and afraid I would lose courage, until she finally ran out of chat in the absence of my usual polite questioning.

She set down her cup and sighed, as if she could not take much more of me, and said, "What is it? What is it now, Claire?"

Question: To squeeze the universe into a ball or to shrink, craven and defeated, from the moment?

I said, "Mum, we need to talk."

Faith: "We have been talking, love, or I at least have been trying."

"No. About important things."

"Oh, Claire."

"I'm serious."

There must have been an edge to my voice or a most unusual determination in my demeanour for she deigned to let me speak but not before picking up her handbag and standing to look down on me. "All right," she said. "We can talk. But I've been stuck in a meeting room all day. If you want to talk to me, come sit in the park so I can get some fresh air before I get on the train."

That threw me, I must admit, for why couldn't we just stay where we were, but at least it wasn't a no. We paid the bill, crossed the road, found a bench, and sat down upon it side-by-side, not face-to-face as I would have preferred, but still, to me it was better than nothing.

"Well then," said Faith, basking in the mild air, her face raised to the warm winter sun.

Big breath. "You know how upset I am about the operation ..."

"I don't know why. It won't take long, and then you won't be in pain anymore."

"I mean about children."

"Didn't they say you couldn't conceive now anyway?"

"Yes. They did ... all of it then, not being able to have children and having to go to hospital."

"Oh."

"You should know this."

"Should I? They won't leave you in pain if that's what you're worried about."

"Oh for God's sake. I am worried about that, yes, but what I'm also concerned about is the way you make me feel."

"Me?"

"Sometimes I think you have no idea how unkind you are to me."

Big sigh. "Oh, Claire ..."

Begging myself not to give up, I said, "Just let me finish. I know you love children. I know you think them the be-all and end-all ..."

"No I don't!"

"Yes you do. Child bearing is at the centre of catholic womanhood. You've always said it ..."

"Oh well, when you put it like that ..."

"So I'm afraid that not being a mother, not being able to give you grandkids, is going to mean that I'll be treated like a failure, like some sort of second-class citizen ..."

"Don't be ridiculous. Not everyone can be a mother. Besides, I'm sure Ruth and Grace will let you love their children."

"What, as an act of charity to the barren woman?"

"Well yes. But I'm sure it will suit them too. Think of all the babysitting you could do for them."

Trying, as always, to upright the capsizing conversation, I said, "You're doing it again."

"What, Claire? What?"

"Making me sound like a burden, like a failure."

"But they would like it!"

"But we're not talking about them. Oh Mum, for God's sake ..."

"Don't use the lord's name—"

"This needs to change ... this ... our relationship. It makes me crazy, and given how much time you devote to being a grandmother and given that will have no relevance for us, we have to find a different way to relate now that I'll never be like the others."

Faith, with eyes closed, soaking up the light, said, "I never thought you'd be like the others, Claire. They have their lives, you have yours."

"But we're not talking about them. Why can't we talk about me? Why even now, even after Sally, can you not show some kindness or sympathy? Why do you always make me have to fight?"

"Oh, Claire. I do feel sorry for you, darling, but I just think it might be for the best."

Starting to lose it, I said, "Best? Best for whom?"

"You, of course. You're thirty-seven, and you're not married. Isn't it better to have the decision made for you?"

I sat silently after that line, absorbing that opinion, which prompted Faith to finally open her eyes and turn her head to look at me to see, thinking back, if she had worn me down or reduced me to impotent silence, which had always been much the same thing.

Finally I said quietly, "Why do you seem to enjoy hurting me, Mum, confusing the issues, making me feel terrible? It's not accidental, is it?"

"Oh," said Faith, cross and disappointed, turning away, "as if I like to hurt you."

"But you do. You do it all the time, so you must get something from it."

"When?"

"Like when I offered to come home and help you after you had your hand operation and you said no because being the childless one, I'd have enough caring of you to do when you were olld."

Faith, sitting up on high alert, said, "I did not."

"Yes you did. I'll never forget it. I was only thirty. Or the time you said I'd never marry because I was too difficult and stubborn …"

"Well you haven't—"

"Or when you took me to see the bridge that Luke jumped from and then told me not to mention it to anyone even though it was so traumatic to see it …"

"There was no point upsetting other people …"

"Or when I told you I suffered severe period pain and you told me you thought I'd always had a low pain threshold."

"I'm not a doctor. How could I have known it was serious?"

"Or when you told me as a teenager that you didn't think I'd have children. Why would you say such a thing to your daughter?"

"But I was *right*!"

"You don't even acknowledge my grief for Luke, and you described my sorrow for Sally as self-pity. Why do you go out of your way …"

Faith then started to rock back and forth, her hands up to her face, with such a sudden change in attitude she left me reeling. "Oh, Claire. I'm only doing my best. I'm sorry you think me such an inadequate mother. Oh, oh, oh, why do you always have to be so hard to please ..."

Big sigh. "I just want this to stop. I can't handle it anymore."

"I'll try to be more sensitive then," said Faith, sniffing behind her hands, "but that's all I can say because I've never meant to hurt you, darling."

"But you keep doing the same things. You must mean it."

"Oh, Claire, I'm not very smart. I'm just your stupid mother. I try to love you all as I always have, but I get it wrong, clearly, and then I get in trouble. I feel so bad because all I do is love you and pray for you and want the best for you all. Maybe I should just remove myself from your life because I never know what to say to you, Claire. I'm either in trouble for not caring enough or for caring too much ... oh ... oh ..."

And there was me, wiped out again.

"Please forgive me, Claire. Say you do. I can't bear it."

So I said it. Of course. What else could I do?

Faith said, "Let me help you when you have surgery, darling. Let me make it up to you."

"How? What do you mean?"

"I'll come back down to the city. I'll help you in hospital and when you go home. I'll be there when you come out of theatre. How does that sound?"

I heard warning bells—not doom bells but a clear warning clang.

Yet as her tears miraculously dried in the sunshine, I lost the will to fight and thought maybe I'd done it. Maybe I had finally cut through and maybe also she could just once be of help to me. I was just about to agree when she said, "I won't be able to stay at your house, of course, but I'm sure I can stay with Grace and can bring you food and do some tidying. Can I do that for you, love? Will you let me help? Then we can put all this rubbish behind us."

Rubbish? Unable to stay in my house of sin? Ah, the heavy cost of Faith.

"I'll put in extra prayers and I'll even get the prayer group onto it, darling, so the surgery will go well and you see it's for the best."

Losing the last of my will to live, I said, "Okay, Mum."

Then she stood up, pointed with joy to a nearby florist, and said: "Let me buy you some flowers, Claire, to show that I forgive you too. I know you're upset. I know you don't mean to make me feel bad."

We walked across the park towards the shop.

"After all darling I'm the only mother you've got and you need me more than ever now."

"What? Why now?"

"Well, now that you can't have a family of your own, of course."

# Chapter 29

# Thomas

**W**hen Claire finally got her cadetship, she became the first independent female professional in her family or even her family tree, ever. She was a totally new creation, generations upon generations in the making. She was the living proof of God's plan rolling out so gently across time, across continents, from the ravages of the Irish famine to the Australian bush to arrive at my funny Claire. Not that she was aware of it then, living, as she was, so thrillingly in her long-dreamt-of future to have much time for the past, but I thought it wonderful.

You are such wonders of creation; the first or the tenth, the last or the second, generations in the making, every single one of you. Your life counts. Really it's so important. What's the lovely piece of scripture that explains it? God has known you from the beginning? Yes. Or: God has been waiting for you from the first day. Both are true.

So Claire was the first free professional female in her long family line.

But what a miraculous aberration was my Claire, for in their world then, there was, in the life plan of all those little souls in the cult designed by Faith and enforced by Joseph, absolutely no place marked *freedom*.

Oh no. While Claire had been marked out for a lifetime of chastity, the rest (apart from Luke) were earmarked for sacrifice at the matrimonial altar to enhance Faith's standing in the parish by bringing forth more little Catholics to help promote her to the role of matriarch, a much more powerful position than that of plain old mother. They were also expected—well, the girls I should say—to settle down without a whimper into dutiful obedience if they wished for Joseph's approval. And they did, for searching for approval was all they'd ever known.

So by the time Claire was hurtling into her future—absolutely astonished to find a world opened up to her by the feminist revolution, a development so long kept secret—the oldest two had been betrothed, bound, and shackled.

Peter, desperate to be first, to forever play the overbearing, overheated role of the firstborn son, chose his small town high school sweetheart, a vibrant, cheerful girl whose father had died when she was young, leaving her vulnerable to the notion of husband as father figure. Peter thought her perfect, just made for bullying, controlling, brow-beating. He spoke over her at the wedding and never, ever stopped. Well, not until she left many years later, a move that shocked him to his core and brought forth keen lamentations that flowed along the lines of her ingratitude, her stupidity, her irresponsibility, her sheer, perverse effrontery.

Not once—not even when his children chose one by one to go with her—did he review his behaviour, reflect upon his shortcomings, or regret his hot-tempered martinetting. Oh no. They were all stupid and ungrateful. Then he simply found another wife.

Oh, Peter. His father's son and perfect in his eyes: another egotist, another narcissist. A man who absolutely believed himself when he shouted over others that there was no point looking back, that self-reflection (of the moral, not the mirror, kind) was for weaklings and fools.

Really, who do these people think they are kidding? At another point in history I'd say no one, no one at all, not even themselves. But now? Well, now I think most of you believe it. If there is no God, no life after this one, why regret a single thing? Yet here is the puzzle to me. If you think there is no God, no life after this one, and so no point looking back, how can you look forward? What do you see there? Age, disease, death, nothing. No wonder you're all so frantic, so neurotic about staying young.

Really, you're labouring under such a limited philosophy, such a bleak worldview that you've become too proud to look back and too afraid to look forward, thereby becoming totally trapped in a present that lacks both perspective and meaning. Honestly. No wonder you're all on Prozac.

But you can change this in a heartbeat. Just think: God is, God is love, God loves me and has known me from the beginning. Think that and the chains of emptiness, of non-meaning, of the cosmic isolation of the capital "I" simply melt way. Go on. Give it a try. I dare you.

And there was Debbie—dear Debbie, passively married at twenty, pregnant at twenty-one to a bad man, a man who even then gave me the shivers, all those years ago when Claire and I first met him. Oh yes, there was much dark fluttering agitation all around that man, which, while clear to me, of course, was not at all clear to Debbie or Claire.

I feel upset about this now as I look back, so sad for Debbie. So many times down here this time with Claire, my powerlessness, my inability to change anything has felt overwhelmingly bleak. This—her marriage to him—was one of them. Claire shared my misgivings up to a point, found him unsettling, vaguely unpleasant, but what could she do either? Debbie was in love. It was time by Faith's reckoning that she was wed. He was Catholic, he held down a stable job, and he stoked the boilers of Joseph's ego until steam came out his ears, making him unable to think straight, not even to protect his precious Debbie. And so the deal was done, a deal that on the one hand produced three fine children but on the other condemned Debbie to decades of secret abuse.

Year after year after year, with not one person knowing, Debbie privately absorbed such pain and maltreatment behind the bedroom door as to take the breath away. A little ragdoll, a passive victim, she was her father's daughter. Unable to leave her catholic marriage, unable to ask for help, to defy her husband, to cause a scandal, she was her mother's daughter also. She did leave finally when she felt the children were old enough to cope with the shock and when she could take no more. But note—it was a decision made with priorities in that order.

I have a soft spot for Debbie for so many reasons, but the main one being that it has often felt to me that Debbie and Claire were—because of Faith and Joseph—two halves of one whole. Where Claire thrashed and fought and shouted, Debbie endured with quiet dignity. Where Claire felt forced to defend herself, Debbie defended her children.

They should have been whole, of course. They should have been strong and stable and entire. But they were not. How could they be? They were fractured, they were damaged, and they were hurt. Yet still they were good. Debbie has remarried since to a good man, and her children are all happy and whole, which is a monumental achievement, a victory won in silence, obscurity and pain.

Not the stuff of legend.

Not the stuff of men.

But it should be; it should be.

And then there was Ruth, who was initially delighted with Claire's abrupt departure and then infuriated by her success. But while she nursed her hatred, she thought long and hard, as she finished her school years and heard of Claire's progress out in the world, of how she could use it, use Claire, how she could make Claire's work, work for her. Ah. She was her mother's favourite, Faith's special child with a heart like hers that held within it a central chip of ice and a mind like hers that turned and turned in search of the advantage.

And that brings us to sweet Grace, a child as unfortunate as any of them in a way, given that her generous heart and gentle spirit were the prey, the nourishment, not only of Faith and Joseph but also of Ruth, her adored older sister. Oh my. What a triumvirate. By then Grace was so shy, so meek, so confused by all she had seen, so curled up in upon herself she could hardly manage to go into a shop to buy a loaf of bread.

Really. Any other parents would have worked to give her confidence, courage, to allay her fears, but not them. Faith used her shyness—as she used all their weaknesses—to bind her more closely, to tangle Grace ever more tightly in her apron strings, demonising all that existed outside the cult, the family, the family home.

It took Grace years and years to realise she had even one drop of merit or meaning in her own right, that any personal worth could possibly exist outside her role as serving girl, as handmaiden to Faith and Ruth. She was a shining sun flower made to believe she was nothing but a silly little weed.

What lies Faith told them all as she looked into their trusting eyes and smiled and smiled and smiled. Even then, as Joseph was perfecting his hollow laugh routine, she was perfecting the dissemination of information, particularly then as they began to leave one by one to go out into the world. And this is how she did it. As the fat black spider in the heart of the family web, the one they rang, the one they trusted, Faith kept to herself any and all information that shone a favourable light on any of them. Oh yes, this she kept to herself.

Instead she spread in a most disappointed, long-suffering tone of voice all that touched upon their personal inadequacies, their failures and foolishness (except, of course, for Ruth). All of them (except for Ruth) she stabbed in the back with the tiny dagger of maternal malice but made sure no one knew by each time saying to each one, "Don't say I said that. It will only hurt them. Keep that to yourself. You know I love you all."

So that no one knew, so that each one thought themselves worthy, the others hopeless. So there could be no love, no collective good will, no truth.

Narcissists hate to praise. Really, they cannot stand it. To them, any praise for another is one piece of praise less for them.

And then there was Luke, growing up as best he could, navigating his way between the Scylla of his mother's manipulations and the Charybdis of his father's contempt. Such a good heart he had too but one that was by then becoming so injured, so fractured he began to absorb the lessons of his father, the standard set by his only brother, the atmosphere in the house, and took to belting Grace.

How terrible that sounds to me—how violent and unnatural for this child, how desperate. But he did. He beat up Grace, pummelling and punching, screaming and shouting while

Faith pretended not to hear. She could have stopped it in an instant—indeed could have prevented it ever occurring—but she didn't. Of course she didn't. Do you know why?

Because she needed to feed Joseph's hatred for the boy so as to isolate him, just as she did with Claire, so she could control him, manipulate him, have him do her will. She let Luke beat the daylights out of Grace (sacrificing them both) so she could tell Joseph when he got home, so Luke was punished, scorned, loathed, so everyone remained in a state of violent agitation, so no one could think straight.

She did it so she could then say to Luke, "You know what your father's like. I know he doesn't like you much. But I love you. You can trust me. You're special to me."

And just as Claire believed her, Luke believed her. Ah, Faith and the long game. What a terrible thing.

Luke hated himself, of course, could not forgive himself or even at times understand what had driven him to such wild aggression. As I said, he was a most gentle soul, a tiny, shining light growing dimmer in that house with them.

Many years later he told Claire that during this time—as his self-loathing began to sprout like a noxious, strangling vine—he once woke up to see Jesus standing at the foot of his bed, bathed in a gentle glow, smiling, calm, and comforting. Knowing Luke as I got to later, I was not in the least surprised.

Really, not at all.

To quote a hero of mine (beloved not just for his genius but for his humility, the mystery that still surrounds his identity, which is, of course, the very antithesis of egotism), there are more things, Horatio, in heaven and earth than are dreamt of in your philosophy.

Take us, for example.

Just the other day, Claire and I were reading (so comfortable, the two of us now, her safe, me inside) about a book that has come out that at last, at last brings some scientific thinking to your understanding of us. And understandably after so much time—so much time!—I was delighted, thrilled, astounded. It seemed such a miraculous advance on your previous obsession with us and dancing and pins.

But as I read on, my spirits sank and sank. Really. It was a dreadful disappointment.

Describing a phenomena known as "the third man" (don't ask me why given we are not men and do not come third, which should, in hindsight, have set off alarm bells), it explains how some people in desperate, life-threatening situations feel a comforting, intelligent supernatural presence by their side. In these cases it happened on a frozen mountainside and in the cockpit of a burning plane, helping, advising, saving. I was so excited until I read the author's conclusion that the feeling of the presence was a function of the brain, a primeval survival mechanism activated by life-and-death desperation, a chemical process designed to help you keep going, to help you survive.

Honestly. He'd collected more than one hundred cases detailing the phenomenon, and that's the conclusion he came to—that we are a chemical process, an illusion. Really. You people. I felt like tossing the paper out of the window.

Why are you so intent upon missing the point? Why cannot it be that desperation opens the mind? Or that desperation transcends the human ego, the capital "I", and allows you to see without the eye?

Both are true. The phenomenon is of the mind—not the brain.

Really. Sometimes I wonder why we bother.

# Chapter 25

# Claire

One of the greatest shames of my life (apart from my treatment of Luke) is my lifelong practice of handing it over to other people, laying it at their feet and hoping to hell they can make something of it. For years I refused to take responsibility for my own happiness, to take care of myself, to meet my own needs, to use my brains more and my heart less.

True, I'd never been taught to believe either that my happiness mattered or that I was deserving of care, but that's no excuse. I'm a voracious reader, after all, capable of thought and analysis, of figuring out from fact or fiction what strategies work and what don't, but I could never find the will or the wit to transfer that knowledge from the world of the intellect to the world of the intimate.

And it's not that hard. Surely you would think that after being hurt and exploited more than once I would have learnt that perhaps presenting yourself as a willing slave or sacrifice, devotee or drudge was not the best idea ever dreamt up by woman. No, not a good idea at all to fall at another's feet whispering, "Love me, love me." Definitely not. But still, some lessons take years to learn and some behaviours years and years to unlearn.

Yet after ad hoc bouts of therapy (which didn't work) and a commitment to healing (which did), finally I understood after being shown a chart representing personal boundaries, a word I'd never used, a concept I had scoffed at often as a piece of modern psychobabble indulgence.

It was a simple diagram that resembled an archery target with circles within circles. The outer ring was marked acquaintance. The middle ring was marked friends and family, and the inner ring—the trusted core—the intimates.

I stared at it when it was shown to me and was too embarrassed to express my shock, too embarrassed to say, "What? We have a choice? We can let people in, in stages? We have the right to ask people to earn our trust? We don't have to let in anyone and everyone who knocks upon our door?"

Instead I said, "Yeah, yeah that old stuff. Everyone knows about boundaries!" while thinking, *Holy Jesus, how have I got this far without knowing we have a choice?*

Don't get me wrong. I didn't let everyone in. Instead I only ever thought I had two choices—not the ten gradations of the chart—that is I let no one in so I didn't have to give everything or I gave everything. I know why I behaved so idiotically now, having let Thomas speak, but I didn't know then. Then I thought I had no rights and therefore no responsibility either.

All I had was hope and need. How very creepy I was.

For example: First love. Four years. I gave up my job and moved to another city to be with him, found no work to be had, and came back. I waited and pined for him to return, which he finally did. We moved in together. We spoke of marriage, children, and love until he spoke at the last to say he didn't love me anymore. Without another word, he walked out of the house and into the arms of a friend of mine. I'd shared a house with her while awaiting his return. I'd heard her pick up the phone of an evening when I was waiting for his call. I'd heard her chat for hours as I lay alone, never dreaming it was him. I'd watched them in private conversation when we were out with our gang, had even once thought I saw them holding hands, but did I see it coming?

Lover two. Three and a half years spent with a man because he wanted me, and I thought: one, I'd make at least one person happy if I let him have me; two, that his obsessive desire for me would make betrayal less likely (wrong); and three, that being shrunk to the size of a private collectable for his bedroom cabinet wouldn't hurt so much.

Lover three. We spent less than a year together, but it took two to get over (a very bad piece of mathematics, that one). I gave him money, only to find he was wealthier than I was. I gave him my heart, only to find his was already taken.

And then Mark.

Can you believe such idiocy, such monumental foolishness? For it never occurred to me, not once, to let them prove they were who they said they were. Not once did I think it might be worth my while to watch, to wait, to see. No. They said, "Oh, Claire," and I said, "What is it? What can I do? What more? Love me, etc."

Creepy. Oh most creepy.

And I went for handsome as if I was living in another age where outward beauty was seen as an expression of inner goodness, a most nonsensical notion if ever there was one. Or perhaps I just thought it might rub off on me.

Yet while I resented them all at one time or another for their perfidy, I don't now. What choice did they have? I was almost begging to be betrayed. Only the weak and ill-intentioned found my big-eyed need in the least attractive. Not that I let any good men in, but if I had, they would have run even sooner and faster, no doubt. All of which is just the romance side of the madness.

I did it too outside the bedroom, specifically and most significantly with Ruth. You know from Thomas how we were as children. I should, in hindsight, have stayed true to what I knew of her, but did I? No, of course not, for one day she knocked upon my door, all smiles and sisterhood, and I let her in.

Within two weeks of that unexpected visitation, I had moved out of my little house with my kind friend because Ruth was in need of both. While she went to university, I subsidised the rent, paid for her dinners at fine restaurants, brought her gifts from my travels, propped her up, pumped up her tyres, helped her become a city sophisticate, and introduced her to her future husband, all over a period of about eight long, long years. Then I did it all over again when she decided upon a whim to pack up and follow me halfway around the world to Edinburgh.

"Why?" I ask myself now, and I can only say that apart from falling for her seeming warmth, I at least subconsciously knew when I was of use and therefore of value to her, my standing improved in the family, and that was not, for me, a benefit ever to be sneezed at. Not long ago Grace told me that Ruth had hated those days of sharing houses and nonsense and stories and secrets but had no answer when I posed the question, "Then why did she follow me to Scotland?"

Though I have her measure now, then I really thought us great friends. And they were good days then, for her need outweighed her malice and tempered that of Faith and Joseph so that for one brief, glorious spell when Luke was well and shining, for one short, golden season, the good outshone the shadows in our family home. I still look back on then with nostalgic longing even though I had no clue as to what was real or what any of it meant.

Now I know I was merely being tolerated because I was playing my habitual role as the willing family sacrifice, but then I thought I was loved. Still, though the warmth was chimerical, the laughter and wine in such a beautiful place, when we all drove to the vineyard in separate cars to sit outside watching the sunset and the stars and pretended, at least, to like each other, it did feel wonderful, as if all that had come before had drifted away on the evening breeze.

But then Ruth's man proposed, and the lights went out. She had no more need of me then, no need for pretending, and a week after the wedding, she came calling to say she didn't want me in her life anymore. This came as a bit of a shock given that I was still trying to get the hair-dresser hair-sprayed bridesmaid knots out of my hair.

Ruth said, "You're drinking too much." (True).

Ruth said, "I have a new life, and I don't want to be brought down by you." (Maybe true).

Ruth said, "And my husband doesn't like you." (Not true.)

She said, "You can come over occasionally, but we're not friends anymore, okay? Right. Got to go."

I almost expected her to finish with, "Because I'm so busy now being a wife and everything."

Ha! Secret wife business.

And what did I do? Yes. Not much at all. You'd think I could at least have said, "Give me back my wedding present then, you ungrateful hound," but no. Not a word came out, and though I felt hurt indeed, I thought perhaps it was fair enough, a tad brutal perhaps, but still, different paths and all that.

I was drinking too much. I did have the black dog of depression snapping at my heels, and I did realise it wasn't up to her to give my life meaning (same lesson for the twentieth time unlearned). What I didn't expect was that we could not be civil either. I didn't expect hate, and I didn't expect her to turn Grace against me either. And I certainly did not expect her to hate Luke when he first became sick simply because she thought he was taking away the attention due to her as a first-time mother. Then finally I disliked her back, and though we were pleasant when forced to be in each other's company, being such a civilised family, our smiles never touched our eyes.

And while everyone knew, not a word was said or could be said, at least not by me. The overnight breakdown in relations had to be my fault, for Ruth was then in the ascendancy, the perfect young mother, the wife of a successful man, the university graduate and part-time teacher, the happy homeowner, and I, against all that, had nothing at all to show for myself.

Now we don't speak at all. Now we don't even bother with the fake smiles, yet still I wonder when she has so much why the need to hate. It's a mystery to me. I see mums and dads and kids and dogs and love and laughter and belonging every day just in my little street and cannot conceive of why anyone in such a space could or would make room for hate. If that were me, I'd be wallowing in the glorious connectedness of it.

I think Ruth had two children by the time of my little procedure and Grace two too, her first a gorgeous little girl. She was my goddaughter, so denoted in a sweet but sorrowful baptismal service that took place only a few weeks after Luke's burial, making me reel somewhat at the endless dance of life and death.

Grace had asked me to be godmother before I became sick so at least that was not an act of charity but I think of love. At least I hope so, but as with so much of my family relations, it's always damned hard to tell. Certainly the innocent bond that was sanctified that day was swiftly strained, but I'll get to that. I'll get there.

But first to my last psychic flash, which was both scary and of course useless, for I knew one day, in one tiny instant, that the surgery would not go well. Specifically, I knew I would not be, as I had been told I'd be, home within six days on basic painkillers. But that was it, that's all I knew, not what would go wrong or how wrong it would be. Just that it would not go well.

Was I going to die on the operating table? Were they going to find it was cancer? Was I going to haemorrhage? I did not know, but while I tried to ignore the thought, it rang true, if only because still, only four weeks after Sally's shocking death, I could neither eat nor sleep, which even I knew was not the ideal preparation for major surgery.

I was so afraid of so many aspects of it—like how Mark would cope with a sick woman in the grandmother ward (not well), if I'd lose a degree of sexual pleasure (I did), or if I'd ever feel like a whole woman again (not really). The psychic information sank easily into the swirling soup of my mind.

I should have been offered counselling in hindsight for I could not talk of these fears with anyone. If I did, I was always told that my worries were groundless, that I'd feel better for it, that it would have no impact upon me other than to rid me of pain. I often wondered had I been a man confronting the loss of his testes whether my concerns would have been taken more seriously.

Still, it seemed, only a few years ago, that a woman worried about the loss of her sexual identity and pleasure was a foolish, tasteless creature—as if all we women need is a vagina to be filled to be fulfilled. Still, the psychic fear I needed to discuss. I rang Grace and asked if she would sit with me for an hour over a glass of wine so I could speak of the fear and talk it away at best, make arrangements at worst.

She said she would. We made a date, and then she threw me completely the following morning when she rang to say she had invited Ruth. I still don't know why she did that for she knew we were estranged. Perhaps Ruth insisted. Perhaps she found the idea of witnessing my distress an irresistible attraction.

I don't know. What I did know, however, was that in Ruth's presence, the one thing that would not be given was mercy. She'd roll her eyes at my fear. She'd mock my worries. She'd say, "For God's sake, Claire, it's just a hysterectomy. Do you have to turn everything into such a drama?"

I knew, for that was her way. Certainly I knew that trying to explain the psychic flash would invite her total scorn and ridicule. So while I wanted to say to Grace, "No, no, no keep her away from me," what I actually said was, "Could you ask her to come half an hour later so I can ask you some medical questions?"

Grace said she would, though she sounded clearly uncomfortable at the request, an attitude she brought to the table when finally we met, as if even at that low hour the issue of supreme importance, as ever, was Ruth's pride.

I told Grace of my fears, which she dismissed, though not unkindly. I told her of my wishes should the worst occur, which she refused to countenance. I also asked her as a nurse to list what could go wrong, which she wisely would not do.

She said, "Claire, they take about twenty minutes, for heaven's sake. You'll be on morphine when you wake up, so you'll be in no pain. You'll be home in five days and well within weeks. I know you feel terrible about Sally … and … and … Luke but really you're overreacting. I can certainly assure you that you will not die."

And I did not have the heart or strength to say that it was not death but more suffering that I feared, that drifting out of this world was not the thing but waking up in it again and having to fight for a future I did not want.

So we changed the subject as we waited for Ruth. And waited. And waited, the atmosphere between Grace and I becoming increasingly strained until it both became clear she was not coming and that she had achieved her goal of making herself the focus of attention.

Then I saw a burning shade of red. Really I went into orbit, for I thought, *You, Ruth, with your husband and babies and house and status and wealth, could you not just once show graciousness? Just once.* And when Grace left I drank more, the wine fuelling a rage that felt a lifetime in the making.

When I got home, I rang her. I said, forsaking any polite preamble, "Where the fuck were you?"

Ruth replied with withering scorn, "You're drunk. I have no intention of talking to you in such a state." But she did.

I asked, "Why say you're coming and then make us wait?"

Ruth replied, "Why should I have come when I was only welcome to come later? You think I'm prepared to be snubbed by you?"

"So I'm not allowed to talk to Grace for half an hour?"

"You know it's not about that."

"What are you talking about then?"

"You want everyone to feel sorry for you."

"I just wanted—"

"You make a drama out of Luke when it was difficult for all of us. You've upset Mum and forced her to come down and look after you …"

"She offered."

"And you should just be grateful at your age that the decision is being made for you."

Then she hung up, leaving me feeling both despairing and demented and wondering for the millionth time why we found compassion so difficult or costly, for it had not even been a year since Luke had left us, and still we could not show kindness. After all, all I'd asked for was half an hour.

# Chapter 26

# Thomas

There is something I need to mention here as we draw towards a conclusion about Claire's birth, that strange mystery of the extra month of cooking time, or Faith's uncharacteristic miscalculation, as she always described it whenever it rarely came up.

You already know it gave Claire a big head, aroused her father's suspicions and dislike, and made her look like a strange little alien. But two other developments occurred during that unscheduled month of extra embryonic development. (I'll explain one here and leave the other for later—though perhaps you've already figured that one out.)

Claire's brain was affected in that month, not just her head, in particular her hypothalamus, that little acorn that sits just above the brain stem. This meant she had a faulty internal thermostat set too low, which had the counterintuitive effect of making her feel hot, way too hot for the Australian interior.

She sweated, she fainted, and she was imprisoned, embarrassed by it. Really, if you have an image of Australian bush kids frolicking in the sunshine, then you may be conjuring the majority but you have never seen Claire.

She wanted to frolic too, but the heat of that sunburnt country simply melted her like she was an ice block, necessitating showers she could not have due to the perpetual drought and changes of clothes that made Faith furious. ("Don't put your stinking things in with the rest of the washing! Don't you ever think of anyone else, Claire?")

It also made her feel for eight months of every year that really, surely, she must have been left behind by a forgetful band of cool-climate gypsies somewhere, sometime, somehow.

Really, she thought this wry thought quite often. It made sense of so much and gave her a certain ironic high-gothic comfort.

Anyway I just mention this by way of explaining that when Claire established herself in her new life in that city by the sea and felt the overwhelming relief that was the coastal breeze, she felt she had finally found her geographical place in the world. Living in that city as a journalist, then, seemed to her really as if she had come home. At last, at last, she felt that feeling of belonging that is so central to your happiness, a core need met at last that triggered a small wave of healing, as I had hoped it would. Then too with the weight of her childhood falling off and falling off—both literally and metaphorically—really she felt like she could almost fly.

In some ways it was her first feeling of true, uncomplicated happiness because Claire found, to her great delight—like many of you do who hold to a cherished dream—she was good at doing what she had long longed to do. Yes, Claire made a pretty good journalist. Not brilliant, note. You would never have heard her name. She didn't have the driven ambition, the single-minded focus to be front-page material, the courage to be a war correspondent, the hubris to be a commentator, the patience or obedience to climb the ladder. But she didn't need any of that because really she just liked to write, and besides, she never got over the simple thrill of having a job that allowed her to wander around asking people questions.

It was that simple to Claire. She loved people. She found them endlessly fascinating— why they did what they did when they did it—and really appeared to me then in those early days in particular to be just an amusing, animated question mark. There was so much to know, so much to make sense of in this world outside the family cult, the Catholic Church, and so much that needed to be jettisoned to make way for the new.

Unfortunately, that included me. And just like you feel it, the abandonment hurt.

I tried to tell her it wasn't necessary. I tried to tell her I was on her side, that I was there for her for better or worse, that I was friend, not foe, even just that I was. But she would not listen.

By then, in an attempt to drown out Faith, to stand upright, to clear her addled head, she had plumped for atheism as her guide into the future. Really, she could think of no alternative given that there was no unravelling Faith's contorted teachings. So she chose to disbelieve in God rather than disbelieve in Faith. I understood, but really talk about backing the wrong horse!

And because by then (knowing herself to be sane) she understood my voice to be related somehow to God (at least she got that right), she ceased transmission. She pulled me off the air. She flooded her head with static. *Oh Claire*, I thought, *you don't have to go that far.* But she did.

Besides, she wanted to have sex, and she didn't think she could do that with me around. She was wrong of course. I could have helped her, eased her way into the world of adult intimacy, but she thought loving God meant chastity, and she was sick to death of chastity. She was twenty years old!

How that makes me laugh to think of. She thought she was old, that time was passing her by, that if not then, then when? Ah the urgency, the rush of youth. Note to self: You can be so funny.

Besides, Claire wasn't just determined to lose her virginity for the sake of it, to become a woman. Oh no. Not at all. Rather, like an academic who has conducted a diligent review of the literature, she had come to the conclusion that sex was the most incredible mystery, so powerful as to make the world go round, the cause of scandal, of murder, of upheaval from the beginning of written history to the pages of the afternoon newspaper, men and women driven to the extremes of passionate madness, of intoxicating surrender and tender domination.

*Oh Claire*, I thought, *don't go that far.*

But unfortunately for my dear Claire, there are not many books that describe bad sex, dreary sex, boring, banal, dutiful sex. No. Who wants to read about that? It would be bad enough, I imagine, to go though it without having to read about it.

So Claire, knowing only literary sex, could not wait. She went to the doctor, she went on the pill (and thus, according to Faith, to hell), she waited for the first month's cycle to pass, and then at the first possible opportunity, at the first party following, Claire had sex.

Oh my. It was, as you can imagine, a dreadful disappointment.

She tried it lying underneath, she tried it on top, she tried it sideways, she tried it with her eyes shut, she tried it with them open, lights on and lights off. Really, though, without knowing the increasingly startled young man, without even knowing his name and without any foreplay to speak of, she found it tedious, inelegant, vaguely ridiculous.

Who wouldn't?

More confused than ever, Claire left after his climax and walked for hours through the sleeping city streets, her knickers in her handbag, her shoes held in her hand, through parks and gardens and along the beach, letting the dawn shed what feeble light it could upon the problem.

*That could not have been it*, she thought. That wouldn't make anyone do anything, she thought, except perhaps go back to reading. If that was it, she should have kept on dancing. But she didn't. Instead, convinced she must have missed something (otherwise the world made no sense at all), she kept on fucking, as you call it, thinking in her upside-down innocence that it might be a matter of practice.

Oh my. My dear girl. You can imagine what I was trying to tell her, can't you? Yes. "Claire, you are missing something. You're right. It's called love," I shouted. "And even if not love, then you could try getting to know them, getting to like them, getting to care about them," I bellowed. "But really," I screamed, "aim for love, Claire!"

But she not only did not listen, she did not understand. Do you know why? Yes—because she had absolutely no idea of mutual love. Really to her, by then, love was a one-woman show. The idea of being loved was beyond her comprehension because she was strangling in the vine of self-loathing that had its roots firmly grounded in the family domain, roots that were diligently fed and watered by both Faith and Joseph without pause or cease for years, even up til now.

Over time then, from this muddle-headed beginning, Claire mistook lust for love, need for love, obsession and control for love, even, not long ago, abuse for love, for that was all she'd known from the beginning. Yet every sexual encounter for Claire was based on her desperate need for love, which made her absolutely hopeless at promiscuity, a needy vamp, confusing the men, poisoning her soul garden, breaking my heart.

Time and time again she chose weak and needy men. She kept believing what they said, and she kept ignoring my advice simply because she felt herself to be nothing. She saw herself as plain, and she knew she was erratic, intense, and awkward. She was confused and confusing: a promiscuous young woman who believed in morality and decency; a stand-up feminist crippled by need; funny and warm and sad and closed, a fractured personality.

She was hard work but easy prey, and she slept around because she could not sleep.

I could have spared Claire so much pain if she had been able to listen. But she wasn't, and I didn't blame her one little bit. I blamed Faith, and I blamed Joseph.

Let us list the cost of their pride and wilful lying. Let's see. They allowed, even encouraged, Peter's bullying brutality, which led to Claire's assault, while Faith's machinations and Joseph's violent dislike destroyed her ability to think straight, stand up in the world, and love well, which for a time lost her God and cost her me. In turn, Peter's bullying also condemned his gentle wife to years of verbal and emotional abuse and later cost him his children, them a loving father. Their warped and callous parenting cost Debbie enormous suffering, turned Grace into a frightened little lamb, destroyed Luke's internal stability and gentle spirit, and fed Ruth's dark hunger for power, for superiority, for control.

Yet take note, through all this, through it all, Faith and Joseph felt themselves to be fine and model catholic parents, secure, confident, pleased with themselves. Pleased with themselves. Perhaps in a way that is the best description of bad I can present. They felt no sense of failure, of guilt, of remorse. None. They could not be blamed for anything, for any sorrow, for any maladjustment, for they had done their best; they had followed the dictates of the church.

Egotists. Narcissists. Liars.

They had so many lies, a veritable internal pantry stacked with lies, with excuses, with misinformation suitable for every occasion.

Lies like: "We never treated any child differently to the others."

Or: "We love you all much more than we love ourselves."

Or: "The happiness of our children has always been the central concern of our lives."

Really you'd think they'd choke. But no, the lies tripped off their tongues then and now with an ease and seeming sincerity made possible only through constant repetition.

In the beginning was the word and the word was God and the word was with God and the word was true. Then came the lie, the liar, the great deceiver, and those who follow after him lie to themselves first and find the lies to be good.

And take note—in all the affairs of women and men over time and at all times, there comes a moral tipping point not just when bad outweighs good (which is, of course, quite commonplace down here) but when bad is *seen* to be good. Remember, God exists in the difference between a bad choice and choosing bad.

When bad is seen to be good, when it is justified, when it is lied about, when it is secretly treasured, the time comes when forgiveness is impossible. Really. I mean it. Impossible.

Remember my description of the soul garden? The point of no return comes not when you can no longer look upon your soul garden for fear, for shame, even for discomfort, but when you can look upon it and see the rusting car hulks, the drying bones, the strangling weeds and think it is good, for it has got you what you wanted, and it is your cherished secret. It is the pleasure, the deceitful superiority of the homeowner showing off the chic renovation while keeping the dungeon a gleeful secret.

And it is, of course, the province of the egotists for whom nothing—nothing on earth—is more important that what they want. You would think, wouldn't you, that as the junk piled up it would be harder to justify and excuse, but not to them. They have only ever done what they found it necessary to do. They have done their best.

I mention this as a way to clarify one of your central misconceptions of God. I've already explained that God loves, that God leans towards you, that God aches to forgive, to heal, to comfort. Yet many, perhaps the majority of you who think of him at all, see him as a cosmic judge, some sort of vicious dictator sitting at the heart of the universe, dishing out punishments. Honestly, you could not be further from the truth.

Let me spell this out. When people get to the point where they see bad to be good, they reject God, not the other way around. At that point, that infernal tipping point, such people will not—will not—suffer the scrutiny of anyone, be humbled before anyone, anyone at all, on earth as it is in heaven. Do you understand?

Just as Faith and Joseph would never stoop even to discuss their actions, their motives, their secrets, let alone apologise for any mistake, no matter how small, so they could not seek even private forgiveness from God. The very idea was anathema, and they snuffed out the candle of their divinity and smashed it to the ground. (And what Faith said in confession every second Saturday is beyond even my comprehension, but safe to say lies, more lies, damned lies.)

They are not to be judged! They are not like other people! They had done their best!

People like them reject him. He never rejects you. Never. You get to choose. It is the point, as I have already pointed out, of this strange and sorrowful and glorious fourteen billion–year experiment.

Faith and Joseph cannot experience the wonderful freedom, the glorious lightness of forgiveness simply because they cannot and will not ask—not for the forgiveness of those they have harmed or celestial, eternal forgiveness. They will not stoop. They will not bend. And over the years, the secrets and the lies and the soul garden junk piled up and piled up.

They chose. They chose the other whose screams of wounded pride still echo through the universe always and forever. They chose the other, and he knows his own.

Your life counts, and the soul counts. Make it count.

What is the lovely Jewish phrase? To save one life is to save the world? Yes. So too is the reverse true. To destroy one life is to destroy the world. Faith and Joseph had chosen to be parents. To bring life into the world simply to use it, exploit it, torment it for the sole purpose of egotistical gratification is a terrible thing.

You may think this overwrought and overblown, but really, God has tried subtlety for eons and look how far that's got him.

# Chapter 27

# Claire

Mark took me into hospital on the appointed day and stayed by me while I was weighed and measured, gowned and bedded, feeling lost and fearful amid the cheerful stoic grandmothers. As I lay there holding his hand, I waited and waited for Faith.

"Where is she?" I asked him in a small voice, knowing he could not possible know.

"She said she'd be here. She's in town; she came last night. She said she'd be here when I came out."

And Mark tried to comfort and soothe. (See, he must have loved me once.) "She'll be here," he said. "She'll probably get here any minute or when you're in theatre, but don't stress. If she said she'll be here; she will be."

But she was not there when they wheeled me in, and she was not there when they wheeled me out three hours later. She was not there when they told me it was the worst womb they'd even seen, not there when they said I'd lost a great deal of blood, not there when they said they feared it might be cancer.

Not there.

They wheeled me into a room and hooked me up to oxygen and monitors and drips and catheters and then allowed Mark in.

"Where's Mum?" I whispered "Is she here?"

"She rang," said Mark. "When you were in theatre."

I looked at him, too battered to speak the question.

"She told me to ring her when you came out."

231

"But she said …"

"So I'll go and call her now, shall I? Is that what you want? Should I do that?"

I gave a tiny nod and sank back into the morphine as he left the building to make the call.

Sometime later Faith arrived, gave me a kiss on the forehead, and sat silently on the far side of the room, gazing at me as if waiting for something.

I did what she expected. Finally, I said, "Where were you?"

"Where was I when, darling?"

"When I came out."

"I'm here."

So tired, I said, "You said you'd be here when I came out."

"Oh that! I thought it would be a waste of time."

I looked at her.

"I thought my time would be better spent helping Grace with her beautiful new baby rather than just sitting around here."

I looked at her.

"And lucky I did. I would have wasted three hours!"

Finally I said, "Why didn't you tell me you'd changed your plans?"

"Oh I thought you'd have enough on your mind without worrying about me."

"But you offered …"

"Oh Claire, please. Let it be, or do you want me to leave? Isn't anything good enough? I'm here now, the operation went well—"

"No it didn't …"

"Of course it did; it just took a little longer than usual, that's all. Now you just have to concentrate on getting well again, and you can't do that if you keep on blaming people for what they do or don't do."

I had no answer to that, of course, but for once, perhaps because of the morphine coursing through my body or my inability to move very much, hooked up to machinery as I was, I did not look away. I did not bow my head in defeat. I did not change the subject. I just looked and looked at my mother, this woman, until finally she said I was clearly exhausted and needed rest and she'd promised Grace she'd be home to babysit her baby so Grace and her husband could have a much-needed night of baby-free enjoyment.

Do you think she used the word *baby* enough? Do you think it accidental?

And so she left, and to this day Faith does not know I had to wait two days to find out if I did or did not have cancer, that I was not washed for three days, and that I was asked my permission to have images of the world's ugliest uterus used in medical textbooks to educate the learned and horrify the unwary.

"How much pain have you been in?" the surgeon and registrars asked me, aghast. "How could you not have known something was terribly wrong?"

I had no answer then. I just looked up at them, feeling like a monumental idiot, for I did not know but I think I do now. I thought suffering was normal. I thought it was my lot.

As I lay there that first night, sleepless, trying to remember to breathe (I overdid the morphine pump in my desperation to find an alternative reality), I could not get Faith's tone of voice out of my head. But despite hours of hazy, drifting thought, I simply could not place it.

I knew it was not the sound of love or worry or comfort, but that's all I knew, that it was awry somehow. Yet while she sounded callous and unfeeling, that was Faith. That was typical; that was how she always sounded to me. No, there was something else, some sharper edge to her voice that I recognised but could not identify.

For the next two days she popped in late morning and again late afternoon, and to this day I do not know where she was in between or what she did. She said she spent her time at the hospital chapel, but not even Faith would sit in church for five hours with no one to see her do it. No witnesses. No point.

But where? The movies? Reading in the park? Eating in the cafeteria? Certainly she did not return to Grace's house. No. She stayed out somewhere to lead others to believe she remained at my bedside, the most devoted of mothers, and to make them believe I was therefore in need of no other comfort.

Yet if I did not entertain her—find the energy to ask of her, that is—she could not even last the twenty minutes she had scheduled. It was bizarre, for she had offered to help me yet clearly had no intention of being of help. What was she there for? What was she up to?

Being too sick and weak to muster the necessary strength for astute enquiry, having on the third day been taken off the opiates and left in dreadful pain, still I did manage to accidentally stumble over the tripwire of her deceit by raising the ever-troublesome topic of Ruth.

I wanted to protect myself. I was too hurt for pretence or defence and could not bear even the idea of Ruth standing by the bedside, gloating at my anguish. I waited till Faith sat in her usual faraway chair, and knowing I'd better make it quick, I raised myself painfully in bed so I could see her clearly. Then I asked, "Is Ruth planning to visit?"

And what did Faith do? She snorted in contempt. She said, "Hardly!"

"What?" I said. "Why hardly?"

"Well, Claire, really," said Faith. "Surely you can't expect her to visit after what you said to her."

I was so shocked my poor old guts lurched, a dreadful, dreadful sensation under those particular circumstances. Gathering my wits, I said, "What did I say?"

"I don't know."

"What do you mean you don't know?"

"I didn't ask."

Trying not to scream the hospital down, I said, "So what do you mean? What are you talking about? What did I say?"

Staring at me, she said, "Do you think I don't know you upset her?"

"How? How?"

"I said I don't know!"

"Then how can you accuse me of it?"

"Because I assumed, Claire, given her upset, that you must have torn strips off her like you did with me."

I stared and stared at her, this woman by my bedside, and I did not look away. I saw her eyes, hard and small and glittering like ice. I saw an expression of triumph on her face. I saw her sitting so fat and comfortable, so safe and sure and cruel. I saw it all at last even as I struggled to understand.

"When?" I said in a voice I hardly recognised, a voice made cold and empty by a dawning comprehension. "When did I tear strips off you?"

And Faith, as if she'd been counting down the days to say it, said, "In the park, of course."

Still with her eyes boring into mine (surprised perhaps that I had maintained my gaze and trying to stare me down), she said, "And that was so hurtful, darling, that I assumed you'd done the same to Ruth, so no, in answer to your question, she will not be visiting."

"In the park?" said I.

"Yes," she said.

"When I was trying to get through to you." It wasn't a question.

"That's not how I'd describe it, darling."

"How then?"

"What do you mean, love?"

"How would you describe it?"

"Oh well as a most unjust attack, I suppose. I try and try to love you, Claire, as you know, but it seems nothing is ever good enough so I assume you did the same with dear Ruth."

And I stared and stared until first Faith started to fidget with rare discomfort and second till I whispered, "Get out."

"What?" she said, astonished.

"Get out. Get out."

And she was shocked—the first time I think I'd ever seen it. She fumbled getting up, she fumbled with her cup of water, and she fumbled with her handbag. And she muttered as she did so to hide her evident confusion. "Yes well. You must be tired. You need to rest, Claire. That's quite the best thing, and I'll be—"

"Get out!"

Finally, out she got, and despite calling on every ounce of strength I still possessed—for I knew it would be agonising—I burst into heaving sobs, holding a pillow to my belly, feeling like my insides could burst out of that primal wound.

Whether the painkillers that could not kill the pain reduced my capacity for forgetting I do not know, but all the hurt of my life at her hands poured like a deluge into my mind. For I knew at that moment that if she could not love me then, when I was so small and sick and hurt in my little pink pyjamas, not after Jess or Luke or Sally or losing the ability to create a family of my own, then quite clearly she never would and had no intention of ever doing so.

Further I knew, in a flash of horrific comprehension that had only taken decades, that loving me had never even been part of the plan. As I lay there in so much pain, I understood I had wasted almost forty years waiting for, working for, and wanting the impossible and she had deliberately led me to believe the lie that she and Joseph were just dying to love me if I could only make myself lovable enough.

And I had believed her, and I had tried. Almost forty years of useless hurt and effort, years lost to depression and self-loathing, of bending to their will, of gazing at them with the eyes of a wounded child instead of looking at them with the cold clarity of maturity.

A wasted, blighted life.

And then, oh then, I wanted to die like never before. I wanted to throw myself off the roof of the hospital. I wanted to swallow every pill I could lay my trembling hands on. I wanted to tear open my wound and let my life force drain away. I didn't, of course, for not only is it a bit hard to die at your own hand in hospital, but I also could neither move fast enough given my shuffling, bent-over grandmother gait to get up to the roof nor bring myself to bring on more pain.

Yet once the idea, the desperate urgent urge for self-annihilation, had finally taken deep root, it took quite some time to dislodge it. Rather I nourished it, fed and watered it as my last best hope.

In the next day or two, the nurses reduced my medication while my temperature and pain rose and rose and rose. They forced me to walk. I told them I could faint. They prepared me for discharge though I lay on my bed curled up and shaking and clutching my tummy, turning from Faith upon her last visit, too agonised to argue. The staff looked at me as if I was hopeless, a liar, a cry-baby, casting their gaze from me to the older women as if telling me to draw my own conclusions.

They said, "It's been six days, Claire. The other ladies are coping. It can't possibly hurt like you say it does."

And I believed them. I had known, via the psychic flash, that the surgery would not go well, so it was all to be expected, and I felt I had no option but to endure as always. In seven days I was home, hobbling and disabled by the pain. Poor Mark had no idea what to do, and neither did I.

He said, "Should I ring Grace? Should it still hurt this much? Should I ask Faith to come over?"

And no was all I could manage. No, dear God, no. Two days later, however, Grace did visit with Joseph, who had driven down to collect the saintly Faith, bringing along with them her new baby, a manoeuvre that seemed to me then, as it seems to me now, a classic piece of Faithism.

Surely, I thought, could I not have a week without babies around not only as a sensitivity measure but also because it was quite clear I could not hold the child or cuddle her. I could hardly stand but stand I had to, for Joseph asked for a cup of coffee. Like my former robotic self I made it as requested. I obeyed upon command.

As I handed it to him and began the long shuffle back across the living room I asked him of his brother who had recently been ill. I did this because I liked my uncle but more because the silence between the three of us weighed like lead upon my fragile mind. Grace took the question as a cue to duck out, with baby, to the nearby shops.

That left just him and me.

Too tired after my one conversational effort to try another, Joseph cleared his throat, put his coffee cup down upon the table, and as if addressing the nation, said, "At times like these, Claire, I think you'll find it's best to think of other people."

I just sat. I sat and stared and sat and stared and thought, *Of all the words in the English language that you, my father, could have strung together at this moment, you have chosen those.*

Not, "I'm sorry this has happened." Not, "I know you've had a tough patch, love, but things will get better." Not even, "How are you?"

No. I should think of other people. As we sat there in the booming silence that it was my job to fill, I could not think of one thing to say. Not one. I just sat with head bowed, waiting for time to pass until my father could bear it no longer, stood up, said he'd go find Grace, that I was clearly not up for a visit, that they'd best leave me to rest. He walked down the hallway and shut the door behind him.

Two days later, my wound exploded, I lost consciousness, Mark called an ambulance, and I was rushed back into hospital with acute blood poisoning from a hospital infection.

The surgeon and registrars on duty were appalled. They said, "How much pain have you been in? Why didn't you tell anyone?"

By then I didn't even have the will or energy to scream.

When Faith rang me at the hospital the following day and said, "Oh you silly girl! How did you get an infection?" I just dropped the receiver and let it fall to the floor, hearing her voice at last at a distance and not booming in my head. I wanted to hurl it out the window. I wanted to wrap the cord around her neck, but I just let it fall and twist slowly in circles, wanting it all to be over …

And as I lay there, I understood that Faith had waited and waited from that day at the park for revenge, that she had offered to help while intending to harm. Then I knew it had all been a lie, that Faith and Joseph had always lied, which meant in turn that I had to rethink all I'd been told about everything but most importantly about Luke.

It was by then astonishingly clear to me at last that if Faith could be so cold, so filled with fury for even a hint of criticism of her in my last-ditch attempt to try and reach her that day in the park, that she could hold the grudge so warmly to her bosom until she could strike back when I was at my most defenceless—and all less than a year since she had lost her son to suicide—then not only did she not love me, but excruciatingly, she did not love Luke.

Faith was not in grief. Faith felt no anguish or remorse or guilt or sorrow. No. She felt none of that.

Yet we had all been so brainwashed in our isolated cultic hothouse family that it took an extreme series of events to open my eyes and free my mind to see the truth and to understand that all Luke had ever said, all we had ignored as the ravings of a lunatic, was true.

# *Chapter 28*

# *Thomas*

As the house emptied, there in that beautiful place, that glorious vine garden, Faith and Joseph grew fat and wealthy and comfortable. Faith was able to attend mass daily, sit on catholic committees, able to rise and rise in that torpid parish hierarchy.

Joseph had given up drinking (too late to do much good to anyone except himself), a development that seemed miraculous to them all, not least my Claire. She thought it incredible, an admirable achievement in the midst of a vineyard and a cause for great respect.

*Oh Claire*, I thought, *you don't have to go that far!*

But she did. She did but only because of lies.

Faith said, "He gave up drinking for me, because he loves me but it's God's work who also loves me and who chose to answer my prayers. All those prayers. It is really God's special gift to me."

Joseph said, "I just stopped because I wanted to, like I always knew I could, a simple choice based on my strength of character. I don't find it difficult in the least."

But both, of course, were lies. He'd done it though hypnosis, the two of them having driven to another city for three sessions that proved successful but that were kept secret, most secret, just another secret to add to their bulging stockpile.

No one ever helped Joseph. He did it all by himself. And Faith lived in God's lap. It was only to be expected. Lies, lies, lies, and none of the children knowing, so tight were Faith and Joseph until she accidentally dropped her guard one day many years later and let the truth slip out.

Claire, when she heard, thought it was bizarre. *Why lie?* she thought. *People use hypnosis all the time.* But of course Claire did not understand egotism on such a scale, really had a very limited understanding of self-interest at all. Yet obviously, without an understanding of egotistical self-interest, she could not understand her parents, her family, her life.

By this time as she honed her craft as a journalist, Claire understood cant and deceit when she heard it in her professional life (how else could she have functioned?), but as soon as she entered the world of the personal, the intimate, she shut her brain down, put it in neutral. She believed that love and logic were oxymoronic, that love was not meant to make sense, that it existed—if at all—in the gap between what people said and what they did, which was, after all, all she'd ever known. Not for a very long time did she understand that people could look into her eyes—without blinking or blushing—and say love and mean hate.

No wonder Ruth found it so easy to walk into her life and take it over.

Dear God. It made me weep. Claire was just starting to find her feet, herself, her place, and then along came Ruth. Even now I can't explain how within weeks she was able to convince Claire that her welfare was Claire's responsibility, but she did. Within a month, Claire had moved out of her happy share house and into a flat with Ruth, and Ruth being Ruth, I was exiled once again, out in the cold, onto the balcony, useless again, heartsore, as the fluttering darkness descended and again shrouded my dear Claire.

Over the next few years, Claire supported Ruth while she studied at university (oh yes, Ruth was allowed university), paying most of the rent, finding her part-time jobs, taking her to parties, introducing her to friends, wining and dining her on Claire's rapidly rising income, keeping her secrets, making her laugh, keeping her safe.

In other words, doing exactly as Ruth required. And doing it all with a glad heart because Claire thought Ruth being at university was a victory for the girls of the family, thought it to be a result of her quiet crusade for equality, but she was wrong. Really, if Ruth had wanted to fly to the moon, Faith would have searched out a rocket and then claimed she found it as a miraculous gift from God.

Oh Claire, lost in lies, supporting her sister who was being secretly supported by her parents and publicly funded by the state. Ruth thought Claire to be a monumental idiot. It was both interesting and painful only being able to watch Claire in these years, her heady twenties. She loved so unwisely. She lusted so bleakly. She worked hard and worked hard to have her parents know how hard she worked but to no avail. They refused to acknowledge her professional achievements. They refused to see the signs and symbols of success.

Instead, Joseph gave her to believe that he thought her a fluke and a flake. Instead, Faith gave her to believe she thought her godless, hellbound, hopeless. At one stage, after hearing of Claire's decision to move in with a boyfriend and abandon Ruth, Faith wrote her a letter telling her she was a whore with a soul stained beyond redemption. She was used linen, and her supposed boyfriend was only after one thing. He would throw her back as soon as he had taken his fill, and no one would then have her. She would never be wed, and she was dirty, disgusting, and foolish.

Really, she covered everything, don't you think?

Joseph refused to allow the young man onto the property and absolutely refused to speak to Claire for more than two years—two years!—to teach her a lesson, to show her what happens to whores (he always knew it!) and to women who refused to know their place. But again, as usual, although she was bowed, she would not break.

She spent time with sweet Grace and thought her lovely, found Luke to be hilarious, smart, self-deprecating, and absurd and wondered why no one had ever said so, why she was only finding out then, so late, why she had only ever heard that Luke was lazy, useless, and foolish. Never for one minute did she think Luke was being demonised as she had been. And not for a minute did she wonder what was being said about her.

Not knowing who and what her parents were, she went right on loving them too and began to bring them gifts as offerings, presents from her travels, friends to amuse them, offering them stories and warmth and attention. It makes me feel physically ill to think of her tireless efforts now, for while Claire thought it good, forgiving, generous, they thought of her as resembling nothing so much as a beaten dog bringing its master old bones, dead birds.

She also suspected that if she tugged on a tangle, everything might unravel, which of course it eventually did. But some things take as long as they take, and Claire had years to go before she found the peace and courage to start the un-weaving. It takes a very strong heart to see hate where there should be love and not be turned to stone.

Good people in this wild, wild experiment with humanity lean towards good. They give the benefit of the doubt, they show pity, they ease distress and they forgive. What did I say at the very beginning, the best driven mad by the worst? Yes. But don't think I see Claire as the best, of course. We've been to some very dark places, she and I. But she aimed for the good, and really that's all God asks.

Throughout all this time, I begged her, shouted to her to stop, to think, to calm, even really to collapse. Yes, really. I wanted her then to break down so she could rebuild. I wanted her to walk away. But she would not listen. She just moved back in with Ruth and let the darkness almost swallow her whole.

For her twenty-seventh birthday, Claire organised a dinner at her favourite French restaurant. At the restaurant, they were given a large round table. At the table, one of her friends produced a video camera. With the video camera the friend shot footage of the raucous, happy gang, particularly focusing on Ruth and Claire.

In that vision, which Claire watched later, she was stunned to see Ruth acting as her carbon copy: Ruth laughing like she laughed; Ruth speaking like she spoke; Ruth smoking like she smoked, using her hands as Claire used her hands, tucking her hair back, throwing her head back, sitting as she did, even swirling her wine as Claire did.

It was not mimicry. It was not flattery. It was identity theft. Claire felt intense discomfort when she saw the film—as did her friend—but could ascribe no meaning to it.

"Was it unconscious?" she asked herself.

"No," I shouted.

"Was it sinister?" she wondered.

"Yes," I bellowed.

"What did it mean?" she thought and thought.

"That takers take and take and take," I would have said if I thought she'd listen, if I thought she'd hear. "Warning, warning!" I wanted to say, but I was outside again by then, and outside no one can hear us scream.

Yet, just as good does not easily recognise bad, so too bad does not see good. Faith, Joseph, and Ruth never for an instant thought Claire's kindness a gift, a choice. They thought her weak, easily flattered, and silly, so it came as a huge shock when Claire finally made a different choice and withdrew her love.

But did it give rise to remorse or shame? No, for narcissists do not do shame. Oh no, all it has given rise to is more of the same, hate and blame, and fear now too, I think, for if Claire is no longer under their control, she is the central witness for the prosecution.

Have you wondered how I know so much at last after all these years? Yes, because Faith thought Claire was so absolutely bound and controlled she let some of her secrets out, feeling quite safe, that her little cultivated worm would never turn. How filled with rage she is right now. Still, it is the rage of the impotent, not the powerful, now, at last.

Now Claire is free of them entirely, but it is a freedom won at great cost, as if she is a lone survivor from a shipwreck, washed up on the shore, too injured right now to go far, certainly not back into society. But that day is coming, I know it, and I build her up and make her strong and get her ready, much as I did in the months leading up to our second dash for freedom. That was a journey abroad when Claire was so thrilled to finally be living her dreamt-of future she dropped some of her defences and let me back in.

And just like now, I advised, I protected, I healed. I also acted as travel guide as we set off to have the time of our lives—well, I should say the time of her life. The adventure was new, wonderfully new to her. To me it was like going home or I should say, as close as it gets to home for me here.

# Chapter 29

# Claire

I don't know why, in hindsight, I didn't act immediately on the knowledge hard won in hospital but I didn't. Perhaps I was too sick and sore, for it took me six months after my little procedure (as Faith still calls it) to walk fully upright without pain (at the start) or fear of pain (at the end). Or perhaps I just sank back into my old ways and tried to convince myself that it was not them but me. But that's just a guess.

What is fact is that during that time, I felt like escaping life would be easier than attempting yet again to escape my family life, and if not for the difficulty in obtaining a gun, I surely would have done it.

Yet all the other options for self-annihilation carried a risk of more pain which held little appeal. I also could not rid myself of the nagging suspicion that such a drastic act might be viewed quite favourably by certain members of the family if for no other reason than that I would not let Luke rest in peace, unknown and unmentioned, in his hillside grave.

My love and grief for him, mind you, were not acts of courage or defiance. No, I spoke of him with warmth and sorrow through naive misunderstanding, for I could not for the life of me conceive how we could physically see one of our number die, hear that last weary, rasping breath, only to put it behind us like a painful episode best forgotten.

I could not get that sound and the ensuing eternal silence out of my head. The rest of my family would not hear of it.

At the first Christmas after Luke died, I suggested, as I lay the festive table, that we make a toast to him, to mark his absence and perhaps to do him belated honour for all the joy and high spirits he had always given at that time of year, but Faith quashed the notion in a heartbeat.

"Oh Claire," she said. "I don't think so."

"Why not?"

"Because I don't think it's appropriate."

"Why not?"

"Because it will just make us sad, of course."

"But we are sad, aren't we?"

Faith, taken aback, replied, "Well yes I suppose so, but we don't have to wallow in it, do we?"

Then too in that first year I'd been shocked to read the coroner's report into Luke's death that was less a report and more like a sentence, giving as it did little more information than that he had died by suicide. I wanted his mental illness recorded; I wanted it known that he'd *been* failed not that he *had* failed. Having been repeatedly told by Faith and Joseph that this was the ultimate cause of his untimely leaving, I assumed they would want that known too.

So quite innocently, I pushed them to write to that coroner, to have the failings of the system that my parents held so firmly to account put on the public record, for what reason I'm now not sure. Perhaps I wanted a researcher in the future to link the suicide numbers with the failing, flailing, hopelessly underfunded mental health system. Perhaps I wanted to shift the blame from me. Perhaps I just wanted Luke's story to be known.

Anyway, whatever the reason, I would not give up, and finally Joseph did it. He wrote a letter to the coroner, which did not surprise me then but intrigues me greatly now. He sent a copy to me, which I have kept, that looks far less like a copy to me and far more like an original (good paper, penned signature), making me doubt he sent it to anyone but me.

In it Joseph describes Luke's visits (voluntary and involuntary) to psychiatric units and the lack of follow-up care upon release. He writes of Luke's refusal to take his medication and the subsequent angry eruptions, and he condemns the lack of dedicated health workers available to track Luke as he began his drift around the state and countryside, one lost soul among so many.

All of this is true as far as it goes, I suppose, and it was what I wanted, what I had asked them to do. But even as I read it then (and even more as I read it now), the words *my beloved son* clanged with furious dissonance in my head as Joseph's final literary flourish. Then I thought he must have meant it. Then I believed he must have sent it.

What a nut I have been. I remember even suggesting that we, the remaining siblings, get together for Luke's first anniversary, only to be totally gobsmacked to hear Peter reply to the suggestion, "But won't that mean we'll have to talk about him?"

Talk about shades of a "good knock to the head." I thought he was merely being a blockhead. But now I am not sure of that either given a strange and startling statement made by Ruth a little time later.

As it turned out I was too sick to do much anyway that first anniversary of the dying day and spent most of it lying in bed, staring at the ceiling, struggling to survive. Yet still at one point I did make the effort to shuffle to the phone to call my parents, who I thought might be hurting for Luke like I was, even then, even after the hospital, even after Joseph's visit. It must have been the drugs.

I said to Faith, "I just thought I'd ring. I thought you might be finding today a bit hard."

"Why?"

"Why? Because … because … it's Luke's anniversary."

"Oh … oh yes … I know of course it is but … I wasn't sure what you meant."

"Right."

"It's thoughtful of you, darling, but remember what I told you? Luke's with God now so we don't have to be sad, and anyway, shouldn't you be trying to get well?"

"What? I … am."

"Well gloomy thoughts won't help now, will they?"

Honestly, during so many moments during that time I thought my mental elastic was going to absolutely snap, that the psychological filaments keeping me tethered to sanity were pulled so tight they could twang apart at any instant, pitching me into madness. I felt mildly amazed an hour, a day, a week later to find I still was who I had always been (for better and worse) and not a gabbling lunatic slumped in a corner.

In other moments of acute and excruciating clarity I wondered if I was not being slowly pushed towards madness and self-destruction.

But those moments were few. Far more frequent were those of roiling, futile confusion and hurt, missing Luke and needing him more than ever and knowing him gone forever and that I'd had a hand in his going. All of this felt so utterly crushing that I became more dependent than ever on the vagaries of Mark's disposition.

A most vicious cycle.

Then only a few weeks after the hospital and Luke's anniversary, Grace rang to tell me I was not welcome to attend the first-ever birthday of my goddaughter, her daughter, because, surprise, surprise, Ruth did not want me there. I tried to fight that, as I recall, even raised my voice in useless protest, but really by then I could no longer figure out what I was fighting for while knowing that whatever it was, I would surely lose.

But I did protest possibly just for something to do. Having gotten nowhere with Grace, I took it to the management, Faith and Joseph, saying I thought it a most disgusting piece of work, expecting nothing, of course, but no longer willing to pretend we were functional, decent, civilised.

In hindsight that was perhaps my first act of not pretending, and it must have gusted like a gentle but icy breeze through their cosy domain, for in a most surprising twist, Joseph insisted that Ruth and I meet to resolve the dispute. Well not exactly. First he suggested I meet with both Grace and Ruth until I pointed out the inherent injustice of a two-against-one arrangement.

Then he suggested I go to her until I reminded him of the gaping wound in my abdomen that still required twice-weekly visits from roving nurses to empty, clean, and pack. Well not exactly. That would have made him faint with disgust. I just reminded him I was still weak, that perhaps Ruth, being well, could come to me. Still, while he could not be described as a fair and honest broker, the meeting did take place, Ruth arriving, pale and agitated, at my house late one morning.

If I'd had the energy, I would have been astonished. As it was, I simply waited. Upon sitting as far from me as possible in my little house while still occupying the same room, Ruth placed before me a demand for an apology.

"For what?"

"You know what."

"For what I said on the phone?"

She glared at me.

"For asking why you kept us waiting when you had no intention of coming to meet us?"

"But it wasn't quite like that, was it, Claire?"

"So you want me to apologise for saying fuck?"

Ruth glared at me and let the silence be her answer.

"But I've heard you say it loads of times …"

"I do not."

"I've heard you."

"Listen, I didn't come here to argue with you, Claire. Are you going to apologise?"

"Of course not."

She went white. Her whole body began to twitch and quiver until I thought she might have a heart attack, as if she was struggling to control a volcanic loathing, which I must say took me aback somewhat, for I had vaguely assumed she'd come to resolve the problems, to ease the tensions between us, to dampen the discord, not inflame it.

But I was only surprised for a minute and surprisingly not afraid.

She said upon my refusal, "Right then. This is what I've come to say. From now on, you are no longer welcome in my house except on Christmas day. You will never be invited to any party, any function, any of the children's birthdays, any social event I'm in any way involved with. Do you understand?"

I looked at her.

Ruth said, "It's about time, Claire, that you realised you reap what you sow."

I sat gazing at her with fascination, but instead of responding to her declaration of intent or the reaping and the sowing said, "Why are you such a bitch, Ruth?"

She began to splutter.

"Why are you so full of rage and hatred?"

She began to choke.

"You malign everyone with your back stabbing. No one is ever good enough. You can't get enough of other people's sorrow. You've spoken horribly about Peter and Debbie. You're manipulating Grace, and you were an absolute rolled-gold bitch to Luke."

At that last reference she made a sound as if she was swallowing her own tongue, stood up, and screamed, "How dare you mention Luke!"

"Why not? We all know how you treated him …"

"How dare you," she shrieked. "You know the rules."

Now that stumped me. "What rules? What on earth are you talking about?"

"You know the fucking rules, Claire. We … don't … talk … about … Luke!"

"Says who? What are you talking about?"

But she gave no answer to that. Instead she grabbed her bag and marched out of the room and down the hallway, shouting, "I only came here as a favour to dad. If I had my way, we'd never see each other again."

And finally finding the wit to respond with the right words at the right time, I shouted back, "Well at last! Something we can both agree on."

When she slammed the door behind her, I feared all my pictures would fall off the walls. That was the last time we spoke with any meaning, if spoke or meaning are the right words to use, but she did mean what she said. I have never been back into her house or invited to a party from that day to this. Though she was most magnanimous in allowing for a suspension of hostilities on Christmas Day, oddly enough that gracious dispensation has never held much appeal. Ha!

But even now, so many years later, I still wonder what she meant by the "rules" or Peter's evident discomfort in talking of Luke. Was she telling the truth, expressing a fact, a decision made, or was it simply a manner of speech?

If it was a decision made then why? Why not talk of him? What was there to hide? And if it was a decision made, why did no one tell me?

Then I had no idea. Now I have quite a few.

## Chapter 30

# Thomas

Even as a child, Claire had three wishes in her life, three dreams that made up the entirety of her personal dreaming.

The first, the greatest, the one she still hopes for, really, after all these years was and is to love and be loved particularly, intimately, and truly. The second was to work with words. The third was to live a life of freedom of both thought and action, to see the world, to experience, to learn, and to wonder.

Now, knowing Claire as you do, you'd know she'd have given up the two latter wishes in a heartbeat for the first (what a funny feminist was Claire!), would have delightedly settled in the suburbs (she thought) and spent the rest of her life attempting to be the most ordinary, acceptable wife and mother the world had ever seen. She would have cooked. She would have cleaned. She would have been a true and loyal wife. She would have loved her babies, crooned them to sleep, cradled them in her arms. Life would be perfect, and she would at last, at last be found to be acceptable.

I doubted it deeply, of course.

I said, "But when would you get the chance to read for hours?"

I said, "But when would you get the time to think for hours?"

I said, "How would you cope with routine when you can be so restless, when you have it in you to go looking for trouble?"

But she ignored the questions, as I knew she would and fully accepted, for there is no place for common sense in the world of the ideal, the happiest of happy-ever-afters. Besides, it was a good dream, and God knows it might have worked with the right man, the right babies, a miraculous alignment of the stars. But the chances of happiness for such a family unit, with conflicted Claire at the centre, would have been outside chances, long odds, as you say.

Still, for better or worse, such a love simply refused to step out of her dream world and into her life. No prince. No knight. No rescue. So, having won a place in the world of words, she finally thought she'd better get on with the third.

I was so excited. So excited! To go back to Europe, my old stomping grounds, as you say, after so long made my heart sing. For that is what Claire had decided. She would throw in her job and spend a year travelling the continent—just by herself.

Oh my. It was a wonderful idea—just the two of us—but really it made me fearful. Claire had such a topsy-turvy innocence about her, such a naivety, such a stubborn refusal to see bad, to understand the full breadth of human nature. I wondered how she would survive. When she decided to make Rome her first destination, I almost lost consciousness.

*Oh, Claire*, I thought. *You don't have to go that far.*

But she did.

She'd longed to see Rome since she had been a little girl—partly from Faith's pontifical persuasion and later from Joseph's historical, hysterical lectures.

While I suspected London may have been a better launching pad for this journey, I did not try to talk her out of it, not Rome, not any of it. No. There were enough people willing to do that.

Faith and Joseph told her she was foolish, that she should not give up her job, that she should not spend all her money, that she should buy a flat given that she was by then, at twenty-eight, unlikely to be wed, that if she wanted to go she should go on a short organised tour, that she would not cope on her own, that she was condemning them to twelve months of needless worry, that she should wait for Ruth, that she was silly, selfish, and thoughtless.

Oh my. They covered everything, don't you think?

But Claire, having bought her ticket and rail pass, having hired a cottage in Province a few months into the journey, having studied the maps, plotted her course and having lost the ability to eat or sleep from fear and trepidation, would not be moved.

How I loved her then, for courage is not fearlessness. Courage is overcoming fear, and Claire was terrified. She lost weight. She lost sleep, lost concentration, and at one stage lost her passport before she'd even left the country. But still she was determined. She refused offers by colleagues to join their travelling band. They sent her glamorous itineraries, but she said no. They sent her estimated costing, but she said no. They cajoled her. They flattered her. They painted fabulous pictures for her, but still she said no. She wanted to go alone. She wanted to be free.

When the day of departure finally came, she felt, really, to say the least, somewhat hysterical for although she wanted to go to the airport alone, to leave alone, to get it done, that she could not do. Oh no. Faith and Joseph were determined to make sure she felt inadequate and incompetent if it was the last thing they did, just in case it was the last thing they got to do.

So the whole family arrived and stood awkward and uncomfortable in the middle of the airport concourse, trying to project appropriate family feeling. Debbie and Grace cried. Luke put his arm around her and wished her a silly bon voyage. Peter talked over him. Ruth, about to be left alone with just her own life, looked upset, as indeed she was.

Joseph said, "You can still back out."

Faith said, "I'll pray for you, you silly girl. What a worry you are to us all."

Good grief. I could not wait for the boarding call.

Finally Claire had to go, left them all, and walked, looking so small and solitary, through the massive doors into international departures. She let out one huge sigh and burst into tears. And the flood gates having finally opened, Claire cried off and on halfway around the world.

She was quiet and discrete, desperate to find the composure she imagined was appropriate for women of the world, but still the tears would not stop. Her neighbours asked if she was all right, was there anything they could do. The flight attendants kept bringing her water, some gently stroking her head as they passed, such unexpected, unfamiliar kindness that it brought her quite undone.

She was ashamed and embarrassed, but still she could not stop. Really, she didn't know where such tears had come from but deep down, I think she knew they were tears of relief, the tears of a prisoner released. And although she did not believe in God then, she allowed a prayer to half form in her mind, which took the vague outline of, "Please don't make me have to go back," which felt to her so treasonous, so disloyal she cried some more.

★★★

Perhaps I should take a moment to describe Claire as she looked then, given that it had such an impact on our travels, which surprised me not at all but shocked Claire to her core. Let's see, let me remember her then. She had long, blonde, curly hair, which she intended to hide under a specially purchased hat. She no longer wore glasses all the time but only when she needed to see, much preferring by then to look upon a world in soft focus.

Really, with such poor eyesight it was a bit silly. She missed so much—like telling facial expressions, like friends waving to her in the street, like deceit—but she was stubborn. Quite literally she would not see what she did not wish to see, a determination I think driven as much by her subconscious mind as her rational thinking.

So she did not wear her spectacles, but she did wear sunglasses almost all the time, knowing her clear grey eyes gave too much away, that they had a sorrow in them she could neither hide nor explain.

Also, my nutty, shy Claire half believed if people could not see her eyes and she could not see people, she could in fact become invisible. In some ways it all had the opposite effect. She looked sort of glamorous and confident behind her sunglasses, and when she took them off, her unfocussed gaze looked more "come hither" than "bugger off."

What else can I tell you? She was of average height, quite slender for her then given her acute-anxiety pre-departure diet of wine and cigarettes. She had a low, smoky voice, and despite the darkness that had gathered around her, she looked younger than she was, innocent, fresh.

But though as I said Claire was of average height, she always seemed small to me, a little young woman, vulnerable and easily hurt. Picturing her on the streets of Rome then, even as we flew towards it, gave me the shivers because she seemed to me uniquely defenceless for many reasons but most crucially because she thought herself ugly.

Oh my. Admittedly a latish bloomer, Claire had grown into a fine-looking woman (that is as much as she will allow me to say), but she could not see it. For Claire was, forever and always, the fat fifteen-year-old, the ugly misfit, nothing like her pretty sisters, a disappointment to them all. Any compliment she ever received simply did not compute, could not go in.

*Surely,* she always thought, *if I am pretty, if I have become attractive, surely someone in the family would have said so.* As if that information would ever be allowed to trickle back, for Joseph would never see it and Faith would never say it.

And there was another reason for this blindness also. As the head of the cult, as the minister for propaganda, Faith claimed the role of family photographer. Now, have you ever noticed how the feelings of the photographer for the subject often overlay the image? Have you noticed that you can spot the loving gaze, the ironic gaze, the passionate, lustful, longing gaze behind a photograph?

It is there if you look for it, really almost as much information about the picture taker as the person pictured. I say this to explain that Faith only ever took bad photographs of Claire. Unconsciously or consciously, her feelings always showed.

Then she would show the clearly unflattering image to all members of the cult, particularly to Claire, and exclaim, "Isn't this one nice? It looks just like you, Claire!"

And Ruth would back her up, leaving Claire, of course, to wonder, *Do I really look like that, all double chins and squinty eyes?*

And if she did protest, if she did manage to say she didn't like it, did not think it a fair representation, the two conspirators would roll their eyes as if to say "you are so vain," or "you might as well accept it" or "this is how we see you; this is how you are."

And Claire did accept it. Of course she did. What choice did she have? She trusted them.

Faith buried the decent photos, blew up the ugly photos, and let it be clearly known to Claire and to them all that she was, like she had always been, a daughter only a mother could love.

Oh and I should point out that Faith had been fat and plain for many years herself by then, her children having taken her comely figure and her teeth and given her varicose veins. But she, of course, was not subject to the same critical gaze as others. Oh no. She was holy. She was saintly. She was not a woman but a woman of God, a creature of another order altogether, which meant she could eat what she liked and place the weight of blame on her children.

Anyway, back to the journey. So little Claire was attractive, alone, defenceless, and naïve, and I said, "Help me, God," over and over again as we approached the eternal city. Though she attempted to sneak in unobserved, really she had no hope. It was the off season and quiet by Roman standards so even as she wheeled her luggage up the street she was noticed, sized up, discussed. If she'd known, she would have swum back to Australia.

Ah that city. We walked and walked and walked. Claire gazed upon the Colosseum (that dreadful slaughterhouse), but not sharing my memories of it, she thought it wonderful, incredible, felt like her heart could burst out of her chest for this one thought alone: *I made it. Me. Claire. I got myself to Rome.*

For Claire it was the most enormous thought, original and profound. For Rome it was very old hat indeed, as old as the seven hills. For me, knowing this town as I did, I just wished she could think the thought without looking like a such a big-eyed, small-town rube.

"And wear your glasses," I also said for the millionth time, for I wanted her to see that she was being seen, that countless male eyes were upon her as she drifted so delighted and dreamy around those ancient stones. But did she listen? Did she see? No and no.

Over the next few days as she tried to get her bearings, Claire was crooned at, lunged at, chased and followed, stroked as she walked, caressed if she stood still, and kissed if she sat, which came as a quite considerable shock. After such moments she scurried like a scared rabbit back to her hotel room. She would look into the mirror at that same old ordinary face and ask, "What the fuck is going on?"

She'd been single for a while by then and really felt herself to be more a brain on legs than woman, so going from the observer to the observed made her head spin. And there was no escape. After only a few days there, she went to the restaurant across the street for dinner one night, being too afraid and too shocked to go further afield. Thinking herself unknown and unnoticed and with only her phrase book to help, she asked to sit at the window to keep her hotel in blurry view, to help her feel safe.

The charming manager, who had seen her, of course, suggested another table. But Claire said please and he agreed, though with a certain look of concern upon his face. She sat, she sipped her wine, and she ate. She looked furtively at the Romans now filling the other tables, let the language wash over her, gazed out the window, and felt calm for the first time in weeks.

Until a group of young boys congregated on the other side of her window, crooning, giggling, blowing her kisses, and making comments and suggestions that, really, can be understood in any language on earth.

Oh my. Claire almost spilled her wine. All the diners were staring at her, at them, laughing and laughing. Claire was horrified. She gazed into her wine, at the wall, into the middle distance, wishing she could disappear, fall into a hole, go up in a puff of smoke. She had no idea what to do, but the manager did. He strode out the back, grabbed a broom, marched through the restaurant like a general passing his troops, went outside into the street, and began to beat them with the handle.

He shouted. He cursed. He let them have it. The boys laughed and ducked and ran. The restaurant was in uproar. Claire thought she was going to vomit. Her face went a greenish colour, and when the manager came back in, put the broom away with a triumphant flourish, and approached her to apologise, I thought she might faint.

"Welcome to Rome, Claire," I said, laughing.

And as the historic city laid its ageless spell upon her heart, it helped bring my shy friend to life.

The chaos, the noise, the dirt and grandeur, the poverty and spectacle, the violent, lawless undertones, and the passionate social interaction were absolutely intoxicating to her. She could not tell by tone or gesture, for example, if people were talking about the weather or a catastrophe, about good news or the last straw, and she didn't care. Everything felt extreme, decadent, corrupt, glorious, frightening, wonderful.

Australia, white Australia, felt very new, very dull, very English in comparison, and Claire had never been good at the stoic composure they had all inherited. No wonder she loved Rome. She did think, however, that it would be easier to experience it as a man. But I told her, having last lived there with a man, that that was not necessarily so. Rome could eat up men and women, the young and old, rich or poor, white or black, anyone, really, depending on the hunger of the times.

The key, I told her, was to blend in, to get tough, to show no fear. And she heard me then. It was like the old days or these days. Remember when I said desperation and fear can open the mind? Claire, safe to say, was extremely open minded. Besides, the others had all drifted away by then, preferring to stay where they knew they were welcome, preferring Faith and Ruth.

And on that note, let me list the differences between us and them. We are gentle, wise, solitary, obedient, and powerful if you let us be, and we never leave. They are aggressive, stupid, and chaotic. They travel in packs and are only powerful if you will it so. They are also lazy and will always leave if they are made unwelcome, uncomfortable. Of course they will; they have millions of options, millions of homes to go to while we have only one. So Claire was becoming too hard for them. I was back inside, and the light of the universe flooded back into her soul.

I never liked Rome quite as much as I did then.

Yes, she heard me. She bought a long, expensive coat to cover her travelling gear. She bought a new hat, new sunglasses, and a cashmere wrap and tried as best she could to look … what's the word? Jaded? Yes. World weary? Yes. Over it? Yes, all of those. Really she did her best to adopt the air of one who has seen it all and been neither surprised nor impressed. In other words, she tried to look like a Roman.

But it took some practice. It certainly did not happen overnight, so dazzled, so breathless was she by this city of cities that not even her sunglasses could hide her big-eyed wonder, not even her wrap could smother her sparking excitement. Really, she could not help but stand out in off-season Rome. One night, not long after the broom beating, Claire, still in shock and preferring to take her evening meals in the privacy and sanity of her hotel room, stood at her window watching the evening draw in, the night magic take hold of her little Roman neighbourhood.

She was losing herself in her dreamy imaginings (as many a young woman has when in Rome) when she was startled out of her reverie when a young man popped his head out of the corresponding window in the palatial building across the narrow street and began to croon to her in Italian. Ha! Claire got such a fright she almost dropped her wine glass as she jumped back into the shadows of her room. Then he disappeared, only to re-emerge at another window on another floor, crooning at her this time in what she thought may have been German.

By then the people in the street—the newspaper man, the tobacconist, the waiters, the florist, the commuters arriving to extricate their cars, really even two machine-gun-toting caribanierie—were involved, engaged in the scene, looking at him, trying to catch a glimpse of her, laughing, encouraging, participating. The young man was shouting down to them, and they were laughing back at him. Claire looked like she might faint.

Then, once again, he disappeared, only to pop out at another window on another floor. Of course by then Claire was, as he had no doubt hoped, hopelessly intrigued and remained standing in silhouette, peeping out the window.

Was it a palace across the road? Who was he to have the run of such an enormous building? What were they saying? What did he want?

Oh, Claire. Only Claire would ask herself that last question.

But as she pondered it, he called to her in English. He said she was beautiful. He asked if she was American. He said his heart was aching for her, and in between each line, he took the advice and encouragement thrown up by the growing crowd below.

"Tell me your name, bella." He sighed. "Let me show you Rome, bella," he groaned like a man in pain.

By then Claire had the giggles and felt that nothing had ever been, would ever be again as preposterously hilariously romantic in her life as this half hour. She felt like she'd stumbled into a comic opera. She felt like the princess in the tower. She felt like she owed it to him, to them all, to do something, though what she did not know.

At yet another window on another floor, he draped himself over the sill and sighed, "Please, bella, I beg of you. Tell me your room number."

The crowd liked it.

He said, "Please, bella, let me call you."

The crowd thought it good.

He said, "Please, bella, let me love you," and really they went mad, clapping, laughing, shouting. "Just tell me your room number. Please, bella. Please."

Well what could she do? Too shy to shout, too shocked to speak, she signed. Finally. She felt it had to be done. With her fingers, she signed her room number.

"Two," the young man shouted to the cheers below. "Seven," he cried to hoots and whistles. "Four," he finished to a rousing round of applause. "Oh Bella," he cried. "You make me happy man."

Looking back, I don't think Claire had ever really been as shocked at herself as she was right then. She'd been trying to be discrete but instead had given the whole neighbourhood her room number. She was trying to be independent, and she'd invited someone in. She'd been attempting to absorb Rome as an intellectual, historical reality and fallen for romance at the very first hurdle.

I can't tell you how hard I was laughing. Really this brief moment, this lovely patch of time healed a lot of old wounds. Life down here, I got the chance to remember, can be great, great fun.

I'd like to go into the details of this trip for your sake as much as my own, to infuse a touch of lightness, freedom, optimism into the story, but really you know all about that. There are stacks of books about travel and adventure, and really I'm afraid of being pulled off the air again.

I don't think that's likely. Don't get me wrong. We're very close now. But still I cannot take this access for granted. Really it is so very rare. Let me just say then that dear Claire had the time of her life, and though she spent the first six months alone—well, almost alone— she was not lonely. Oh no. At home she was lonely. Here she was simply alone, which was, of course, a very great leap forward.

She floated around Venice, swooned through Florence, adored Vienna and Salzburg, and really loved it all—getting on and off the trains, choosing where to go and when to go there. She trod the ground of heroes in Greece, sat on Austrian mountaintops, and lounged around in Corfu. She got her drinking under control, she spent days and days walking the streets of cities she had dreamed of, and she slept like a woman satisfied.

And she wrote. She wrote separate letters to Faith and Joseph, the first about churches, the second about politics. Only later, much later, when she asked why Joseph had never written back, Faith told her he would never write to her, just in case she was found to be the better writer.

But still she wrote. She wrote to Nan and Pop about country life, to her sisters about social life, and to her brother Luke, to her great surprise and delight, just about life. These letters, really, were the start of their friendship, a friendship sparked by the chance at last to communicate directly without Faith's interference. They found each other funny. They found each other quirky, philosophical, curious, and warm, characteristics that were profoundly obvious to everyone who knew them both outside the cult, outside the family. But for them, such revelations had been almost eighteen years in the finding. Faith would have burned those missives if she could have for a friendship between these two was the very last thing she had in mind.

But still a friendship bloomed. They wrote about science and nature, philosophy and religion, everything from the nature of the universe to the cricket, and they were shocked to find themselves such a surprise, as if they were sibling strangers. With eight years between them, Claire tried to remember Luke for herself, the little boy she left behind when exiled to boarding school, the sweet-natured lad she met on weekends on the vineyard and could find no shadow of the person Faith and Joseph clearly believed him to be. Yet still she could not, would not think, *They lie, they have lied, they are liars.*

That friendship that could only blossom when the two of them were on opposite sides of the world should have lasted each other's lifetimes, but it didn't, as you know. How could it with Faith forever lurking in the middle, at the core of it, them all?

After a few months, when Claire was bone weary, she made her way at last to the cottage in Province for a month of staying still. There's not much to say about that time. She didn't have an affair and didn't meet odd locals. It didn't change her life or allow her to see the world in richer hues.

None of that. It just pleased her. She spent that month sitting at her outdoor table gazing up at the ruins of a twelfth-century castle and living on, through a combination of her limited vocabulary and cooking skills, bread, ham, cheese, olives, tomatoes, walnuts, and eggs. She walked the hills, beating off crazy French farm dogs with a stick while the owners looked on impassive. She walked every week to the wine cave to have her plastic container filled. She read and she read and she wrote and she lay in the sunshine in European springtime meadows so contented that she began to doubt her doubt in God.

Oh my. How happy we were. The locals thought her somewhat nutty, staying in a honeymooners' cottage alone, coming all the way from Australia to sit and read for a month, but they just shrugged their shoulders in that Gallic way and left her to it.

Then she went to England, then to Scotland, then to Edinburgh. She fell in love with it and fell in love. Well, not love exactly but something she thought was close enough, something with meaning, and that was an advance from her former practice.

I liked him, he liked her, and he made her laugh, which is a sound I can never hear too often. She loved the weather. She loved the old streets, the brooding lanes, the castle and the crag. She loved snuggling with her Scottish beau for whole cool afternoons, and she really loved that he was a chef. Oh yes. You can only have so many ham and cheese sandwiches, no matter how good the bread.

Really, she felt she was in heaven.

Then. Then Ruth turned up. Oh my. Not able to pull off the character impersonation without Claire to provide the scripts, Ruth had fallen out with her boyfriend, which had caused severe bruising to her ego. This necessitated the balm that only Claire could give; that is, Ruth was low and needed to be carried. Wanting also to win him back, she needed access to her template. She needed her confidence restored. Really Ruth just needed, and when Ruth needed, Ruth got.

And Claire, being happy, ignorant, and kind, gave, of course. She found Ruth a room, which Ruth found too pokey. She helped find her a job, which Ruth found too dull. She shared her friends, whom Ruth found too Scottish and a local pub, too smoky. She took her to Egypt, where Ruth complained of the heat. She took her up to the highlands, where Ruth complained of the midges.

Oh my. Claire was made to feel really that if she was any kind of sister, any kind of decent host at all, she would tilt the earth on its axis for the comfort of dear Ruth.

You should see the photographs taken of the two of them then. All of Claire show her larking about, silly, joyful. All those of dark-eyed, dark-haired Ruth show her in various expressions and poses of dissatisfaction and annoyance, with a coldness about her that had nothing to do with the climate.

The truth lies in the eyes. Every con artist knows it. Watch the eyes.

But Claire, refusing to wear her glasses, did not see and so did feel all she was intended to feel, which, as you know, drove me to distraction. She did feel sorry for the heat of Egypt; she did regret the midges and the wind in the highlands. Honestly.

I said, "Claire, she's a university graduate. She knows about the heat of Egypt."

I said, "Claire, stop feeling and start thinking."

I said, "Claire, don't you remember you were happier without her?"

But she could not hear or would not. But before you write her off as an idiot, remember she had been blamed for so many things, beginning with her birth, that it simply felt normal, to be expected, and all her freedom and peace simply melted away in the cool Scottish air.

I was so upset. I was shouting, "Shut up, shut up, shut up." Really, Ruth reduced me to that level of undignified frustration. I thought if Claire had only a bit more time just with me, just a bit more time without her spirit being drained by Ruth, if she'd had time to exorcise the ghosts of the cult that trailed after her sister like a putrid miasma, we could have gotten somewhere.

I wanted her to realise how capable and resourceful she was. I wanted her to realise she was not ugly, hopeless, foolish. I wanted her to see she belonged in the world, not squashed into the narrow confines of the family role forced upon her by Faith and Joseph, but I ran out of time. Really, Ruth swept in with the others in tow, and my voice, my quiet voice, was drowned out by her bleating.

It causes me anguish to think of it still. Really I felt I was almost on the verge of a breakthrough, that I could have changed Claire's life, changed all you know was to come, changed it all. But no, that was not to be. I wept and asked for guidance and was told, yet again, most frustratingly, most hopelessly, simply to witness. And that was hard. To be so close to truth and freedom yet, once again, to lose the ability to transmit, to transform, to be pushed back into silence.

We are so easily discarded or disregarded, but though we never leave, there are times when we very much want to. Ruth's arrival was one of those times.

# Chapter 31

# Claire

I tell the story of Ruth's rant for two reasons. One is to explain the continual chaos that made clear thinking almost impossible and two for what happened next, which relates to both that weird sister of mine and my old friend Death, who had not quite finished his dance macabre through the chambers of my house and heart.

As I slowly began to heal, my dear friend Kate, who had been my boon companion both at home and abroad, slowly began to die. She told me not long after Ruth's pleasant visit that the cancer that had afflicted her in childhood had returned, as the surgeons had said it might. I knew she would not survive a second time, knowledge that sent me not into fear or sorrow but into the most monumental rage of my life.

Can you guess with whom? Yes, with God, of course. I shouted (inside my noodle), I cursed, I blamed, and I heaped imprecations upon him in whom I refused to believe, lashing about internally in search of answers I would not heed until the worst thing happened, and I mean that literally.

Worse than the loss of Jess, Luke, Sally, worse than seeing Kate begin her painful decline, worse than the operation or leaving Mark (though that was yet to come). The worst was that Thomas left. And just to make that even harder to appreciate, I did not know him as Thomas then. I only knew the voice had some connection to God, though what that was or how it worked I did not know.

One day the voice was there like it had been from the beginning (whether I liked it or not), and then it was gone (whether I liked it or not). The desolation caused by the silence felt absolute, eternal, and annihilating, if for no other reason (and there were many) than because it felt like I had extinguished the spark of the divine by my own idiotic, enraged internal blustering.

At the beginning of the booming silence, I shouted (silently) profound sentiments much along the lines of, "You come back here and listen to me! Come back and answer the charges. This is all your damned fault! You can't pursue me all my life, take away the people I love one by one, destroy my hopes and dreams and even my illusions, and then just bugger off. You can't. You can't."

But he could.

I shouted (silently), "I'm doing my bloody best here, you know. I've tried to live a decent life and I *deserve* some fucking comfort." But I didn't apparently.

I screamed (silently), "How could you leave me in my hour of greatest need?"

But I got no reply. Not a word. Not for months and months, and it felt hellish, not least because it was such an excruciatingly personal and solitary anguish, for I could hardly explain to Mark, for instance, that the voice in my head had not only left but left me devastated, now could I? Only Luke would have understood, but then I was still labouring under the misapprehension that he'd been psychotic, so even that thought only provided a scratchy sort of comfort, for perhaps all it meant was that I was psycho too.

Now I realise—way too late—that he'd been through a similar experience himself, just before he decided on a life in the priesthood, but I was too smug to listen. I remember he told me one day, as we sat contentedly in a beer garden, that he had felt the acute absence of God, and to my shame, I think I teased him; gently, of course, with great love and good humour.

I think I said something like, "But you're a scientist, Luke. Haven't you been told that God is dead?"

And I can picture him laughing and throwing back his head as he replied, "Many times, by many different professors, in many different ways. The only problem is that I don't think anyone has told him."

But I should have listened. So many times he tried to tell me things of great importance.

Anyway, as those months passed without my dearest friends and without the voice and with no reply to my incessant demands, I shifted tack, as is the way of these things, to begging, pleading, grovelling. As I listened to my music of an evening (Mark's absence in those days being positively encouraged, the beginning of the end perhaps), I whispered such gems as, "I'm sorry. I'm sorry. I'm not angry anymore. I'll be good now. Please talk to me. Please come back. I won't shout at you anymore, I promise. I've learnt my lesson."

But I hadn't apparently, for not a whisper did I hear in reply. Not for many months, which felt like years.

But don't think that during this time I merely sat staring vacantly into the darkness, as if in a catatonic stupor. No. I fought with Mark when he did come home while in between trying madly to prop us up to atone for all my sadness, sickness, and strangeness.

And I launched myself into my saving Kate campaign, which I knew to be futile (given that she needed oncologists, not me) but which I could not resist. I knitted her hats for her chemotherapy. I babysat her delightful toddler son while she consulted the consultants. I gave her husband a break from the bedside as she endured her first, second, and third surgery. I raced to her house upon her call when she was too sick to supervise her son. I even, on one mad occasion, offered her a kidney if that might be at all helpful, which at least had the effect of making her laugh and laugh and laugh. I even said yes, with an aching, wretched heart, to her request that I deliver the eulogy at her funeral should it come to that.

Poor Kate. She probably wished me a million miles away at times, but I felt a bloody-minded compulsion (at least at the beginning of her end) to at last, at least do everything possible to love, support, and help a loved one I would lose. At the time it felt heroic, but now I fear it smacks more of the egotistic, for I was doing it for me as much as her for I could not face the burden or the fear of any longer asking, "Why didn't I?"

So I rushed around buying gifts and flowers and calling more than I should have as much to meet my own needs as hers (of which I'm most ashamed) and as a way to ignore the internal silence that felt more dreadful every day, as if whoever, whatever the voice, it was now gone forever and for all time and it was all my own damned fault.

For months and months the emptiness continued, even after I had the about-time lightbulb moment of realising that if nothing I did or said made the slightest difference perhaps I should stop doing or saying anything at all. You could call this acceptance, a willingness to humbly wait, but that suggests a depth and maturity I did not possess. That was not me. I had just run out of ideas.

You probably think I'm mad writing of this, for it's far more in Thomas's line than mine. Yet he asks me to and so I do (having learnt my lesson). Yet my cooperation far outstrips his, for after all the questions I have put to him about this time, all he will ever say is that he was instructed to be silent. More he will not say.

And when I ask, "Are you Thomas or God?" he says both. He says, "I act as a two-way radio so of course we are both. Not 'or,' Claire, but 'and,' like the wave-particle duality of quantum physics that sits at the core of all creation."

Well maybe. Who am I to argue? All I know is that his leaving felt catastrophic, and only later did I realise the experience was not one of madness or of punishment and certainly not unique, for it was described centuries ago as the dark night of the soul. The medieval mystical monk St John of the Cross coined the phrase (if you can use such a term for the musings of mystical monks) to explain the loss, the absence, the aching hollowness that can at times occur between God and humans as that of the lover pining for the beloved.

I wouldn't put it like that. I'd say it's more like losing the only good and true thing you possess, the shock element being the discovery that you do not, in fact, possess it; that it comes from a different source, that it can be taken away. St John says it's God's way of burning down the ego into ashes, destroying the self, and purifying the soul in readiness for the mystical union with the divine.

I wouldn't put it quite like that. I'd say it's as if the last remaining supporting beam that props up the entire haphazard, shambolic jerry-built personality has been forcibly removed to allow the whole mess to collapse into the dust.

Yet while God might think that necessary, it isn't very pleasant, for while you're going through it, while you can feel the hammered-together piles of driftwood that make up a lifetime of attitudes and coping skills and history come apart spectacularly (at times) or with slow inevitability (at others), it feels like the utter destruction of all you've ever been or known. And all without a glimmer of hope that it is for a purpose and without even the slightest comfort that anything, anything at all, will replace one solitary board, one window frame or tea pot of the house that you had cobbled together. You can no longer find comfort in identity (woman, writer, sister, daughter, lover), for those roles no longer have any absolute meaning, for you aren't those things or just those things anymore. You are nothing. No thing.

For me, it lasted about a year, though it felt like ten, and at the end all I could do was to endure it with silent (at last!) humility, acceptance, and a shivery sort of hope that all would somehow, sometime be well. And then, when the emptiness (St John describes it as aridity) felt both normal and lasting, when I felt that while I could never be who I was once, it was of no great matter, the voice came back as if it had never gone but also as if two different people were now engaged in a conversation of much greater maturity, far deeper intimacy, far warmer friendship.

I'll never forget it. I was in the garden (of the spooky house just before it got spooky) when I found myself in my internal dialogue of old before I was even aware of it, as if it were the most natural of daily discourses. I felt a gratitude as light as a butterfly and as profound as the sea, which is when I began to accept it all, all the deaths and the one approaching, all the anguish of the past and the present.

Don't get me wrong. I didn't get filled with wisdom, and it wasn't an epiphany. It was just the tiny spark of starting to change or more accurately the even tinier spark of knowing

I wanted to change. This was no born-again tambourine and beaming smiles thing (Mark and I being increasingly at each other's throats). No, it was more just the humble realisation of how bleak and dull and limited life is without the beauty of the mysterious.

Just one little step and it reminded me of Luke telling me not to get so dark that I couldn't find the light. If he'd been with me then on that afternoon, I'd have said, "As it turned out, dear brother, it was more a matter of a general power outage than a matter of choice."

That's when I knew I had to leave that house and Mark. That's when I knew there was no point resisting the call to change, yet I am no mystic monk and still have bad days ("no, no, no that is not right, that should not be!"). At least now am far more able to let such feelings pass through and pass rather than using them to construct an emotional lean-to that requires such wasted energy to support. For I have been fighting or forced to fight since I was born and old habits and all that. Yet I try, and as Thomas tells me time after time, that is all that's ever asked.

Now I understand much that has hitherto eluded me. Take the meek shall inherit the earth, for instance. If Jesus used the word *meek* to denote the humble or the humbled, those who have learned or been forced to learn to accept life, who have had their egos blasted in the furnace of fate, but who can then find intense joy in the smell of rain approaching, the distant laughter of a stranger, or blossoms in the hair, then I think I finally get it. The key word is inheriting the *earth*, I think, not the world.

Last New Year's Eve, for instance, I spent in my little flat in the darkness caused by a power failure caused by a spectacular electrical storm sweeping across the city. I watched out my large front windows, listening to the booming thunder, refilling my wine by the flashes of lightning with only a little spider on the ceiling for company. I felt utterly alive, of the earth on that night of change, not of the world as I had always spent it. Never in a million years (do I exaggerate?) would I have expected to find myself in such a place both physically and emotionally—content with nothing. Who would have thought?

I know it must not seem as if peace and non-resistance reign triumphant in my heart from all I've written, but please remember as I said at the start that writing this was not my idea and not my choice, at least at the start. I said no many, many times. I would have preferred to tell a different tale—a gothic mystery perhaps—but he asked and asked and asked, so I said at last yes (having learnt my lesson).

Such a little word, but one that has come at some cost, I might add. In the eighteen months of writing, which at times has felt like taking a potato peeler to my skin, I've become sick, as if it were the result of bringing poison to the surface. I am so poor the thought of my five thousand–dollar wedding dowry sitting forever unclaimed in my parents' bank account calls to me at times like a siren song, and like Ulysses, I have to strap myself to the mast of freedom to resist its practical allure.

And I've lost hair too and am now the proud owner of a bizarre little bald spot in the lower back of my head, which Thomas finds most amusing. I suppose it is, for if, as the scriptures say, even the very hairs of my head have been counted, well then, God certainly has considerably less to keep track of now.

# Chapter 32

# Thomas

After another six months in Edinburgh, after discussing and then abandoning the proposal of marrying her lover for the purposes of residency rather than romance (which my little romantic could not bring herself to do), after Ruth had convinced her future host and husband to come for her (thereby having no further need of Claire), and after going through almost all her money, gradually, sadly Claire accepted that there was nothing for it but to go back home.

One late afternoon, a few days before her departure, her lover (let's call him Scott—yes, why not, he was one) asked her to go with him to their local pub. So downhearted was she, however, that she shocked him (and me) speechless by saying no. Claire said no—to the pub. Really, I couldn't believe it. Neither could Scott.

"No?" he said when he had regathered his wits.

"No," said Claire. "I'm tired, and I've got the blues."

"Well a night out will cheer you up."

"No, I just want to stay in and curl up and pretend I don't have to go home."

"But you never want to stay in."

"Well I do tonight."

"Please, Claire. Just come out for a little while."

"No."

"Please."

"No."

"Pleeeease."

Claire sighed. She looked into his pleading eyes. She sighed again. "All right, all right. But I'm not dressing up. This is it. If I go, I go like this."

Really you should have seen what "this" was. Having spent the wintry afternoon despondently packing and lying on her bed staring vacantly at the ceiling, she was dressed accordingly in torn old jeans, a shapeless old T-shirt, and an over-shirt two sizes too big. She wore no makeup, and her hair was clumped like a big fat bird's nest at the back of her head.

She stared at her lover with a dare in her eyes.

He said, "Well you might want to—"

She said, "It's this or nothing …"

He said, raising his arms in defeat, "Fine. Okay. Go like that."

So she did.

She pulled on some whiffy old socks, her clumpy walking boots, and an old coat and stood ready at the door—ungracious, cranky, making a point. They walked into the crackling cold night, down the hill, into the pub, and straight into her surprise farewell party. For minutes she stood staring at the crew of about twenty, paralysed by the conflicting desire to run straight back out again, back home, to clean herself up, and the desire to embrace them all. Finally, eventually, she simply emitted a tiny, strangled squeak, and everyone understood, having gotten a look at her by then, all that meant.

Someone took her old coat, someone brought her a whisky, someone found her a seat, someone handed her a cigarette, and someone even offered the use of a comb. Such kindness. Such warmth. How I wished she could have stayed there in that cold, clear climate. Then later (how this makes me laugh still), when she had stopped shaking and overcome her shyness, Scott asked her to accompany him outside.

And what did Claire say? She said no, of course. She said it was too cold. She said she couldn't find her coat. She said they had no need for such privacy, that he could say whatever he wished to say inside, near the fire or in a quiet corner. At each refusal, the poor man rolled his eyes to heaven.

"Please, Claire. Please. Just come with me, please, dear God please."

Well, what could she do? She gave him a glare, she found her coat, and she clumped outside. She was momentarily disconcerted to find her friends out there too. She looked at him, he looked at her and then he said, "Look up, Claire."

Finally, at last, she did as she was asked, and what did she see? Fireworks, rockets, sparklers, Catherine wheels bursting into colour over that age-old skyline. Her face lit up with joyful wonder.

As they cracked and boomed and blossomed overhead, she said, "What are they for?"

He stared at her.

"The fireworks," she shouted, "what are they for? What festival?"

He shook his head in astonishment. They looked at each other in great confusion, their faces bright in the light of the rockets, until finally he shouted, "You! They're for you! They're our going-away gift."

Luckily he was standing so close to her he could catch her when her knees gave way. Really, she had never been so delighted, so moved in all her life. I tell this little tale so you can see, like I did, how different her life could have been without them—her loved ones—sucking the very marrow out of it.

It was beautiful, and as she stood there warm and safe in a Scottish embrace, looking up into the sky, I knew she would have given anything, anything at all, to be allowed to stay, and I felt much the same.

But that was not an offer made to us. No visa, no money, no choice, so two days later we found ourselves with very heavy hearts flying over the ocean, through an endless night back into her old life.

Oh dreary, dreary day, though still perhaps that is more an observation based on hindsight than on what I felt then, for I hadn't entirely given up on the hope that she could build a different life upon her return. Really, she had done so much, had proven so much, if only to herself, had developed strength and self-contained tenacity, had withstood loneliness, fear, and isolation, had made good friends in foreign lands, and really had flourished in the cool of Europe despite Ruth's best efforts.

Surely, I thought, this must mean something. Surely Faith and Joseph could not disappear all this. Surely Claire could stand up now.

And she had Luke by then too, dear Luke, no longer just her little brother, but by then, through the old-fashioned medium of the thoughtful letter, her friend.

Luke met us at the airport at 5:00 a.m., which came as another delightful surprise to Claire, who had expected, at that grim hour, to simply drift back in alone to sleepwalk back into her homeland. It was a very Luke thing to do, which is to say it did not involve setting an alarm but rather sitting up all night, happily occupied, awaiting her arrival, done without fuss or fanfare and with all expressions of gratitude shrugged off with his typical good-natured grin.

Too wired to sleep, Claire opened a bottle of wine upon reaching his flat, and the two of them—feeling really as if they were meeting for the first time—sat talking and laughing for hours. It felt like a good omen to me. It felt like Luke could bring with him the fresh winds of change that Claire so needed to blow away the strangling cobwebs of her past. Dear Luke, really he had that effect on people, even on me, that charismatic glow that he had even from birth creating a subliminal sense of warmth, comfort, and security, making people feel that really nothing bad could happen when Luke was there.

Do you know who he always reminded me of, or then at least? I'll give you a few clues. He loved nature (was studying ecology at university), he was happiest outdoors, he had no interest at all in money, clothes, or status, and he knew the names and habits of almost every Australian creature of the air, the land, and the sea.

Have you guessed? Yes, he made me think of a modern, antipodean Francis of Assisi. What a hilarious friendship. St Francis of Assisi and Don Quixote. One who could not see bad and one who would not. Really, talk about the blind leading the blind. Still, though, they were good, and I loved them for it.

Luke's innate integrity, his merry nonsense, his "no-worries" generosity of spirit, all made him seem like he embodied light, that he was light. People, just as they did when he was young, flocked like moths to his flame. It must, even then, have felt enormously burdensome, I think now, to see such hope and expectation in other people's faces, to feel the need to shine, to cheer, even at times to save.

And even I did it. Even I wanted miracles from him, I am ashamed to say. Still, I couldn't help it. There was a magic about Luke that seemed to make everyone think, *All shall be well and all shall be well and all manner of things shall be well.*

Well, as you know. Wrong. Wronger. Wrongest.

After a couple of days of sleeping, catching up with friends, and walking those familiar streets, Claire went home to the vineyard. There she was given one day to tell her stories and show her photos, and then it was back to business. Joseph was appalled by her tattoo (which she got in Edinburgh as a joke—an Edinburgh tattoo). Without words, which was his way, he gave her to understand he thought it whorish, disreputable, disgusting.

Then they started on her future.

"How much money do you have left?"

"Not much."

"How are you going to support yourself?"

"I'll get a job."

"You don't expect to just walk into a job, do you?"

"Why not?"

"You throw a good job away, you spend all your money and think you can just pick it all back up when you feel like it?" Insert hollow laugh here. "That's a bit arrogant, isn't it, Claire? Where are you going to live? How will you afford a car?"

It was so intense and relentless that it was very clear they had missed Claire a very great deal indeed. Yet after this, after she left there a wreck and she did, within days, walk back into her old office and into a job. Afterwards Faith and Joseph rarely mentioned the journey again to ensure the idea never sank in that she had seen much more of the world than they had, so she was not, could not be, more adventurous, capable, and resourceful than they were. As if they had already rewritten the story for the family annals under the title "Claire's dreadful waste of money."

Of course, such a negation of her experience and revisionism—while only to be expected—tipped Claire off-balance, just as intended, and her spirits sank, just as they had intended. Not that I could advise her in that house, of course, but if I could have, I would have. I would have told her to shout, "Fuck off, fuck off, fuck off." Not very intellectual, I know. Not very sophisticated, but by then, I clearly understood it was all deliberate, that it was exploitation and predation, so what else was there to say? Of course it is a very hard thing to say to your parents, to people who claim to love you, to people you should trust. No matter how old you are, you are forever their child.

Claire could not. Instead she sank into a depression, her feelings of hopeless entrapment made worse from having known the taste of freedom.

She tried to fight off the encroaching darkness by doing what she had always done— running from it, hiding from it, ignoring the lengthening shadows, and my spirits sank to see it. If she'd been capable of listening to me, as in the days in Europe (which felt to us both like a lifetime past), I would have begged her to slow down. I would have said, "Stop. Stand still. Turn to face the dark. Look at it. Look into it. See from whence it comes."

For perhaps the one upside of evil and oppression is that it can look so small, so deformed, impotent, and ugly when you turn to face it. Instead, when you run, deny, and pretend, it looms up behind you like a giant, tentacled monster, engorged on fear and anxiety. Turn and stand and look, however, and watch it shrink back from a steady gaze. Don't get me wrong. You might still be looking upon pure hatred, but more often than not hatred located is hatred castrated.

But Claire could not, would not listen, for she was so busy pretending all was well at first by hanging out with Luke as opportunity provided. But then he left town, and though Claire was deeply enthused at his plans to get a post science degree and travel the country, still she feared the removal of his much-needed light.

Then she found herself forced to defend his choice and then his absence to Faith, Joseph, and Ruth.

Faith said, "Surely he should have tried to get a job after graduating instead of floating around the place. Honestly, that boy."

Joseph said, "He's so damned selfish. Do you know he hasn't even called his mother for more than a month? He doesn't care that we might be worried. He doesn't care about anyone but himself. He's not a patch on Peter and never has been."

Ruth said, "He'd better be back in time for my wedding. But even if he makes it, I bet he won't have anything appropriate to wear, and we'll all be running around after him as per usual."

Claire stood up for him stoutly, of course, but thought, *Who wouldn't want to run from this? Run, Luke, run, and don't come back.*

Then she threw herself into another foolish love affair which, as these things can often be, was not so much an act of pushing back the shadow land as embracing it. Oh if only she'd stood still, it would have saved her so much pain.

For it was in the throes of that grim lust that a life was sparked and then extinguished in a decision born of a boiling, combustible mix of panic, self-loathing, and despair. Oh Claire. She knew the night it happened, I think. Certainly she knew within days but could find no quiet internal space to give the fact some thought, let the idea, at least, take hold.

All she could think was, *No, no, no, I can't, I can't, I can't,* and her body responded likewise. She turned green, threw up six times a day while keeping everything in so tight even as she wished to expel it all. She felt idiotic at thirty-two to have made such a mistake and could not for many years even understand how it came to be given their use of condoms.

Only later did she find the clarity to remember the horror of conception, that it had been an act not of love but domination and that she had allowed it to avoid another fight, for the dreadful sin of laughing with another man over dinner. Later she wondered if he'd put one on at all in the darkness of their union or sought to teach her a lesson she would never forget.

I longed to tell her just to sit still and wait, just to calm. For I believed then, as I believe now, that nature would have resolved the matter, as it sometimes does (given it was her first pregnancy and her chronic illness), thereby saving her years of guilt and anguish and more years of sorrow and self-loathing after the removal of her womb when, on top of everything else, she had to hate herself all over again for that panicked, incoherent choice.

The pain you cause yourselves down here at times takes my breath away (metaphorically speaking).

Claire's squirming with discomfort to write down these words, for still and forever she feels great shame for it, such shame that once, on a desperate whim, she raced into a catholic cathedral, up the aisle, and into the confessional box to blurt, "I had an abortion," only to hear in reply through the grill, "You're a murderer then." It wasn't a question. In reply she sobbed, "Yes, yes I am, that's exactly what I am," and no amount of Hail Marys could wash that thought away.

But I write this for a purpose, not just to reveal Claire's secrets, for I am telling this to her as I tell you. Her greatest regret lay in the chaos of her decision making. That is, she had not been able to sit with the life within her as an adult woman and think and feel and weigh. She could not then locate where the manic "I can't" came from and so put it down to callousness, selfishness, shallowness. But it wasn't any of those, in my opinion.

I thought then, as I still think now, that subconsciously she could not bring another life into the world to be treated with scorn, shame and malice, as she knew it would be. For just as she later heard Faith say, "I knew you'd never be a mother," so too could she hear her sigh with contempt, "I always knew you'd end up as an unwed mother, Claire."

And too, she could still hear Joseph's "whore!" echoing down through the ages. She knew all that would inevitably flow to her but more crucially to her little one given that she could not even defend herself. So many lives destroyed by pride and domination.

But as you know, she did at last in her own quiet way, in very different words, tell them to fuck off, and on that day, the day she cried freedom, she thought her bones were going to melt.

One of the moments of the greatest getting of wisdom down here is to know when there is nothing else to say. That is, finding the courage to accept that you cannot change other people and the even greater courage to cut your losses, accept that there will be no justice, no happy ending, and simply walk away. Yet like all moments of wisdom, it hurts a very great deal, and our hearts ache for you. Really, they do.

I just want to break off here for a moment to quote something Claire and I read in the paper this morning. I can't resist. It's so idiotic, so muddle-headed, so illustrative of the prevailing zeitgeist around these parts. It is from a letter to the editor about narcissism.

Part of the letter read, "The devastating impact of this condition leaves sufferers and their loved ones socially marginalised, emotionally impoverished, and profoundly traumatised by the consequences of the narcissist's behaviour."

The writer then goes on to describe it as an "awful condition—whose causes remain largely unknown and untreatable."

Did you note the key word in the first sentence? Yes. Sufferers. Ha! That this condition leaves sufferers profoundly traumatised. Oh really, people, switch your brains on. Or what about the bit about the causes being unknown? Oh my. Has the writer, I wonder, never heard of pride, vanity, selfishness, and deceit or the timeless human lust for power and control?

What's the bet the writer is a psychologist? Do you think Faith and Joseph were traumatised or pleased with themselves? Do you think they were marginalised or the pillars of the parish? And one last question. Do you think this awful condition could be cured through a strict regimen of remorse, shame, regret, and humility?

I do. Honestly, how you've lost an understanding of human nature is beyond me. It seems to me like you're marched backward into an emotional dark age. Repeat after me— bad is not mad. It is rational, for it achieves a purpose. Bad is not weak; it is strong, tireless, tenacious. And most importantly bad becomes evil, and evil cannot back down; it can only be defeated. How can you defend or protect yourselves or each other if you don't believe people to be capable of evil?

How can you choose if you don't believe there is a choice? Sometimes life really is very simple. Good and bad. They have been part of the deal since almost the beginning, whether you believe it or not. And as I said earlier, all bad comes from the bloated ego. No one ever, ever does bad for altruistic reasons.

Note: very few humble people commit atrocities.

# Chapter 33

# Claire

I wish I could write that I travelled Kate's final journey on planet earth walking strong, true, and kind beside her, but I can't. No I can't, for after fifteen years of friendship, it failed over a ridiculous, petty disagreement that took only five minutes of talking but resulted in eight months of silence (the rest of her life, as it turned out) and years and years of thinking to untangle.

But to explain it, I'd best explain us. Kate was the yin to my yang. Airy, cheerful, flighty, and free-wheeling, she was the summer sunshine to my more autumnal twilight. Though we shared neither music, nor literature, nor movies, nor passions, we had our profession in common, many mutual friends, and a crazed sort of dreamy romanticism about life and love that bridged the gaps and provided passage between her world and mine.

At times, though, we drove each other nuts but never for long and never without amusement sooner rather than later—except for this time. The last misunderstanding, surprise, surprise, involved Ruth, who had met Kate through her husband, whom she had, in turn, met through me.

It caused me great discomfort, the friendship between Kate and Ruth, for I did not understand it then, but now I do. Then I thought, *How can you (Kate) not be loyal to me as I knit for you, sit with you, and mind your baby boy when you know what she (Ruth) is like?* Isn't that small? I'm ashamed to write it, yet still at times being unable to remove Ruth from the inner sanctum of my life made me feel crazed with frustration (as it once apparently did Thomas).

But now I understand why Kate loved Ruth, for she was the mother of three, the happy wife (then), of comfortable means and rising status (then), and so represented life, love, success, and feminine fruitfulness. I, on the other hand, without ever wishing, wanting, or welcoming it, had somehow become the Mistress of Death.

And Kate did not want to die, would rarely acknowledge the possibility of death even as the treatment options were gradually exhausted one by one. Through her sunny though fragile demeanour, she made all of us who knew her make believe that all would be well even, indeed, that she would be well.

Anyway, the collapse of the friendship came about one day after she had asked me to help her find a venue for a party and then proceeded to have it without inviting me. I was hugely hurt, of course, but even more confused, and when I asked her why, Kate said, "Because it was mainly for children."

I said, "So?"

Kate replied, "It was my four-year-old son's party!"

"So?"

"You're uncomfortable about kids since the operation."

"Maybe in the first week or two but not now. You know I'm not. I'm mad about your little boy."

"Well I only asked parents with children. I didn't think you'd want to come."

"But why did you ask me to help? Why get me involved?"

"I changed my mind. All right?"

"Am I not acceptable without children?"

"Don't be ridiculous."

"But I just don't understand this."

"Oh, Claire. I just thought it was for the best!"

"Best for whom?"

"Everyone!"

"Everyone? Everyone who? Did no one want me there?"

We looked at each other across my dining table as the silence lengthened and gathered in the air between us. Finally she stood, put down her teacup, and said, "All right. I wanted Ruth there, okay? I wanted Ruth and her husband and her children there."

"So?"

"So. I know you hate her …"

"She hates me …"

"And I know you can't stand to be in the same room together, and I didn't want that stress."

"As if you thought we'd make a scene?"

Kate just looked at me.

I said, "But Kate, we never make scenes. That's half the problem with my family. No one does pretend pleasant like we do. That's all we do. You know that."

"I'm sorry if you're put out about it, but I thought it was easier ..."

"But it wasn't even necessary, Kate. Or did she say I couldn't be there? Did she make you choose?"

And then she cracked it. She picked up her bag and said, "I shouldn't have to explain myself to you! In case it's escaped your attention, I'm dying of cancer. I don't need this shit!"

And then she too marched down the hallway and slammed the door behind her, but this time I had not one word to say in return. Indeed all I could think was, *What the hell just happened? How could one question go so haywire?*

Then over the next days and weeks I rang to apologise, but my calls went unanswered. I e-mailed apologies, which sparked no reply. I passed the message through her husband but heard no word back. It was a staggering development, it seemed to me, a horrible twist, and over the next eight months, all I heard of her rapid unstoppable decline I heard third hand until Ruth's husband phoned with the last word on her passing.

Once again I thought a death should have meaning, that it could and should change the living (would I never learn?). Upon hearing that her funeral would be held in another small country town, I rang Ruth (would I never learn?) as both a gesture of peace and a recognition of mutual grief and more practically to ask for a ride to the service.

She said no. She said, "We're leaving very early."

I said, "That's okay. I'll get a cab to your house. I'm not asking you to go out of your way. Just tell me a time to be there and I'll be there."

She said, "No. It doesn't suit."

I was annoyed, of course, but hardly surprised and mostly, to be perfectly honest, quite considerably relieved because I was not sure how to show my face at such a gathering, for everyone would know.

Once Kate and I had been joined at the hip, as had often been said of us. Once we were as close as sisters, but in her last months I'd been banished in one angry exchange. I kept imagining walking into another funeral in another church, facing another sea of faces, but this time knowing that behind most, the mental machinery would likely be grappling with the overwhelming, unanswerable question: "What hellish, unforgiveable thing did you do to upset your dying friend?"

A fair question, you must admit, for who fights with dying people? I do, apparently.

And because I couldn't explain it to myself, I had no hope of explaining it to others. So when Ruth said no, I sort of breathed a sigh of relief, for I had at least tried. Later when Ruth's husband rang to say he'd organised a lift for me with mutual friends, I could have boxed his ears for his kindness.

Thankfully it wasn't as excruciating as I had feared, not only because most people were gracious and appeared glad to see me but also, of course, because most of my grieving had already been done in exile. Then, when Ruth rose to speak in my place with a strange, hooded gleam in her eye, it mattered to me not one jot for I had never wanted to do it in the first place.

Yet that look caught my attention, for it was one of grim triumph. At first I thought I'd misread it until I noticed how often she looked up from her notes to make sure of my attention. Until I caught this look, I had blamed myself mostly (why did you mention it, you idiot?) and Kate sometimes (why could you not forgive me before you left?), but that look gave rise to thoughts of a very different nature.

Watching her rather than listening, I did know Ruth felt like she'd won. I realised that much of the performance was aimed at me, and a shiver went down my spine as I sat and looked at her, turning over in my mind the coldness of it, the implacability of her hatred, the lengths she was prepared to travel, the depths she was prepared to plumb to make me suffer and to make me pay. For I knew she'd never much liked Kate, had heard her say it often enough when Ruth and I still spoke, but there she stood at the altar, claiming a love and tenderness of the very highest order.

It is a frightful, unnerving thing to have an enemy. It is a frightful, unnerving thing to be hated, for it is not rational so cannot be rationally dealt with or diffused. As I watched her up there and later mingling bravely at the wake, I wondered what it would take to satisfy or assuage such loathing and really could think of not one thing.

My love for her over ten long years was clearly insufficient. My acceptance of her dislike of me was obviously pointless, and my sorrows and loss did not do it. When I backed down before her, she despised me. When I stood up to her, she detested me, and when I gave ground, she used it for a victory dance. No, I thought at last. The only thing that I could do that could possibly please Ruth in this life would be to remove myself from it, much as Luke had finally pleased her.

Nothing else would do.

That, I think, is the nature of hate, for it is my mere existence that constitutes the insult. Scary, don't you think? To be hated just for being alive. In some ways that could be the single-sentence story of Luke and me within our family cult. I'm sorry it's taken so many other sentences to get here, but it is a most painful fact for me to face, for him as much as for me.

And only now do I understand the full meaning of those words, for while I didn't really understand at the start of writing this book, when I simply put down what Thomas said to put down, I know now that Joseph did indeed hate me for being from the beginning. I know because now I remember. Now I recall incidents, moments, events that until now I had neither the courage nor the will to scrutinise.

They have plagued me over the years, these memories (like the image of the red-handled bicycle pump), posing questions I could not or would not bring myself to answer, but now I can and shall write them here in memory of Luke, knowing as I do that all that happened to me, one way or another, happened to him too, for we were entangled, like those crazy electrons, and perhaps will be forever.

When I was only about four years old, I'm pretty sure Joseph tried to kill me. I could never prove it, of course, could never ask about it or expect an honest answer if I did, so you will have to judge. You can decide.

Do you remember Thomas's hellish hamlet description of the town where I was born or taken to? Bleak, boiling, ugly, plonked onto plains that spread out for mile after mile in each direction, even seeping around that one weird hill.

Some of the flattest land on earth, when it came time to teach me to ride a bike, Joseph found the only road with ditches and a concrete culvert and promptly, with one mighty push, sent me crashing into it. I had been expecting a replay of the teaching method he'd used with Debbie—that is, I thought he'd run alongside the bike, holding the seat, offering encouragement and advice, staying close till all was clearly well, for isn't that how it's done?

Certainly that's what I had seen, for I was so thrilled for dear Debbie, so excited for her as she took off down a flat, empty road, and couldn't wait till it was my turn. Whether it was deliberate or an act of his subconscious, I will never know. All I know is that I fought like a little fury to get my feet back on the pedals, wailing, "Daddy!" as I went sailing head first into the concreted drain, which must have been, really, the only one for miles on those rainless plains. I was fractured, bruised, cut and bleeding but was given no medical attention. Rather it became a joke: my awkwardness, my clumsiness, my hopeless inadequacy. But I knew right at that moment of the violent, outrageous push that it was meant one way or another—that my father did intend to do me harm.

The other memory that haunts me still will only ever remain vague, yet the element of sinister intent is as palpable now as I know it was then. I don't how I came to be there, for again I was only four or five years old, but one afternoon I drove with Joseph alone, an unheard-of event given his aversion to me, to a dried-up riverbed in search of firewood.

Even now, the thought of that place, with its long-dead trees, the absence of any birdsong, the silence only broken by slithering and scuttling, the strange shadows and sickly light, makes my guts clench.

It was a dead, forgotten, abandoned place, and when we got there, when Joseph had driven down through the scrub to the bottom of the decline, turned off the car, got out, and pulled the chainsaw from the back, I wanted to close my eyes and wait in darkness till he was done. But that I could not do. He told me to get out. I said I didn't want to. He shouted at me to get out of the car, so I got out.

Then as he walked towards a stand of dead gum trees, he told me to go for a walk. I'll never forget it, for the very idea of walking around there was terrifying, not least because I was so small amidst such towering death and dark decay. I remember Joseph said it at first as a kindly sort of suggestion, saying something along the lines of, "I'll be awhile, Claire. You go for a walk, and I'll call you when I'm done."

But I would not go.

He said, "Claire. Do as I say."

But I would not. I said, "No thanks, Daddy. I'll just stay here with you."

He shouted, "Do as I say!"

But I would not go. No matter how many times he shouted at me, I would not move.

Joseph said, "Do you have to be so difficult, so lazy that you can't even be bothered to go for a walk? I don't want you standing there staring at me while I work."

But I would not move.

I said, "It's okay, Daddy. I'll look over there, away from you. I just want to stay here. I don't like this place."

And I would not budge from the side of the car, not when he shouted, not when he said I should think of it as an adventure, not when he finally turned his back on me in disgust and sparked up the chainsaw. No, I stayed by the car like my life depended on it, as I think perhaps it did. What adult would push a little child to go walking off into such an isolated, desolate, godforsaken, snake-infested place except one who wanted to leave the child there?

For my father was not the type to want blood on his hands. Plausible deniability has long been more his style. So much better, as he later did with Luke, to find a method of removal that could be blamed upon the child if enquires were ever made. "I told her not to go wandering off, but she's such a wilful thing!"

# Chapter 34

# Thomas

So, we're almost done. You almost know it all but still not quite everything.

Luke, to the chagrin of his critics and delight of his friends, did make it back in time for Ruth's nuptials, and Claire was thrilled to see him, needing his warmth and light (post-abortion) like never before. But he didn't stay in town for long. He should have, but he didn't.

No. For Joseph couldn't stand to see him so handsome, tanned, and carefree, and Faith couldn't bear the freedom and peace that swirled like an aura around him. So they pushed and cajoled him to come home, offering love and comfort but planning contempt and control.

Faith said, "Why don't you stay with us and get a job in a factory just to save a bit of money, love, while you decide what to do?"

An eminently reasonable plan, had it been sincere. Yet to them it had more sinister intent, for if he agreed, Joseph could look forward to months of sneering ("I didn't ask you here, it was your sainted mother's idea") while Faith could bask in the renewal of her power and influence, for which she was most desperate. For right then, it seemed to her, post-university and pre-profession, lay her best chance of pushing Luke towards the priesthood, and push she would to see through this grand design that had been decades in the planning.

She cooked him special meals. She bought him new clothes. She made him feel beholden, and she heaped him up with pious tracts to serve as a heavy moral contrast to his free and easy drifting. Then, just as she had with Claire all those years ago, she crooned that she knew best, that she knew wherein his happiness lay, that he owed it to God to give his life, that she had known he was special from the moment of his birth.

Dear Luke, he couldn't stand it, and like Claire upon her return from freedom, he felt as if he was drowning in the dark, hot waters of their need. But whereas Claire tried to soothe her anguish with wine, Luke chose drugs. In particular, he chose LSD in the hope of glimpsing a different reality, I imagine, obtaining the tablets from Claire's horrible ex-boyfriend without her knowledge.

Luke bought it during a trip to the city, took it back to the country, chose a mate to share it with, selected a glorious star-spangled night, and went down to his beloved river to sit on the bank in the dark to trip out of their skulls.

Oh my. They took too much, being both impatient and desperate, and did not come down for days, leaving both young men frightened, chastened, changed. When Luke told Claire not long later, she went into orbit. She shouted at him she was so fearful.

She said, "What in God's name were you thinking of? Your mind is so precious! Oh God, Luke. Three days of tripping, how nightmarish."

"It was," said Luke meekly. "It was terrifying. I felt like I was in hell."

"I bet. Are you all right now?"

"Mostly."

"What do you mean mostly?"

"I still kind of get these weird flashes and colour changes …"

Claire groaned. "Oh Luke, what have you done?"

I'm not sure, even now, if the LSD led to his sadness and madness. Maybe it did. I'm more inclined to believe the sadness and madness came first, were the catalyst for the drug-addled attempt at escape from the clutches of Faith and Joseph, from the pain of the past and for fear of that future being so relentlessly laid out before him.

The question, to me, has always been why he felt the need to take it or to take so much, not whether it played a part in all that was to come. To me, it suggested despair, and I wish Claire had never told Faith of it, even though she did it for the best of reasons, for I knew how Faith would use that knowledge.

I knew she'd store it away in her witch's kitchen to pull out if needed to poison Luke's name and to place the blame for his suffering squarely upon Luke himself and even others, as it turned out. I knew. I could hear it in Faith's voice the day Claire told her, the breathless, "Did he really?" sounding as if a prayer had once again been answered.

But the link between the drugs and his death was never clear to me, for it took two years for Luke to first become depressed and another year to become erratic, bursting with rage and misery at Faith ("She a liar, a monumental egotist, a blasphemous hypocrite") and

Joseph ("He abused me as a child. He destroyed my life. He's hateful and cruel."). Then it took another year to lose all hope altogether.

Then Luke's ranting did seem unhinged to Claire, particularly given that Faith and Joseph were busy delivering the performances of their lives as worried, stricken parents, lying about their attempts to help him, their dealings with his doctors, their heartfelt prayers for healing. But they don't now, do they? Now his words echo like those of a prophet in the wilderness, and I know Claire would give anything to have that time back, to listen to him, not them.

But finally she did. She thought it was too late, but it wasn't. She heard his voice, clear and constant, as well as mine, and between us Luke and I made her listen, made her see. We pulled off her sunglasses, metaphorically speaking. We threw open the curtains, and we made her look upon the reality of her life, not the one she had so long wished for.

It was painful but necessary, and I feel I've done now what I was sent to do. So, I think, does Luke, whose spirit will soon soar with the eagles, where he belongs. This only gives Claire a scratchy sort of comfort, for she'd like to feel him close for just a little longer. Yet still, I think Claire has now almost done what she was born to do too, but before she could, there was one last thing I asked of her before we began this mad collaboration. Can you guess?

Yes. I asked her to tackle Faith, to confront that most artful dodger, for I knew Claire had to know the truth, to sacrifice her illusions, to have no doubts if we were ever to proceed, for Faith was her mother and not easily discarded. So first she wrote a long, painful letter, to which she received that wretched six-sentence reply.

Then Faith, shocked to receive no hurt response, began to leave a series of wheedling messages on Claire's answering machine. ("I love you, darling. I want to talk to you now. Why won't you talk to me?") She ended with one she was clearly reading and had clearly prepared.

She said (clearing her throat), "Claire, I don't know why you won't talk to me, but given that you won't, I just want you to know how difficult you are. For example, I have a *beautiful* photo here of Ruth with her brother and other sisters. Now I'm sending a copy to everyone, but what do I do with you? If I don't send a copy to you and you see it somewhere, you'll say I'm being cruel or heartless. But if I send one to you, you may not want it. See how difficult this is? I find it impossible to know which way to jump with you sometimes. So. I just wanted to explain that. I want you to know that I love you, and now I just want to talk to you. Bye."

What a melange of malignant mischief. Oh my. You should have seen Claire's face as she sat listening to that motherly malice float out of her message machine and into the air.

Yet even then, she couldn't quite believe it. She couldn't believe Faith had brought up Ruth again, for time without number, as if she sought to play them against each other still, as if they were children; as if Faith believed Ruth to be Claire's eternal Achilles heel, which of course she did, having designed it so.

Claire couldn't quite believe Faith would have the audacity to describe her as difficult again, for the millionth time, this time without Claire actually having to do anything at all to warrant the descriptor. But even beyond the pain of hearing at last so clearly some of her mother's sly tricks, she understood that if she was still found wanting then—after surviving the loss of Jess, Luke, Sally, and Kate, after accepting childlessness, enduring great physical pain, and finding the courage to leave Mark—then, with no shadow of a doubt left to cling to, Claire knew it was by design. In a cataract of recollections, she thought of all the misery and wasted effort involved in her lifetime's attempt to please Faith and Joseph.

It hurt, but she was strong enough at last. She was ready to know, for she did not sink but rather felt as if for the first time in her life she was standing on solid, unshifting ground. And as angry as she had ever been.

Really, it was thrilling at last to see her righteous fury, and I pressed Claire passionately to call her mother, to confront her enemy while her mind was focussed like a white-hot laser, for I knew if she did, everything would, at last, tumble into place.

She heard. She rang. She told Joseph in a cold, unfamiliar voice that Faith could call her back if she wished when she returned from her Sunday stroll and sat back down to wait, resisting the urge to calm her thumping heart with a glass of wine, knowing it was a medicinal luxury she could not afford. For she felt she had one last dragon left to slay, which made me laugh not only because it meant that she had finally, finally given up waiting for a prince to come along and do it for her but because her imagery was so far removed from mine.

I thought, *Pluck the leach off, Claire. You can do it.*

Ha.

Forty minutes later, Faith rang and said with absolute complacency and confidence as she settled into her lounge chair and took a sip of tea, "Well then, darling, and where do we go from here?"

"Nowhere. That's it."

Faith, as if choking on her biscuit, said, "What? What do you mean?"

"Your letter and your message were the most contemptuous, dismissive communications I've ever received."

"Oh. I didn't mean that. I was just trying to let you see how difficult you can be."

"About the photo?"

"Yes."

"About something that hasn't happened?"

"What do you mean?"

"Have I actually done anything, Mum? Have I made a scene? Have I said a word? Have I even received it?"

"No, darling. That's my point. I didn't know what to do …"

Claire: "But nothing has actually happened. Has it?"

"But you can be so difficult …"

"I haven't done anything wrong, though, have I, given that the situation has not arisen, has it?"

"Well …"

"Has it?"

"No."

"So now we've got to a point where I don't even actually have to do anything to be blamed, is that right?"

"What should I have done?"

"What about asking me if I wanted a copy like a normal person?"

"I suppose so."

"But then you'd have had nothing to use against me would you, nothing to twist or manipulate or blame me for?"

Faith, starting to panic, said, "It's not like that."

"Yes it is. It is exactly like that. And the letter was incredible. You couldn't have given it less time or effort."

"That's because I didn't know what to say."

"You could have taken all the time you needed."

"I did."

"You couldn't bring yourself to write more than a few lines and made no reference to anything I wrote. You gave it two minutes."

"No I didn't. I thought about it for a week."

"Stop lying! I got it back in less than a week."

Faith, who missed not a beat in being caught in a lie, said, "Well I did my best."

"No you didn't. You gave it the time you thought it deserved. It was a choice."

"That's because I thought it was all wrong."

"Wrong? It was about my feelings, my experience, my life. It can't be wrong."

"Well silly then."

"Silly? When I wrote how close I came to suicide—you think that's silly?"

"No … no … not silly. I meant all the motives you gave me were wrong …"

Claire sighed. "I didn't ascribe motives, Mum. That was the point of the letter. I asked you why you treat me the way you do. And you didn't even both to answer."

"Well I just didn't know what to say …"

"Well the good news is that you don't have to worry about that anymore."

"Don't say that!"

"And I hope you realise that if you'd counted on me as part of your old-age care plan, you had better think again."

"Why would you say that?"

"Why do you think?"

There was a pause while Faith regrouped. "I'm a stupid woman, Claire."

"What?"

"I'm stupid. I've never held down a job. I've always stayed at home."

Claire, hearing bells of recognition at this familiar tactic, asked, "What's that got to do with anything?"

"I'm just saying if I've let you down you shouldn't judge me because I'm not very smart."

"But this isn't about brains though, is it? It's about love."

"Well … yes … but my memory is going too, it's terrible. I'm afraid I'm going to end up like Nan."

"Oh stop it. This is ridiculous. It's all about excuses, all prevarication, so you never have to take responsibility for anything you do, so you can refuse to listen to a word I have to say. You never even acknowledge how much I loved Luke."

Faith, in her most patronising, practiced tone, as if she had been waiting to use it, said, "Well, love, I suppose that's because you weren't with him much in the end …"

"But what did I do instead? Who supported you when he was sick and troubled?"

"I don't know."

"You don't know?"

"Well you did then I suppose."

"Yes I did, and the fact that I didn't spend more time with him is something that I'll regret for the rest of my life."

"Oh yes, we all do."

"No we all don't. I do."

"Yes, we both loved him."

Claire said, "And we both grieved."

Faith, who couldn't even acknowledge this, said, "Well I don't think your grief can compare to a mother's love."

"So it's a competition, is it?"

"I'm just saying ..."

"Oh enough. I've treated you with love and respect my whole life, and you cannot give it back ..."

"That's true ..."

"Even at my lowest point, in the hospital, you made me cry when it was agonising."

Faith, heaving a big sigh of not this again, said, "Oh really, Claire ..."

"You couldn't even be kind to me then."

"I was there."

"No you weren't. You were never there."

"You needed to rest!"

"More and more excuses. And the fact that you couldn't even stand up for me when Ruth was being her usual malicious self ..."

"But you're grown women!"

"I was sick and heartbroken."

"What should I have done then?"

"Stood up for what you say you believe in. How about that for an idea? Compassion to the sick and weak, justice perhaps ...

"Well yes, when you put it like that, but I thought you'd work it out."

"So justice has age limits then, does it?"

"No."

"And back to the subject. I notice the only thing you referred to in my letter related to Ruth, so let's get this sorted out once and for all. Why do you think I want to be her friend?"

"I thought you did."

"Why? When have I ever said that?"

"I just thought you did."

"Why would I? I was her friend, as you well know. I know how she treats her friends. Do you know the last few times I've seen her she speaks over me whenever I try to say something? Did you know she passes food and drink to everyone but me and turns her back upon me whenever she can?"

"Oh."

"It's pathetic, of course, and kind of laughable, but still, it is a disgusting way to treat anyone, don't you think?"

"I didn't know it had got that bad ..."

"And why would that be, do you think?"

"What?"

"Could it be because I'm never allowed to mention it, am given instead to think I should not only be willing to accept such crap but do it in the hope that she might like me again?"

Pause. "I'll speak to her then."

"Don't bother."

"Don't you want me to do something?"

"No. Of course not."

Faith, confused, asked, "Why not?"

"*Because it's too late!*"

Faith made a noise like noxious gases being released.

Claire said, "I don't care what Ruth thinks of me from now until the day she dies, do you hear me?"

"Yes."

"And speaking of death, I want you to know that taking you and dad into account when I was contemplating suicide is my last gift to you …"

"Well I'm sure we appreciate that …"

"Sure you do, particularly when you describe it as silly, which strikes me as a very strange thing for a mother to say who's lost one child that way …"

"I didn't mean that. I do care."

"Which is why you always ask me how I'm doing, how I'm coping, about leaving Mark or not having kids …"

"I don't want to rub your nose in it."

"Rub my nose in it?"

"Yes."

"So asking me is rubbing my nose in it?"

"You know what I mean …"

"No, I don't actually. I only know what you say."

Faith, changing tack, said, "Well at least I call you. Do you know, love, it's always me who rings?"

"And why not? We only ever talk about you. You can at least press the numbers."

Faith gasped again, as if finally realising Claire had been watching, paying attention, but for how long?

Scrambling, she said, "Your father and I do love you, Claire …"

"Yeah right. Did you show him my letter as I asked you to, to make sure there was no more confusion?"

"Um … no …"

"No?"

"He didn't want to read it."

"Why not?"

"Um … he thought it was too personal."

"Too personal? Before reading it?"

"You know what he's like."

"So he thinks we're a corporation now, not a family then?"

"I don't know! Look, I'm sorry that you think I'm so hopeless. I'm very sorry that I can never please you. I'll just pray to die now then. I suppose, there's no point me staying around."

"Nowhere I haven't been …"

"It's not like I have much influence with your sisters."

"Influence?"

"No, no I mean I'm not that close to them."

"What rubbish. Don't be ridiculous. Besides, that has nothing to do with me. They're the relationships you made. I'd never have created a family like ours—that's your doing."

Faith gasped again. "Yes, well," was all she could say.

"Anyway, there's nothing more to say."

Faith, in a panic, perhaps the first of her long life, said, "But what's going to happen now?"

"Nothing. All you have to do is take me off the fortnightly phone roster. I don't want it."

"I can't do that, love."

"Yes you can."

"But I *need* to talk to you."

"Well I suppose I can't physically stop you calling, but I don't have to pick up, do I?"

"You can't do that!"

"Of course I can."

"Oh, oh let me make it up to you then."

"You can't."

"Let me come down and stay a few days with you."

"*God no!*"

"Well let's be friends then if you think I'm such an inadequate mother."

"But we're not friends."

"Aren't we?"

"What do you think friendship is?"

"I don't know. When you listen to someone and give advice …"

"Is that it?"

"Isn't it?"

"You really don't have a clue, do you?"

"But you've got to give me another chance."

"I've given you chances. I've tried time after time to get through to you, but you treat me with contempt. No more, Mum."

"But what will happen when we see each other?"

"I doubt that's going to happen any time soon, but if it does, we'll be pleasant. You should be delighted given that pleasant is your holy grail. But there will be no more intimacy between us. And that should please you too no doubt given that you think me so difficult."

"No I don't!"

"You've said it about four times in the past hour."

"But I didn't mean it!"

"So you were lying?"

"You can't just walk away from us."

"Listen, Mum, you had your chances and now it's too late. Luke and I were the beating heart of our family, and now you've lost us both. I hope you're happy."

"Oh …"

"I'm going now. This is horrible. I don't know, Mum, something went very wrong between us a long, long time ago. I've spent my entire life trying to put it right only to discover none of it was my fault. And now I don't care anymore."

"Your father and I do love you, we do respect you …"

"Yeah, yeah, yeah."

Then Claire hung up and sat as if in a catatonic state. She was astonished she had not cracked it, that she had not raised her voice, used lashings of low-level coarse language, or crumbled into dust from sheer frustration. She was shocked to have found herself able to resist the temptation to ask her mother a million questions, knowing she would only be inviting more strangulating lies.

But mostly she was stunned to find that Faith could not say sorry, just once, about anything, for that's all it would have taken to melt her resolve. But Faith could not do it, not even then, and that proved to be a great revelation.

Finally Claire pulled herself out of the stupor and poured herself some of that longed-for wine. And while she sipped and felt herself for the first time ever to be somewhat new (a battered phoenix rising?) and just a tiny bit fabulous, I darted up to Faith on wings of sunlight to glimpse her response to the rebellion. I found her still sitting in her lounge room (I could only look in from outside, of course) and can only relate what I made of the reaction by the expressions that passed across her face.

First was a black rage, which seemed to me to encapsulate the notions of, "How dare she? No one talks to me like that. You can't reject me, you wretched child. I'm your mother; *you are mine!*

Then came a softening of her features as if she was thinking, *It's only Claire. Claire! What am I worried about? Claire is too soft to hold out on me. Who else does she have? She'll come round.*

And then, at last a bitter, glittering smirk, as if to say, "And when she does, oh won't we have some fun then …"

And with that thought, she got up and got dinner underway, for there was never any need for Faith to go hungry. I didn't stay around, but it wouldn't at all surprise me if she mentioned not one word of this to Joseph, for it was a touch humiliating, after all. No need to let him know that she had not been victorious; he might throw it back in her face some day. For that was how Faith thought and was very much the type of thinking encouraged in the cult Faith built.

# Chapter 35

# Claire

So at last it's up to you to play judge and jury, for now you know as much as I do. But as I present my case built on years of observation and heavyhearted deductions (no confessions being forthcoming), bear these questions in mind.

What is murder? Does it have to be one act of destruction at one moment in time, or could it be endless acts of cruelty over an entire lifetime until no more could be endured?

You decide.

This is what I think happened to Luke, an opinion I have reached after at last finding the courage to strip away all my parents' self-serving claptrap, all their lies, denials, and false feeling; in other words, now that I can see them.

You've heard their version of events. This is mine.

I think that from the time I first took Luke home following his breakdown in the forest, Faith began to plot at first his isolation (to limit the possible contagion of truth infecting the family) and later his destruction (if no other solution could be found), for he represented the threat of enormous humiliation. Also, if he wasn't going to be a priest, if he'd been rejected by her beloved catholic church, if he was broken, then she had no further use for him, so best to move him on somehow, for hadn't she done the same to me?

I'm pretty sure she thought, *If he's going to talk of abuse, best for everyone that no one should listen and better still if he just stopped talking.* She was always such a believer in doing what was best.

That's when Faith and Joseph fell over themselves in their hurry to have me leave the country for the shores of Ireland, offering me money and a trip to the airport, both of which represented unprecedented support. That's when they started the rumour that Luke was not sad and sick but psychotic and deranged so no one would listen, so he'd never be heard.

I think they lied to him about my leaving, wanting to estrange us, the two outsiders, wanting us at odds so he had no champion, no defender. I think she did not tell him I did not want to go but rather that I did.

I can picture Faith saying something like, "Now Luke, of course Claire wanted to leave you behind. What can you expect? You're not her burden. And don't think she cares for you specially. She was just looking out for you because I asked her to. And you've got yourself into such a mess you can't really blame her. Yes. She said that—not me. All I know is she couldn't wait to go. You know what she's like. You weren't counting on her help, I hope."

As I write it, I can almost hear it, for there had to be some rational explanation for why Luke looked at me with such wounded eyes, the eyes of the betrayed, when I returned months later, a look so confusing and painful to me I could neither meet it nor understand it. I should have, of course, but when I asked Faith what it meant, she said it was just a symptom of the madness, and I believed her.

She said, "He hates everybody, Claire. It's the disease. Don't bring it up with him. It will just cause more upset. It's not personal." But it felt personal.

I also think they lifted not a finger to get him medical help but called the police quick enough when Luke stood up to his full height, loomed over, and shouted at that quaking bully Joseph. This, of course, they also explained as being for the best, the best way for him to get treatment by locking him up in a mental ward (for how could anyone in their right mind find Joseph wanting?) and certainly the best way for them to stay safe, which as always was best for all.

It was horrifying for them to involve the police, but that, of course, was as nothing to Joseph's rage, I suspect, at being shown to be so craven when finally confronted by that son whose gentleness had for so many years acted as a spur to his sarcastic tyranny.

I think if the law had allowed it, they would have sectioned Luke then for the term of his natural life. Faith knew that Luke was a suicide risk as the years unfolded. I know because I told her of my fears, both actual and psychic, yet she did nothing to prevent it. She asked no one else to help and later denied she'd ever heard my warnings. Instead, she once said in my presence, "Do you know, Claire, I think it was God's special gift to me that I never saw it coming. I think he spared me that suffering."

And then she gazed into my eyes, daring me to call her a liar, which of course I didn't.

I think too that she pushed Luke towards the precipice, day by day, encouraging the idiotic malice of the exorcism, telling him that he might be possessed while stirring the chaos by declaiming that his suffering would not be happening if it were not God's will. At the same time, she let him know he was too erratic, dirty, and miserable to be around the beautiful babies and so to stay away from family events, keeping him from those of us who loved him while shedding crocodile tears at his absence.

I remember it all calmed down somewhat when Luke went to that last monastery, and I had such hopes for him there, picturing him with a band of brothers, those precious few, mystics like him, calm and loving. I didn't know then that he was being worked as an unpaid farm slave. I didn't know he was given only a shed to live in and was refused a place in the cloisters of his dreams. It never occurred to me that they could treat someone so.

Then, when he rightly became angry, they pushed him out with only a train fare in his pocket after six months hard labour, sending him back to his original persecutors. It makes me want to cry to write it, for where the hell was I?

Anyway, that's when the shit really hit the fan, it seems to me, when Luke returned to the new town of Faith and Joseph's retirement, where rural isolation could no longer be counted on to hide the family secrets, and where Faith was busy establishing herself as the Most Pious Woman in the Parish. Luke's arrival and subsequent welcome into that catholic society must have horrified her. For of course he went straight to the local church upon his return, that crazy diamond, the very last place Faith then wanted him to be.

When I think of him there, particularly during his last days, do you know who I also think of? Yes. You would have guessed. Cool Hand Luke, that glorious, flawed outsider who would not be broken, who refused to accept cruelty and injustice even at the cost of his own survival. I can only watch that film very occasionally, not only because golden Luke looked like him but to my shame, because even such celluloid suffering brings me undone. And when I think of Luke quietly, uselessly seeking consolation in that church, I think of Paul Newman's Luke and his final discussion with God.

He says, "I know I got no call to ask for much, but even so, you gotta admit, you ain't dealt me no cards in a long time. It's beginnin' to look like you got things fixed so I can't never win out. Inside, outside, all 'em rules and regulations and bosses. You made me like I am. Just where am I supposed to fit in? Ol' Man, I gotta tell ya, I started out pretty strong and fast. But it's beginnin' to get to me. When does it end? What do ya got in mind for me? What do I do now? All right. All right. On my knees, askin'. Yeah, that's what I thought. I guess I'm pretty tough to deal with, huh? A hard case. I guess I gotta find my own way."

Then the police cars arrive outside, and he looks up and says, "That's your answer, ol' Man? I guess you're a hard case too." And then he dies, of course, in a hail of bullets but it wasn't, as you know, that quick for my Luke.

First, on the Thursday night before he plunged to his eventual death, he had a last supper with Faith and Joseph, the first time he'd shared a table with them for years. At the time, or not long later, Faith told me it had been his idea, and maybe it was.

I'm more inclined to believe now, though, that she was behind it somehow. I even think she might have asked him over to dine to prod him with barbs of cruelty, to destroy any lingering hope of being loved and cared for or finding sanctuary or that justice would ever be done, for it's a bit of a coincidence that he broke bread with them one evening and then tried to kill himself the next, don't you think?

I do now. Now I don't believe in coincidences. I think they served him up one last dish of malice that he could no longer stomach. And this is why I believe it.

I think that despite her denials, Faith knew Luke was the mystery man on page three of her local newspaper as soon as she saw it, for why else would she have flown out the door to clean his flat, as she claimed, at nine thirty on a Saturday morning? Faith didn't even do church cleaning on a weekend, for they have long been sacred.

So she knew, but given that the report described not a young man in his twenties but a man in his forties, with no identification upon him and a smashed-in head, how did she know unless she was expecting it?

We all know how much credence to give her claim of a miracle in finding Luke's suicide note in the chaos of his flat. Clearly she found it because she was looking for it, but now my doubts go even further, for since I've walked away from her, Faith has sent me at least six meaningless, manipulative cards. A few were addressed to me in a different handwriting, as if she thought to trick me into opening them.

It made me laugh to see it first, but then it made me pause, for the deceit gave rise to a most bleak suspicion. I've only seen Luke's suicide note once, Faith refusing to show me for a long time, claiming it was too upsetting for her, for me, for everyone to handle.

But I insisted at last. It said only, "Dear Family. I can't take the pain anymore. Please forgive me. I hope we meet again."

It was gentle and gracious, like I'd expect from Luke even at that sad hour, but then again, so would she. No blame. No anger. No outrage. Just the way she would have liked it; just the way she would have written it herself.

Of course, I would have liked to see where she'd so miraculously stumbled upon it, would have liked to have read everything he wrote, but surprise, surprise, an unknown woman destroyed everything.

And I mean everything. Not even a coffee cup was spared the annihilation of Luke's worldly belongings. Do you find that suspicious? I do. I most definitely do, for despite her denials, she must have known who did it. She must have given permission.

So what did she want destroyed? His journals? His written claims of abuse? His handwriting?

Then, in the next miraculous development, Faith met the police as she was driving home. Now my mother, fearing risk to her most-precious reputation, would never have involved the police unless she absolutely had to, and now I think she felt that need because of the line in the newspaper saying city detectives were on their way to town to determine what happened to the tragic figure found dying and bleeding on the road.

I think she felt desperate to head them off, to stop them from entering Luke's flat, to stop them from reading his writings or even comparing the note. So I don't think she miraculously found two policemen; I think she went looking for them. I also think, of course, that Joseph knew it all, was in on it all, sanctioned it all, but stood back, as he always did, to let Faith take care of family business.

They knew, for that bitter, set-jawed look upon their faces as they walked up the steps of the city hospital to identify their son was not one of heartbreak at what he'd done but more like rage that it was not done well. Then they blamed him at his funeral, they buried him in private, and then they shut down any further mention of his name.

Hardly the behaviour of loving parents; hardly the behaviour of innocent people.

I wonder if it sounds strange to you to hear how painful it is for me to write this of them, my parents. I loved them and came close to choosing death over clear vision because I think I always knew or suspected that if I looked at them too closely, I could well be appalled at what I saw. It's hard to see hate where love should be. It's hard to know that those you are biologically designed to trust can prey upon such innocence.

And in the writing of this, there have been many times when I have doubted it myself, for shouldn't evil loom physically large, suck the leaves from the trees, wither the flowers and crops, and cause the lakes to boil? Could it possibly look like two grey-haired old people, sitting so smugly in the front row at mass?

Even when we began this collaboration, I wasn't entirely comfortable with Thomas's views on Faith and Joseph, for I thought he was being too harsh. Still, I comforted myself instead with the knowledge that such a strange tale as this would be unlikely to find a publisher, so I gave him his head, or mine, as the case may be. But just when I started to hold more doubts than usual, not that long ago now, three things happened to quash them.

First, Faith sent me a birthday card that included a hundred-dollar cheque (that I promptly binned after noting wryly how my value had increased since my departure, my normal going birthday price having previously been a quarter that sum, as if she thought to buy me back). In the card she wrote that she still loved me, still thought of me, and that they would *love* (underlined three times) to have me back in the family.

I binned that too.

Then two weeks later I was chatting to my darling godson (Debbie's firstborn), who told me he was going up to the country for the weekend.

"That's nice," I said. "What for, an engagement party or birthday or just to see your mum?"

The dear boy paused. Then he struggled for words until he came out with, "Um … no … for Gran and Pa's fiftieth wedding anniversary party."

"Oh," I said. "Right."

"Didn't you know?" he asked quietly.

"No, my dear, I did not," I said and felt so awkward for him I swiftly changed the subject.

So the day came and went, and I thought about it as I drifted lonely as a cloud in town, thinking of all my cousins, nieces and nephews, aunts and uncles, brother, and sisters and the terrible price of truth and freedom.

And though I knew it was typical of Faith to send the card claiming love while refusing me an invitation, still it hurt. That squeezed-heart feeling, my constant companion, meant it took a few days for me to think past the perfidy of her actions to the oddness of them.

Surely, I thought, it would have served her purpose better to invite me on the understanding that I would most likely decline. Then she could have had a field day at my stubbornness, my unforgiving nature, my recalcitrance and ungrateful hard-heartedness, don't you think? She could have revelled in it, in front of a large audience, all there to pay her honour, her and Joseph, for their heroic virtue and marital adhesion.

No, there was something most definitely wrong about it, but given that I was unlikely to find an explanation or be given further information, I put it out of my mind. Until.

Until about two weeks later I came home to find a message on my answering machine left by my ex-sister-in-law, Peter's first wife, a dear woman I had not spoken to for years and years.

She said, "Oh, Claire. I just want you to know that we love you, me and the children. I've always loved you. I hope you know that. Remember you were my bridesmaid? I really care for you and hope you know you are always welcome with us. The kids are always asking after you and wish they got to see you more. Anyway, I'll go now, darl, but call me if you get a chance, for I'd *love* to talk to you."

I think I stood motionless in the middle of my little lounge room as the words spilled over me, thinking, *What the hell?*

Don't get me wrong. It was lovely to hear from her, but the effusive outpourings struck me as most bizarre. It sounded like she thought I had cancer or some terrible affliction. It sounded like she thought me at death's door.

For the next two days, I wracked my brains trying to understand it, think my way around it, aware as I now am that if something sounds odd, there's every chance a lie has been put into circulation. But I couldn't figure it out, so took the most practical step of ringing to find out.

We went through the warm preliminaries, filling in the gaps of the years, discussing the kids, until she said, "We really do love you, Claire."

Trying to figure out how to frame a sentence that wouldn't sound rude or dismissive, I said, "Thanks for saying that. It's lovely to hear, but it kind of sounds like you think I'm distressed or in trouble of some kind."

She said, "Oh no. I'm just so upset about what's going on with your family."

Well that threw me. My departure shouldn't give rise to this level of anguish surely, I thought. "Oh right. Um. What do you think is going on with the family?"

"How they're blaming you, of course."

"Blaming me?"

"I think it's disgusting."

"Blaming me for what?"

"For Luke."

With a touch of a shriek, I said, "Luke? What do you mean blaming me for Luke?"

"For giving him the drugs, for causing his death."

I was speechless for a minute. "How do you know this?" I asked quietly. "Where did you hear it?"

And in reply she explained my sisters had told her kids this at the anniversary party to explain my absence; that I was held responsible, and Faith and Joseph in all good conscience could not forgive me for it and thus could not invite me to their special day. It was, she said, the hushed and shameful talk of the day, raised whenever my name was mentioned, as if I was the ghost at the gathering.

Goodness me. It took a minute to absorb, but then I rocketed into orbit. I told her that not only was it a lie, that I'd had nothing to do with the drugs, but also that I had walked away from them because they lied but I don't know if she believed me. For theirs was such an horrendous lie it sounded like the truth, and my defence was so plain it sounded just like a lie.

When I hung up, I sat in the dark, harrowed to my bones by the knowledge of how bottomless was their treachery: that they could dig up Luke to point his bones at me; that they could have my kith and kin believe me to be a drug peddler; that they could claim to have rejected me (for no one could ever be seen to have rejected them); and that my mother could twice use the information I'd so naively given her in trust to us harm both again.

And that meant that anyone who had witnessed my profound grief at Luke's funeral would now put it down to my dark guilt and not to the glorious wonder of Luke. Faith and two birds, as usual. I knew she was up to something, of course, but not even I thought she could be so black.

Yet perhaps even more painful than all of that was the understanding that Faith and Joseph had corrupted everyone, all my remaining siblings, all of whom knew I'd hand no hand in the drug deal or that such belated nonsense had anything at all to do with the reasons for my leaving. They knew. Did no one feel morally bound to object? Did no one feel the dirt of the grave upon their hands? And all of them believing themselves to be good, successful, decent people.

To slander the living and the dead, to conspire with and corrupt others, only for the sake of an afternoon party, finally forced me to see my parents as the malignant narcissists they are.

All so they could shine at a gathering held to celebrate love, commitment, and family feeling, or more to the point to honour the less-than-traditional vows, as Thomas suggested, the promises they made to keep each other's secrets, to support each other's lies, and to protect each other's egos till death do them part.

I felt like driving up there with a shotgun, to be honest, but having eschewed the body-bag approach to problem solving when I left Mark, I let the feeling pass through and pass. I'm not sure, but I wouldn't be at all surprised to find that it was right then, sitting in the dark, when my hair fell out.

★★★

Some states in America have a crime on their statue books known as a "depraved-heart murder," under which a person can be prosecuted for wilfully failing to reasonably prevent the destruction of another. I believe my parents are the depraved-heart murderers of their son, my beloved brother, for the mere sake of their obscene egos and not a jot more.

The only thing I remain unsure of is Luke's allegation of abuse by my father, for it is such a heinous thought I cannot think it. He was so little. My mind cannot absorb it.

I know those days were dark and sinister in that house then. I know that almost everything Luke said has proved to be true—well, except when he described me as a modern-day Magdalene, but we can't all be right all the time—yet still I cannot believe it.

You'll have to decide on that and the ultimate questions of: Does the deliberate destruction of one of us say something about all of us? Does evil matter? Should we stand up to it or hide away from it? Does peace require justice, not only in law but in fact? Does writing a book in atonement for personal cowardice ease the misery?

Well that last one I can answer: yes, it does.

I can, in fact, almost picture Luke giving me that sunshine grin again.

Like the two children in that story I invented the night my life seemed to hang in the balance, he went his way home and I've gone mine. He got there first, yet still I believe he continues to light my way, for we are, as we ever were, entangled.

# Chapter 36

# Thomas

Not much more, you'll be glad to know, just one last piece to put into the puzzle.
*(Damn. I wanted to have the last word. Ha! C)*

Do you remember me telling you ages and ages ago, or pages and pages ago, that there were three consequences that flowed from the extra month of cooking time that went into the creation of my friend Claire? Yes? The first, as you know, was that the time anomaly sparked Joseph's baseless suspicions, which gave him an excuse (as if he needed one) to hate her.

The second was the alteration made to her hippocampus that deranged her internal heating system, causing her to swoon and melt, a huge irritation for her in this sunburnt country.

Now to the third, for I did promise to tell. Have you guessed? Yes, Claire was born with an enlarged God-spot, as you call it, which is located, if you wish to go looking for it, in one of the most ancient parts of the human brain, speaking in terms of evolution, just above the brain stem near the thalamus.

That's why she's always been able to hear me so clearly, whether she wanted to or not. That's why we've been able to undertake this wild collaboration, which if nothing else has proven to be one of the great adventures of my long, long existence. Really it's been thrilling.

Would she surrender to the oddness of the project? Would she be brave enough to hear things she didn't want to hear? Would her rational mind win out over her mystic understanding? But more than all these loomed the question, would she be brave enough to tell the truth at the cost of all she'd hoped for?

Really, every day we've worked on this together has felt like the equivalent of participating in an extreme sport (will she make it, will she crash?), but in this case, it's been more about accepting an extreme reality.

To me, after having been so long told to bear silent witness, it has been a joy not only to be heard but to be understood, particularly given that we've both had much to learn in terms of translation, for it is much easier to communicate in pure thought forms than grammar. Also, English, as you should know by now, is not my first language.

Or second. Or third. Ha!

It has made me feel brand-new, as you say, which is saying something. In some ways I'm sorry I was so angry with you all at the start. Not that my opinions have changed. Oh no. I think I simply forgot how tremendous and exquisite is life on earth—how important, beautiful, and funny.

So Claire can hear me because her head's not normal but not subnormal, as she has often thought. And I think it is this, this enlarged God-spot, that gives her glimpses into the future and allows her to sense the dead.

So now you know it all, and I wonder what you will make of it or take from it, this story of good and evil, love and hate, humility and ego. But if I could leave you with one thought, it would be this: You don't need priests, gurus, or swamis to find your way to God. You don't need cults or creeds or closed communities. All you need to know, you already know. God is within. He is in your brains, your minds, your DNA.

Yet while you may not be able to hear us or him as loudly as Claire does, still you can hear us. You know it. But God is subtle, and we are gentle. You have to listen, you have to allow us in, and you have to choose. Turn down the volume of your lives and you could be amazed at what you hear, the music of the spheres, the timeless wisdom of the cosmos. And in the quiet of forever, in which you belong, tend your soul garden.

That's not so hard, is it?

Not Sunday service or money to buy salvation or searching for answers you already know. You don't need intellectual, psychological, or emotional oppression, not any of it. God wants you to think with all your might. He gave you freedom to find your own way home, a design built in from the beginning at the very flaring forth, the central point of all that was, is, and will be. You count, and every choice you make counts.

But you are not alone. Let us in. Rescind the invitation to the others if you feel their fluttering presence and one of us, yours most truly, will be there beside you in a heartbeat.

God leans towards you, and if you pray the right prayer, he can deny you nothing. It's so simple: I love you, God. Thank you, God. Forgive me, God. Help me please.

Nothing life changing, though in fact it is.

For God exists. I should know. I've known him (almost) from the beginning. And he can be so funny.

Claire knows, for as I told her recently, I think it is no coincidence that she lost a small circle of hair right over the exact spot on her head that allows me to tell her anything at all. She thought it was caused by them, her family, and the acute anxiety that has always been their calling card, but I don't. I think it is far more likely that spending two years listening to a voice most people have never heard, let alone believe in, might cause a few hairs to loosen their grip, don't you?

It's as if clear access had to be provided, as if she needed a little less interference to help her believe the unbelievable. For even now, after almost two years, this experience still fills her with wonder. One day I picture her thinking, *Did we really do that, Thomas and I? Did we really write a book?*

Then, knowing her, I expect she'll say, "Can't you tell me now, after all these years together, who you are?"

And I'll reply like I always do, "Who do you say I am?"

And she'll laugh to hear it. Or I hope she does, for that's a sound I could listen to for eternity.

*The End*